Hidden Lives

Cassell
Wellington House
125 Strand
London WC2R 0BB

PO Box 605
Herndon
Virginia 20172-0605

First published 1998

Published in association with

Latin America Bureau (Research and Action) Ltd
1 Amwell Street
London EC1R 1UL

Save the Children
17 Grove Lane
London SE5 8RD

Rädda Barnen
Torsgatan 4
S-10788 Stockholm

British Library Cataloguing-in-Publication Data

A catalogue record for this book is available from the British Library.

Library of Congress Cataloging-in-Publication Data

Green, Duncan.

    Hidden lives : voices of children in Latin America and the Caribbean / Duncan Green.
       p. cm.
    Includes bibliographical references and index.
    ISBN 0–304–33689–0 (hardcover) 0–304–33688–2 (paperback)
    1. Poor children—Latin America—Social conditions. 2. Poor children—Caribbean Area—Social conditions. 3. Child welfare—Latin America. 4. Child welfare—Caribbean Area. I. Title.
HQ792.L3G74 1998
305.23'09729—dc21   97–34290
                                                    CIP

ISBN 0–304–33689–0 (hardback)

       0–304–33688–2 (paperback)

Cover photograph: Julio Etchart/Save the Children

Typeset by Ben Cracknell Studios

Printed and bound in Italy by Giunti Industrie Grafiche

Contents

Books from the Latin America Bureau

The Latin America Bureau (LAB) publishes books on contemporary issues in Latin America and the Caribbean. Current titles include:

- *Introductions to Latin American and Caribbean society and culture, economics and politics*

- *Country guides – Bolivia, Venezuela, Jamaica, Cuba, Colombia, Mexico, Argentina, Brazil, Ecuador and the Eastern Caribbean*

- *A series on Latin American and Caribbean women's lives and experiences*

- *Latin American authors in translation: from street gangs to salsa, from rubber tappers to guerrilla radio stations*

LAB is also publisher of Duncan Green's *Silent Revolution: The Rise of Market Economics in Latin America* (co-published with Cassell) and the bestselling introduction to the region – *Faces of Latin America*.
Other highlights from the LAB list include:

- *Return of the Indian: Conquest and Revival in the Americas* by Phillip Wearne (co-published with Cassell)

- *Religion in the Megacity: Catholic and Protestant Portraits from Latin America* by Phillip Berryman

- *Machos, Maricones and Gays: Cuba and Homosexuality* by Ian Lumsden

For a free LAB Books catalogue, write to LAB, Dept HL, 1 Amwell Street, London EC1R 1UL or call 0171 278 2829.

Acknowledgements

An enormous number of individuals have been involved in the writing of this book. First and foremost are the children themselves, who spoke openly and without apparent surprise to a strange gringo who appeared among them for an afternoon and then promptly disappeared again. In view of the dangerous circumstances in which many of them live, children's names (but not genders) have been changed throughout. In many cases, their trust came from the presence of local workers from a variety of non-governmental organizations (NGOs) and local representatives of Save the Children, whose dedicated accompaniment of children across the region provided me with a bridge to children in the most difficult of situations.

I cannot begin to name all of the people who made this book possible, but would like at least to thank the following: for the initial idea for the book and support throughout, Sylvia Beales and Peter Oakley; for their generous financial support, Save the Children UK, Rädda Barnen, CAFOD, the World Council of Churches, the Columban Fathers and Christian Aid. For help with the fieldwork and/or invaluable comments on draft sections of the manuscript: Denise Allen, Gustavo d'Angelo, Katy Barnett, Emma Cain, Patricia Cervantes, Adrienne Clements, Ana Dourado, Isa Ferreira, Tobias Hecht, Elaine Henderson, Edda Ivan-Smith, Andy Jowett, Martin Kelsey, Leif Lahne, Rachel Marcus, Chris McIvor, Brian Milne, Rocío Mojica, Hermione Singer, Jez Stoner and Ricardo Villanueva.

To my mother Jean,
my children Calum and Finlay,
and my wife Catherine

Introduction

Any visitor to Latin America and the Caribbean is struck by the number of children. They are everywhere – hanging out in gangs on street corners, darting between shoppers' legs in crowded streets and squares, dragging protesting younger brothers and sisters in their wake, quietly working on market stalls, thrusting hands through car windows in search of a few coins, sniffing glue on park benches or confidently setting off to school in immaculate uniforms. It is not just the numbers (37 per cent of the population of Latin America and the Caribbean are under 16, compared to just 21 per cent in the industrialized world[1]), but their visibility. In the North, most children inhabit a relatively private world, at least until their teens. They spend most of the time at home or in school, and if they venture out in public, they are generally accompanying adults, or being ferried to and from friends' houses or various activities. Such a closeted world also exists in middle-class Latin America, but that only accounts for a small proportion of its children. Most children are poor, and for them, the street is part of daily life from the time they can walk.

Hidden Lives may therefore seem a perverse choice for a title, but although children are ever-present, their lives largely remain invisible. They are seen, but not heard and almost never listened to. Consequently, adults have little idea of what their lives are like, what choices they make, how they see their futures or what they want. Unfortunately, this even applies to many adults who play an important role in determining policies which affect children's lives. Save the Children likens this 'invisibility' to the situation regarding women and society two or three decades ago, before the increasing awareness of women's specific economic and social contribution began to transform planning and policy-making.[2]

Images of childhood

Visitors also frequently remark on the precocity of Latin American children. Serious-faced eight-year-olds serve you in the market, tiny girls boss their baby brothers and sisters in mimicry of their mothers. In the shape of working or street children, this early maturity is often seen as 'unnatural', caused by poverty and neglect which have 'robbed them of their childhood'. Such children evoke enormous pity and sympathy among kind-hearted

Westerners, and have become a central part of the region's image in the West.

In making such judgements, adults draw on their notions of what childhood *should* be like – in the words of one author, 'the mythic walled garden of happy, safe, protected, innocent childhood'.[3] Yet unlike the facts of biological immaturity, 'childhood' is a social institution, a reflection of cultural values and social behaviour, rather than something innate. Moreover, a particular child's experience is hugely influenced by factors such as class, gender, and a country's position in the global pecking order, all of which are socially determined.

In historical terms, it is the privatized world of Northern children that is the aberration. The image of 'normal' childhood has changed rapidly in the North over recent centuries. In a ground-breaking study of childhood in Europe,[4] historian Philippe Ariès showed that prior to the seventeenth century, children were seen (and dressed) as miniature adults, adults and children played the same games together, and child sexuality was accepted as natural. Ariès concluded:

> In medieval society the idea of childhood did not exist; this is not to suggest that children were neglected, forsaken or despised. The idea of childhood is not to be confused with affection for children ... . As soon as the child could live without the constant solicitude of his mother, his nanny or his cradle-rocker, he belonged to adult society.[5]

From the fifteenth century on, children began to be seen as different from adults, amusing creatures to be dandled, coddled and cooed over, although the new fashions annoyed stick-in-the-muds like the French essayist Montaigne, who grumbled:

> I cannot abide that passion for caressing new-born children, which have neither mental activities nor recognisable bodily shape by which to make themselves loveable, and I have never willingly suffered them to be fed in my presence.[6]

Once established as different from adults, children were gradually removed from their society, largely through the introduction of formal education, at first among the middle classes, but then spreading across the social spectrum.

As late as the eighteenth century, childhood in Britain still resembled the lives of children in the Third World today. Daniel Defoe said in 1724 that all children over the age of four or five could earn their own bread. Apprenticeship was compulsory after the age of 12 and some began as young as seven. Boys of 11 joined the army.[7] Up to that point, family life in Britain had been lived far more in the streets, and had not yet retreated behind the front doors of its nation of shopkeepers.[8]

Since that time, children's lives and adult conceptions of childhood in the North have changed radically. As economies developed and became more complex, child labour gave way to the need for skilled workers and school became the 'natural' place for children to be. Initially, school life was relatively brief. In 1833, a British Royal Commission declared that at the age of 13, 'the period of childhood ... ceases'.[9] But the length of childhood has grown inexorably, reflected in the periodic raising of the school leaving age.

As children began to be seen (and treated) as separate and different, so adults began to see them as vulnerable and in need of protection, although this was always tempered by the rival view that children, as inheritors of original sin, were in particular need of correction. Hanna More, a conservative writer during the industrial revolution in Britain, wrote:

> Is it not a fundamental error to consider children as innocent beings, whose little weaknesses may, perhaps, want some correction, rather than as beings who bring into the world a corrupt nature and evil dispositions, which it should be the great end of education to rectify?[10]

This dichotomy, between children as barbarians who must be controlled, or as innocents in need of protection, is reflected in their portrayal in literature – on the one hand the frail vulnerability of Oliver Twist, on the other the instinctive savagery of the children in *Lord of the Flies*. But whether as sinners in need of correction, or innocents requiring protection, the new notions of childhood effectively disempowered children:

> The modern conception of childhood – which dates from the 16th century and stresses the innocence and frailty of children – forcefully ejected children from the worlds of work, sexuality and politics, and designated the classroom as the major focus of children's lives. Children were no longer allowed to earn money or to decide how to spend their time; they were forced into dependency on adults and obliged to study or play. Cute, contented and dependent, but without autonomy in important decisions concerning their lives, children 'should be seen and not heard'.[11]

Such views have been entrenched by the way in which children are studied and understood. In the countless books and papers written about childhood development, most portray children, 'like the laboratory rat, as being at the mercy of external stimuli: passive and conforming'. Studies generally ignore the rich and separate world of children, preferring 'a conventional view of socialization as a moulding process carried out by adults. Little attention is paid to childhood as a phenomenon in itself or to children as active participants in their own rearing process.'[12]

Media coverage of children has further distorted the picture. Lurid tales of organ trafficking and child adoption rackets make good television, whereas children wrestling with the mundane tasks of everyday life do not. This book deliberately eschews some of these more sensationalist angles, since they only affect a tiny number of children.

The view of children as passive, helpless creatures in need of protection, education and health care has dominated official thinking at government level and within organizations such as the UN for much of this century. One afternoon spent in the company of children from any poor community soon dispels the fundraisers' portrait of the silent, suffering victim, and in recent years a new approach has started to gain ground. Children are increasingly being seen for what they are, human beings with their own ideas and experiences and their own inherent human rights. In Latin America, this is often described as seeing children as *subjects*, rather than just *objects*. While these rights include the more traditional conceptions of the right to protection or education, they also include previously unacknowledged rights, such as freedom of expression and the right to a voice, at least in the decisions which directly affect children.

This new official view of children was recognized in the 1989 UN Convention on the Rights of the Child, discussed in detail in Chapter 8. In the words of one expert, 'More than any previous treaties, the Convention recognises the child's capacity to act independently, bestowing not just protective, but also enabling rights, such as the right to freedom of expression and association.'[13] In Latin America and the Caribbean, many child rights activists see the Convention, and the changes it has spurred within the region, as a watershed in the lives and prospects of the region's children.

About this book

This book is written in the spirit of the Convention and its new approach to the lives of children. At its centre is an attempt to portray the lives of children through their own words, based on visits by the author in 1995 to Jamaica, Honduras, Nicaragua, Peru, Colombia and Brazil, backed up by previous visits to other countries, secondary sources and interviews. Giving children 'the word', as people say in Latin America, entails a different approach. It means trying, as far as any adult can, to see their lives through their own eyes, suspending judgement in order to understand what their lives feel like from the inside.

Hidden Lives is about poor children, the most hidden of all. It does not dwell on the lives of middle-class children, although they constitute a sizeable number (although always a minority) in some of the more developed Latin American countries. Both outside and within the region, poor children are the least understood; their opinions on work, education and child rights are seldom given a hearing.

Listening to children makes it impossible to portray them as a single 'object', whether as hero, victim or villain: children's experiences are multi-faceted. Most of the stereotypes are wrong. Street children argue, laugh, play, have sex, steal and sniff glue, as well as lie awake at night in fear of their lives. Many of them are on the street not because they have been abandoned, but because they themselves have decided to abandon impoverished or abusive homes. Working children often insist on going to school, even when many parents feel (not without reason, given the state of the Latin American education system) that they learn more from work than from sitting in class.

One of the aspects of life in Latin America and the Caribbean which continues to inspire outsiders is the energy, inventiveness and solidarity with which poor communities confront the difficulties that surround them. Given the failings, corruption and incompetence of many state services, such self-help is often essential to survival. *Hidden Lives* tries to give at least a taste of that daily battle, and the extent to which Latin Americans are helping themselves. In particular, the book looks at some examples where these self-help initiatives are involving children in fighting to improve their lives.

Hidden Lives starts where children begin their lives, in the family – not the neat nuclear myth which dominates even Latin American television advertisements, but the messy, fluid, multi-faceted families of the poor, where children grow up and learn their values. One of those values is the need for hard work, and Chapter 2 deals with the thorny issue of working children, intentionally steering clear of the term 'child labour', with all its negative connotations, until the subject has been better explored.

Although the majority of working children are domestic servants or work on the family farm, the most visible child workers in Latin America and the Caribbean are those who work on the street, and *Hidden Lives* goes on to explore the myths and realities surrounding the 'street children' of the region, whose sufferings, particularly at the hands of police and the death squads in Brazil, have provoked world-wide condemnation. With both working and street children, talking to the objects of all the interest leads to unexpected, and perhaps controversial, conclusions.

Children in Latin America and the Caribbean live in a violent world, and the book goes on to explore two causes of that violence: crime and politics. Children commit crimes as well as suffer from them, and Chapter 4 investigates the lives of child criminals such as gang members and under-age prostitutes, both male and female. It also shows the treatment meted out by authorities to under-age suspects. *Hidden Lives* then examines one of the more brutal ways of dealing with child criminals and other 'undesirables' – murder, otherwise known as 'social cleansing'.

Latin America has long been associated with political violence in the shape of military dictatorship and guerrilla warfare, and Chapter 5 looks at the effect of political violence on children, whether in 'displaced' families fleeing the violence of Colombia's paramilitary hit squads, as child combatants in guerrilla armies, or as victims of military anti-guerrilla campaigns in Central America or the Andes.

Children's lives are deeply affected by the economic policies pursued by governments, and Chapter 6 explores the impact on children of the current wave of free market reforms sweeping across Latin America and the Caribbean. Chapter 7 then focuses on the state of children's health and education, examining the challenges facing the region's dilapidated social services, as well as particular issues such as the spread of HIV/AIDS. Even within tight restrictions on spending, improvements can be made, and *Hidden Lives* explores some of the many exciting new experiments in community and child-run health and education schemes which are trying to overhaul existing systems.

Much literature on children in the Third World falls into the trap of devoting inordinate amounts of space to projects run by innumerable NGOs. All too often, the formula is: outline a problem, and then describe the project that will solve it. While they can help challenge and improve government practices and bring much-needed help to a limited number of individuals, NGO projects on their own can never hope to cater to the mass of the region's children – there just is not enough money. NGOs increasingly believe that acting as advocates for children and lobbying governments, rather than simply running small projects, is more likely to make a difference at the national level. Projects can also help in testing out new techniques which, if successful, can then be adopted by state structures. *Hidden Lives* tries to avoid excessive reference to projects. However, Chapter 8 is an exception, revealing some inspiring results of the new approach to children's rights, in the shape of a new generation of projects run *by* children, rather than *for* them. The chapter explores the debate over children's rights and participation in the decisions which affect their lives, before going on to examine the UN Convention and its impact in the region.

In many ways, writing a child-focused book is an impossible task – adults cannot see through a child's eyes without to some degree projecting their own anxieties, values or needs. But other adults all over Latin America and beyond are busy prescribing solutions for the many difficulties faced by its children, and if they want them to be effective, they have to try and put themselves in the children's shoes, learning to listen and suspend judgement in order to understand their lives, choices and desires. Children in Latin America and the Caribbean do not face a neat choice between a 'normal' protected Western childhood and their own. Instead, they must grapple with the daily threats, opportunities and choices taking place in their own worlds. Unlike adults, children are rarely outraged or discouraged about the lives they lead, and invariably have clear ideas about how they could be improved. They need empathy and support, not pity. In trying to uncover the hidden lives of children, this book is intended as a contribution to that effort.

Notes

1 UNICEF, *State of the World's Children 1996* (New York, 1996), p. 99.

2 SCF UK, *Towards a Children's Agenda* (London, 1995), p. 33.

3 Allison James and Alan Prout (eds), *Constructing and Reconstructing Childhood* (Basingstoke, 1990), p. 2.

4 Philippe Ariès, *Centuries of Childhood* (London, 1962).

5 *Ibid.*, p. 125.

6 Cited in Ariès, *op. cit.*, p. 127.

7 Martin Hoyles, *The Politics of Childhood* (London, 1989), p. 18.

8 Judith Ennew, 'Outside childhood: street children and rights', in Bob Franklin (ed.), *The Handbook of Children's Rights* (London, 1995), p. 201.

9 Cited in Harry Hendrick, 'Constructions and reconstructions of British childhood, 1800 to the present', in Allison James and Alan Prout (eds), *Constructing and Reconstructing Childhood* (Basingstoke, 1990), p. 42.

10 Cited in Harry Hendrick, *op. cit.*, p. 39.

11 Bob Franklin, 'The case for children's rights: a progress report', in Bob Franklin (ed.), *op. cit.*, p. 7.

12 Allison James and Alan Prout (eds), *op. cit.*, p. 18.

13 Jo Boyden, 'Childhood and the policy makers: a comparative perspective on the globalisation of childhood', in Allison James and Alan Prout (eds), *op. cit.*, p. 193.

CHAPTER 1

Home Sweet Home

The Family

Delilah can reel off the names of her ten children, but she has to count up their fathers on her fingers. She reaches five, including the rapist who left her pregnant with her youngest child in the Jamaican tourist town of Montego Bay. One father, the only one who gave her money for the children, is dead; another has emigrated to America; the others are nowhere to be found. As each 'baby father' abandoned her, finding a new one was the best option:

> *The first baby father and me, we used to drive a car and live happy. Then we mash up and he go to 'nother woman and leave me with four children. Easiest way to get money was to find another man and have more children. Me not even care about family planning at that time.*

Now, looking back, she regrets becoming a 'baby mother' to so many men and wishes she had not had her first child at 16. Life is hard for a single mother in a Jamaican shanty town:

> *Sunday we not eat nuttin. Me borrow money from a neighbour. Sometimes the children run away to sea or market to hustle food. Days and I don't see them. Two run away on Saturday. Me fret when they run away. Can't sleep at night — it's all the pressure.*

She worries constantly about the older boys:

> *Vincent [14] have sickle-cell — have to buy tablet at drug store and he need plenty vegetable and milk but me can't afford it. Give him plenty beetroot and carrot. When it bad for a week, he feel pain in all his joints and him refuse food.*

> *Clive [12] act strange. Me think he mentally abnormal. Anything good, he destroy it. Him not learning at school. When me leave baby with him today, he cut the baby. Sometimes I lick [hit] him with me hand.*

Delilah is trying to keep her family together, but the forces ranged against her seem overpowering:

I live in one room, rented in Norwood [a Montego Bay shanty town]. The rent now due long time – I may have to leave. Get water from neighbour but have to steal it. If they catch me, they fling rock-stone. No electric. One bed broken, but have to sleep there anyway.

When they don't go to school, they just run away. I only got one girl and she run away too. Kids don't have clothes – sometimes they steal. Vincent ran off last night and I had to get up at 2am and go find him. I found him dancing and drinking alcohol – it will kill him, with his sickle cell.

Vincent, a tongue-tied beanpole in Bermuda shorts and laceless shoes, feels he had little choice about leaving home:

I ran away 'cause I was hungry. Nothing at home to eat. My big brother beat me up when there no food. When I got hungry, I went to the market to look for food – I didn't find any so I stayed hungry over the weekend. A lady gave me something to eat, some banana and a cake. I get more food at the market than at home.

But the lure of the streets is not just about food:

When I run away I can go to the show house to see movies and ask the gateman if he can let me in. I go to dance hall – I like dancing, reggae music.

With painful clarity, Delilah can see her son drifting away from her, and feels helpless as the cycle repeats itself:

If my sons running away from home now, when they become a big man, they gonna run away from them baby mother too. They not show me any love now – they'll be the same then. The treatment they get as a youth, as an adult they use it themself. Only way to stop it repeating is the children need more love from me. Sometime I neglect them and I don't know what to do. Then they're gone.

Families in Jamaica are in constant flux. Nuclear families, where mother, father and children live under one roof, are in the minority. Most children grow up in other arrangements – being raised by a single mother, a grandmother, an aunt, or in an extended household spanning the generations. Adults come and go. Children are passed from one household to another, often to relatives, but also to neighbours who need help at home or on the market stall. As one study of child labour in Jamaica concluded:

There is thus a constellation of blood relations who may be involved, at one time or another, in parenting a particular child. These include grandparents, parents, aunts, uncles and even older siblings. In

Chores start young: collecting firewood in Peru.

addition stepfathers, stepmothers and a variety of step-siblings may be incorporated into the household. Both fostering and unofficial adoption are common. It is not unusual for one or both parents to migrate to another area, or even overseas, leaving a child in the care of a grandmother, aunt or friend.[1]

Such a pattern creates a 'shifting population of children' who 'learn to think of themselves as independent proto-adults'.

To a lesser degree, such fluidity can be found in family structures across Latin America and the Caribbean. There is no such thing as *the* Latin American family. Any attempt to specify what is a 'normal' family arrangement and what is 'abnormal' among the numerous different ways in which children are raised and socialized usually says more about the person doing the specifying than about real life in Latin America.

Children in Latin America and the Caribbean grow up knowing that they may have to move between homes and be raised by a range of adults. For a child, any family structure brings with it a combination of good and bad, benefits and risks. Moreover, no particular situation completely determines his or her chances. A large household full of different generations of adults can provide more stimulus, companionship and love than the harassed parents in a nuclear family, or it can leave a child feeling utterly lost, passed from uncaring adult to uncaring adult; a grandmother no longer in work can make a wonderful full-time parent or become an exhausted and irritable tyrant; *regalitos* (little presents), as Colombian children given away by their parents are known,[2] may be just as loved as any other child, or may end up as little more than slaves in their new homes.

Yet for all its diversity, the family remains the basic unit of Latin American society, taking the crucial decisions over a child's early life in terms of work, schooling and even whether they should be given away to another family. The starting point for any study of Latin America's children must be an attempt to unravel the true nature of the rapidly evolving, varied family structures in which they are raised.

Shrinking families

The pace of change in the Latin American and Caribbean family is startling. In the 1950s, the average Latin American woman had six children. Now that figure has almost halved.[3] The causes of such a rapid fall in childbearing include the more widespread availability of contraception, the spread in girls' education, and the rate of urbanization. Since World War II, the region's exploding shanty towns have eclipsed its rural villages. In the shanty towns, large families can be a liability: women have to go out to work as maids or in the markets, and since they have left their families in the countryside, there is often no-one at home to look after the children.

Diversity has increased both within and between countries. Poor countries such as Bolivia, Haiti and Nicaragua still have large families, while those in Argentina, Cuba and Chile more closely resemble 'Northern' family models.[4] Within each country, family size depends greatly on income and women's education: poor, uneducated women have much larger families than better-off or more educated ones.

Although woman-headed households have always been a feature in many Latin American and Caribbean countries, family breakdown and the number of woman-headed households have been rising in recent decades. As more women raise families on their own, according to one authoritative study:

> Men are increasingly seen as shadowy figures, drifting in and out of the family and avoiding responsibility. In the absence of a productive role within the family, they become isolated from it. Increasingly, home is a place they reject.[5]

Some of the explanation is economic. Over the last 15 years, Latin America and the Caribbean have been going through an economic upheaval known as 'structural adjustment' (see Chapter 6). This has entailed a reduction in the role of government and an increased emphasis on the market. In social terms it has meant a sharp rise in job insecurity, an increase in the number of women in paid jobs, and increased economic pressure on families through rising poverty, unemployment and falling wages. At the same time, the spread of television and the rising proportion of the population who live in the cities have brought consumer society within sight, if not within the grasp, of Latin America's poor.

Falling wages, coupled with the rise of consumer expectations, have made it impossible for most men to play the traditional role as sole breadwinners for their families. As in Europe and North America, male unemployment has risen, just as more and more women have gone out to work, leading to an increased questioning of male power within the home and the loss of male self-esteem. Across the region, men have reacted to this loss of identity, not by taking on a greater role in the home, but by turning to the bottle (always a prominent feature of male lifestyles in Latin America), and violence, and often by abandoning the family altogether.

In the shanty towns inhabited by Latin America's dispossessed millions, women have always played a prominent role, often as single mothers. The recent rise in marital breakdown has merely reinforced the supremacy of the mother figure in the hearts of the region's children, captured in the commonly heard saying 'you've only got one mother – your father could be any sonofabitch'.

For good or ill, the mother is the central point of emotional reference for any Latin American child. In some cases, particularly in the Caribbean, men may be left looking after children when mothers migrate in search of work. In general, however, fathers are peripheral figures in the adult–child relationship, absent except for the fear they induce. Children who have left home, often with good reason, continue to brood on their relationship with their mother, as in the case of Gabriela, a 19-year-old from Brazil:

> Sometimes she gave me a good beating when I deserved it, because that's what all mothers do – if a kid deserves it, they have to give them a good hiding. When my mother started beating me, I ran away, to the street. And then my mother upped and died. I went on the game and bought her a good coffin. At least that's one thing she couldn't complain about.[6]

Single mothers face a bone-wearying task in raising a family and putting food on the table, in countries with only the most threadbare of welfare 'safety nets' to help them. Forced to spend long periods earning money, single mothers are less able to develop and maintain reciprocal networks with their neighbours, sharing and exchanging childcare, food and other help, even though they need such support more than anyone. They are frequently left isolated and exhausted by their solitary struggle.

One classic account of the daily grind is a diary kept in the 1950s by a single mother in a favela in Rio de Janeiro, published in English as *Beyond All Pity: The Diary of Carolina Maria de Jesus*.[7] Carolina records the daily feuds and brutality of favela life, and the endless round of grinding anxiety in raising three children by scavenging for paper and tin to sell, or for food to eat:

> May 13: I feel so sorry for my children. When they see the things to eat that I come home with, they shout 'Viva Mamãe!' Their outbursts please me. But I've lost the habit of smiling. Ten minutes later they want more food.

> July 20: What an ordeal it is to search for paper. I have to carry my daughter Vera Eunice. She is only two years old and doesn't like to stay at home. I bore the weight of the sack on my head and the weight of Vera Eunice in my arms. Sometimes it makes me angry. Then I get a hold of myself. She's not guilty because she's in the world.

> May 20: How horrible it is to see a child eat and ask: 'Is there more?' This word 'more' keeps ringing in a mother's head as she looks in the pot.

May 22: The money didn't stretch far enough to buy meat, so I cooked macaroni with a carrot. It was horrible. Vera was the only one who complained, yet asked for more. 'Mama, sell me to Dona Julita because she has delicious food.'

June 1: It's four o'clock – I've just made lunch. Today there was lunch. We had rice, beans, cabbage and sausage. When I cook four dishes I think that I'm really someone. When I see my children eating rice and beans, I smile stupidly. I watched the boys playing ball. They run around the field showing off their energy. I think: if they could drink fresh milk and eat meat …

August 3: Today the children are only going to get bread and beans with farinha [manioc flour] to eat. I'm so tired that I can't even stand up. I'm cold. Thank God we're not starving. He is helping me. I'm confused and don't know what to do. I'm walking from one side to the other because I can't stand being in a shack as bare as this. A house that doesn't have a fire in the stove is so sad!

Whether women are actually worse off as single mothers depends on the alternatives on offer. Many women faced with drunken, abusive, unemployed men in the home are better off without them, both emotionally and materially. This is even more the case for children: although woman-headed households earn less than others, a far greater proportion of the income is spent on food and other essentials for the children, whereas men typically retain a proportion of their wages for their own personal use. Some studies suggest that children may even eat better in woman-headed households as a result.[8]

Country life

Just as in any European or North American family, children growing up in Latin America and the Caribbean play, work, bicker, fight and learn about themselves and their world, but, in general, they spend more time working and less time playing than children in richer countries. In the homes of the poor, chores start early, especially for girls, and increase steadily as the years pass.

In the countryside a girl's life can be particularly arduous, according to Ana, 13, a skinny, poised girl from a peasant family in Brazil's parched interior:

I live with my mother, father and nine brothers and sisters, aged between two and nineteen. I get up around 6, brush my teeth, have a coffee and feed the hens. Then I have to fetch water and it's getting further and further away with the oxcart. We get it from the wells with two big oil drums – that lasts us through the day.

Hands that rock the cradle: shanty town families in Spanish Town, Jamaica.
Jamaican families rarely conform to the nuclear family model.

Then I have housework to do, sweeping, cleaning, making the beds or doing the washing. Just the girls – the boys work in the fields. After I've done my chores I go to the fields and feed the animals with left-overs. I also have to look after my little brothers and sisters at the same time as doing the housework.

The girls cook lunch, beans, rice, eggs. Some days we have meat, but not much at the moment. We eat better when the rains come. After lunch I go to school. Our house has three rooms. I share a room with five others – each of us has a hammock or a bed. Two of the babies died at 9 months and a year. One from diarrhoea, one from a urinary infection. That was a while ago.

I get back from school around 5 and go out to look after the animals and help with the hens. I do my homework in the evening by gaslight. Sometimes we visit friends after dinner and chat and play.

I want to have fewer kids than my mother – it wears you out to have so many. Four's a good number – two of each!

In rural Guatemala, adolescence barely exists. Indian children are considered adults after their tenth birthday, according to the Nobel Peace Prize winner, Rigoberta Menchú, whose autobiography gives a fascinating, if somewhat idealized, insight into Indian lifestyles.[9]

When you reach the age of ten, your family and the whole community holds a meeting. It's very important. It initiated me into adult life. I'm no longer a child, I become a woman.[10]

At the meeting, her parents and older brothers and sisters explained what an adult's life would be like:

They told me I would have many ambitions, but I wouldn't have the opportunity to realise them. They said my life wouldn't change, it would go on the same – work, poverty, suffering … . Suddenly they treated me like an adult. My father said; 'You have a lot of responsibility; you have many duties to fulfil in our community as an adult. From now on you must contribute to the common good.[10]

According to Rigoberta Menchú, boys are favoured over girls even at birth, when male babies are greeted with special celebrations and feasting. The different expectations are established straight away:

When the baby joins the community [at a ceremony held forty days after the birth], with him in the circle of candles he will have his hoe, his machete, his axe and all the tools he will need in life. These will be his playthings. A little girl will have her washing board and all the things she will need when she grows up. She must learn the things of the house, to clean, to wash, and sew her brothers' trousers …[11]

Thereafter, girls in rural homes generally fare worse than boys, as this interview with a Paraguayan peasant woman makes clear:

It starts at birth. When a baby girl is born people say that she's going to be a burden on the family, that she's not going to contribute anything, but it's completely untrue because women have always worked more than men. It starts from the age of four or five when we have to help our mothers with the housework and the younger children. Peasant children begin to work at five years old, looking after the animals or collecting the crops or helping in the home, but whereas the little boys can find time to play, the girls never do. I was the oldest of 11 children, so when I was seven I had to help in the fields; there wasn't time for going to school, let alone playing.

The men have this idea that a woman isn't trustworthy. When we're ten years old the father says 'now you're grown up I can't trust you any more'. After that girls can't go out alone so they can't go to school. They say 'girls only pretend to study but really they're going off with men'. They say girls don't need to study to get married and have children. The only thing we are taught is that we're inferior to boys. I was often top of the class but I couldn't continue studying. There was no way out except to go to the cities, to find work in the houses of rich people.

A girl has to submit herself to her father or brother or husband because they say she can't look after herself and she needs someone to tell her what to do. There's a lot of violence in the homes but it's hidden. The women don't want to talk about it. Women are beaten or raped by their husbands or older brothers or fathers. They can't speak out or defend themselves because they are women.[12]

In the Haitian countryside, hundreds of thousands of rural children are routinely given away as part of the practice of *restavek* (from the French *rester avec*, 'to stay with').[13] Poor rural families give their children to a family living in one of the larger cities, such as the capital, Port-au-Prince, in the hope that the city will give them a better life than the parched, barren world of rural Haiti, where 80 per cent of families live below the poverty line. Those in search of restaveks, either a member of the employing family, or an intermediary, travel to the countryside to find suitably desperate peasant families, who normally give the children away for free. Restaveks are seen as unpaid labour, a commodity to be ruthlessly exploited. Children

Daughters and mothers: a young Honduran girl looks after her baby brother.

as young as four or five are given away, often losing all contact with their original family. Without schooling, health care, or anywhere to turn to for help, restaveks are little more than child slaves.

Marie is about seven years old (she does not know her real age). She is one of four restaveks in a middle-class Port-au-Prince household. From 5 a.m. every day, Marie works her way through a mound of chores, takes the family's five-year-old son to and from school and runs errands. The mother regularly beats her with a leather strap. The two other restavek girls (overall, roughly three-fifths of the restaveks are girls) perform similar tasks, although, since they are older, they do the cooking as well. The remaining restavek, a boy, does heavier manual work such as cutting wood. The restaveks do not go to school, eat leftovers or cornmeal rather than sharing in the family's meals, have ragged clothes and no shoes, and sleep on the floor. They are not even allowed to bathe in the water they carry to the house from a nearby well.

Shanty town life

Life for children in the shanty towns of urban Latin America is little better. David, 11, lives with his mother, three brothers and malnourished baby sister in a smoke-blackened wooden hut on the outskirts of the Honduran capital of Tegucigalpa. Sunlight burns through the chinks in the rough-hewn planks, forming globs of colour on the uneven trodden-earth floor. Flies buzz in the heat. Everything smells of sweat and smoke. The two single beds are draped in dirty blankets – 'we keep each other warm!', laughs David. The tin roof, held down by rocks, is rusty, so a plastic sheet slung across the room acts as a second line of defence against the rain.

The shanty town is well-established, and over the years some residents have upgraded their shacks into brick houses, adding second storeys, even garden walls hung with flowering creepers. Other families, like David's, remain trapped in poverty. Twenty-two thousand people live in this shanty town, 70 per cent of them under 18:

We started selling wood when I was six. We cut firewood and drag it down here, bundle it up and sell it. We also clean out the ditches and run errands, or sweep for people. I like hauling wood – it means I can help mum buy coffee and bread. It's better to work as well as go to school. We give half the money to mum and I use the rest to buy food – tortillas and salt usually. When I'm hungry, I like everything. I'm hungry a lot.

Sometimes we get home tired from school and we can't be bothered to collect wood, so we play – we've got lots of friends round here. We play ball, checkers, marbles, chess.

I like reading and studying. I do my homework with a candle on the floor. If God wishes, I'll make something of my life – become a solderer or a shopkeeper. I wouldn't want to live on the street – it's really ugly and I'm too shy.

If I had a magic wand, I'd make this place pretty, so that my mother could take time off and relax – she works too hard. I'd make the house big and have more beds and a television. I'd really like a bike one day, if God wishes.

Despite their workloads, shanty town children have more time for play than in rural areas, although the environment is often more dangerous for playing in. There is little or nothing in the way of parks or playgrounds, but they do not let that stop them. In every Latin American or Caribbean *barrio*, the sky is dotted with kites, ingenious home-made constructions of sticks, plastic bags and paper, rising like quivering slivers of beauty and hope out of the grime, as they are expertly coaxed aloft by barefoot children weaving between the houses and stagnant drainage ditches. Shanty towns are always full of children racing about, chasing animals or indulging in another favourite pastime, lobbing prodigious rocks at each other (and unfortunate bystanders). They are noisy places, full of children's voices and blaring radios; public places, with kids in and out of their neighbours' houses, demanding treats or dodging blows.

In the past, living conditions in the shanty towns, although difficult, have been better than in the countryside. Infant mortality and malnutrition rates are lower and schools more readily available. These have been some of the key factors in driving the continent's urbanization in recent years, as millions of families have fled the impoverished countryside for the limited blessings of the city. In recent years, however, poverty has risen sharply in urban areas, while economic austerity programmes have entailed cut-backs in state services such as schools and health clinics.

The dark side is, if anything, darker than in rural areas. The proximity of the city brings the twin scents of excitement and danger. 'The street seduces them with its freedom,' says Jesús Pérez Espinoza, who works in the Honduran town of San Pedro Sula trying to prevent children from abandoning their homes: 'They can be free of parents or older brothers and sisters; it offers them money; they get curious about *resistol* [glue], try it and that's when they start to fall.'

Boys, especially, flee their overcrowded, hungry shacks for the exhilaration of street life. Often, parents encourage them, relying on their wages from working on the streets, although, once on the street, boys may end up abandoning home altogether.

The violence of life in Jamaica's shanty towns can be intoxicating for teenage boys. 'When war is sweet you have to laugh' says one teenager in

Montego Bay, describing the gang war currently ripping his neighbourhood apart. The boys love the excitement, seeing 'the men dance'. 'I love the charging', says another – invading enemy territory armed with knives and bottles. The boys proudly admit to taking part, gathering bottles for the 'big men' to throw, although they are careful not to waste the soft drink bottles, which carry a deposit on them.

Girls have fewer choices – parents are more insistent on keeping them at home to help with the domestic chores, and often keep them on an oppressively tight leash, as one young Mexican woman recalled in Oscar Lewis' classic study, *The Children of Sánchez*:

> Girls do not confide in their mothers. If girls say they have a boyfriend, they get a beating; if they ask for permission to go to the movies, they get screamed at and called sluts, prostitutes, shameless hussies. These words hurt and that's why, when a boy makes an offer, they accept. Many girls go off, not because they are hot, but to spite their fathers, mothers, and brothers. The girls are like holy water fonts, everyone lays hands on them. He who doesn't hit them for one thing, hits them for another. Mexican daughters are really mistreated at home. That's why there are so many unmarried mothers.[14]

Middle-class children

According to UNICEF, 'most of the region's children are poor, and most of the poor are children'.[15] Nevertheless, a significant proportion (though much smaller than in Europe or North America) belong to the middle class, with parents who earn a regular salary and can afford to feed and clothe their children. Their parents worry about familiar issues like mortgages, keeping their jobs and finding the right school for their children, although the school is more likely to be private in Latin America (as is health care), given the dilapidated state system.

Middle-class children look different from poor children. They are taller, they wear the latest US trends, and their skins bear none of the scars and blemishes which pock the arms and legs of the poor, the legacy of untreated cuts and infected mosquito bites in the dank shacks of the shanty towns. In the more comfortable homes, middle-class children in Latin America are like well-off children in the USA, only more so. Children, especially boys, are not expected to do anything for themselves – maids (or sometimes mothers) pick up their clothes, tidy away the dishes, and clean their rooms.

In Brazil, the rise in violent crime has generated a kind of apartheid between middle-class and poor children.

In Recife, [most] grow up not in houses but in flats [behind] a wall beyond which the kids normally venture only when accompanied by adults. They are shuttled by car from home to school. The street is known to [well-off] children as a place through which they pass in automobiles travelling at high speeds. [They] stay at home until they marry.[16]

In recent years, many of the free market economic reforms currently in vogue in Latin America have hit the middle class hard. White-collar jobs, especially in the public sector, have been cut, while the growing gulf between state and private provision in health care and education leaves parents with agonizing choices and an uphill struggle if they are to give their children a decent start.

Tobias Hecht, a US anthropologist who has spent years with the street children of Brazil, believes that middle-class and poor families have a fundamentally different relationship with their children. Among the families of the better-off, children are *nurtured,* pampered by parents and maids who shower them with attention, toys and encouragement and expect little in return. In the families of the poor, children are seen as *nurturing*, expected to help their mothers by taking part in the domestic chores and, especially with boys, by bringing in an income from an early age. Poor children share this world view, eagerly awaiting the day when they can go out to work and fulfil their proper role.[17]

Other authors put this difference down to Latin America's history. Lewis Aptekar, who studied family structures in the Colombian city of Cali, contrasted the male-dominated families of the Spanish (or English, in parts of the Caribbean) colonizers, with the mother-centred structures of both the indigenous inhabitants and the imported African slaves, who together form the bedrock of the poor in many countries. The European model is the nuclear family, with the father at its centre, while the African/ indigenous model is built around the mother, with other female relatives such as aunts and grandmothers likely to play a greater part than the biological father (who is often absent) in raising the child.

These ethnic differences have become inseparable from differences of class and social status. Given the region's history of conquest and slavery, black or indigenous families are far more likely to be poor, as were mixed blood (*mestizo*) families as racial intermixing increased, while white families are more likely to be prosperous. As a result, better-off families are more likely to exhibit 'European', nuclear forms, while the poor are more likely to have women-headed or more fluid family structures. This could explain why Latin America's own elite show so little understanding of family life

Environmental concerns: poor children in the Haitian capital of Port-au-Prince grow up next to polluted canals.

among the poor, often being the first to castigate them for their supposed promiscuity and fecklessness.

The prominence of women-centred families also suggests the need for a reappraisal of the stereotype of the submissive Latin American woman, oppressed by the machismo of her partner and society at large. This portrait may apply more to middle-class and rural families than to the urban poor, indigenous or black communities.[18] While women in the shanty towns face an array of problems, such as domestic violence and greater poverty (in the case of woman-headed households), and have often been abandoned, rather than choosing to be on their own, strong, independent women are not seen as an aberration. In countries such as Jamaica or Brazil, they are often the norm, and accepted as such, unlike in many middle-class or rural families, where machismo forces women to conform to the stereotyped roles of submissive, dependent wives and mothers, at the mercy of men.

Domestic violence

Sarita's serious demeanour belies her six years. She comes from an Andean peasant community in Peru where her parents decided to send her to an aunt's, hoping that she would be put through school. It nearly killed her:

> I had to look after the baby – I was three years old and I had to carry the baby on my back in a blanket. They beat me with sticks because I couldn't cook. They both used to beat me at the same time. I had blood on my chin and ears and head. They said I'd stolen their money. One day my dad and granny came to visit and asked why I looked so bad. They told them I had fallen over with the baby and they went away again.

> They broke my hand and foot. A señor who was a doctor cured my foot and hand. Now my foot only hurts when other children at school step on it. When they broke my hand and foot they left me there on the floor and stopped giving me food. I died for a time, then I woke up.

After her aunt abandoned her in the locked house, Sarita was discovered when the neighbours heard her sobbing. Police had to break the door down. They found her unconscious (which is what she means by 'I died for a time'), her wounds covered in congealed blood. Since her rescue, she has been adopted by a child rights worker in Cusco.

The UN Convention on the Rights of the Child obliges signatory states to take 'all appropriate measures … to protect the child from all forms of physical or mental violence, injury or abuse … while in the care of parents or any other person who has the care of the child'.[19] However, in most parts of Latin America and the Caribbean, beating children is seen as an acceptable form of punishment, though not usually with the sadism inflicted on Sarita. As one street child explained to his friend, 'she beats me because she's a mother'.[20]

In the fluid world of the Latin American home, the worst beatings are often handed out by stepfathers and stepmothers, rather than parents. Battering by stepfathers is the commonest reason given by street children for leaving home. Physical abuse is worse in poor homes, where the stresses of life can tip parents and other adults over the edge, as a local priest explains in Cusco:

> *Peruvian society is very authoritarian, and when you live in poverty any mistake or accident becomes a disaster and is severely punished. If a kid loses a sheep, he heads for the hills and won't come back. The responsibility is too great for that age.*

In Peru, parents and teachers beat children not only with belts, but also with a vicious-looking version of the cat o' nine tails.[21]

Of course, not all families beat their children, but the greater the stress on the family, the greater the likelihood of disagreements, quarrels and fights. Unfortunately, it is precisely families with numerous small children that face the greatest difficulties in the daily struggle to survive. The phenomenon is neither new, nor confined to Latin America – a much-loved Victorian nursery rhyme captures the agonies of the single poor mother in Britain a hundred and fifty years ago:

> There was an old lady, who lived in a shoe.
> She had so many children, she knew not what to do.
> She gave them all soup without any bread.
> And whipped them all soundly and sent them to bed.

In rural areas (and older, more established, urban communities), the extended family can act as a buffer, helping young couples through the hard times with money and offers of childcare. Family support also exists in the shanty towns, where recent migrants usually stay with relatives or friends until they get established. But life in the shanty towns is more unpredictable and frantic than in the rural villages; job insecurity, crime and family breakdown can all suddenly undermine a once-stable home. Children who grow up on the city streets often rebel against the values and constraints imposed by their more conservative parents. Amid the endless negotiations over how to spend limited income, and the conflicting demands, angry, frustrated men often end up beating their wives and children.

The cycle of domestic violence passes down through the generations, as 'children learn that it is OK to hit people you love; for powerful people to hit less powerful people; to use hitting to achieve some goal; to hit as an end in itself'.[22]

Power and conflict within the family mirror broader power relations, with adult men at the top of the pecking order, and girls at the bottom. Disabled children, especially those who cannot speak, are particularly at risk, both because they can add enormously to the family's workload, and because they cannot bear witness to their suffering. Men take the lion's share of income and food, and sons often imitate their fathers in using physical and verbal intimidation against younger brothers and sisters. In such circumstances, woman-headed families are often less violent, more egalitarian places, although mothers also beat their children, while the eldest son often takes over the paternal role.

While domestic violence is often seen as nothing to be ashamed of, families make great efforts to keep sexual abuse a secret from their neighbours. Although figures are impossible to verify, sexual abuse is undoubtedly widespread. Thousands of children, particularly girls, live the same daily torment as Márcia, a 10-year-old from a Recife shanty town:

My mum and dad were fighting me and I started feeling sick, so he started beating me around my legs. I had to go to hospital. Sometimes my father lies down beside me when I'm watching TV and touches me between the legs. Then I go to sleep with my mother.

Once I was sleeping in the same bed as my mum and dad, but mum left and he started touching me. When I told my mother she threatened him with the police, but he's always beating me and my sisters. He does it when he's drunk – he often beats my mother, too.

I would tell the police, but I don't want them to beat him, at least not too much. I don't think he loves me, but I love him.

My mother went to the police three times, but he always says he earns all the money. All of us have been to the police, but mum always refuses to prosecute. Despite everything he does to her, she says she still loves him, and she depends on him for money.

Again, poverty both increases the likelihood of abuse, and makes it harder for the mother to leave the father, once the truth emerges. The majority of children suffering sexual abuse are girls (over 80 per cent, according to statistics from Honduras[23]). Mothers often find this so hard to accept that they blame their daughters for 'egging on' the father, and the child may be the one who is punished or expelled from the home as a result.

In the short term, children suffer physical and mental injury from both physical and sexual abuse, including frequent bouts of depression and

Heavy duty: girls collecting water for their homes in northeast Brazil.

anxiety. The loss of self-esteem can be crippling – a study of child prostitutes in Central America showed that half of them were initially abused by a father, uncle, brother or stepfather.[24] Abused children are also more likely to become drug users or to attempt suicide.

In the longer term, sexually abused children, especially boys, are more likely to become abusers themselves, when they have children, or to engage in sexual activity with younger children, once out on the streets.

Rebuilding the community

For the pessimists, the traffic is all one way. The Latin American family is fragmenting, broken by the pace of economic and social change and the destruction of old community structures in the drift to the shanty towns. For some local critics, these 'cities of outsiders' represent:

> the final stage of a process of destruction of many very important ties in an individual's life, cultural, social and psychological ties. Often the family is destroyed, the community is destroyed, the relationship with the land in the interior of the country is destroyed. It is a process of destroying these people.[25]

But this apocalyptic view of family and community collapse in the cities ignores the new structures that are emerging, at both state and community level, which compensate, at least partially, for the loss of traditional forms of family and community life. Across Latin America and the Caribbean, numerous initiatives are trying to curb the levels of domestic violence and abuse.

In Peru, dozens of child rights 'defensorías' are trying to raise public awareness and concern, at the same time as taking up particular cases of abuse in the courts. A similar process is happening with the 'conselhos tutelares' in Brazil, which has also established a network of women's police stations, staffed by women police officers. These have made denouncing cases of violence in the home far easier for women who were previously accustomed to mockery and disdain when they complained to policemen. Public education campaigns run by NGOs have also helped break down the taboos surrounding the private world of the Latin American home, breaking the silence that surrounds some of the horrors that go on within.

Furthermore, families in Latin America are seldom passive. Self-help is the only route to survival, and in many shanty towns people are coming together to build new communities out of the rubble of the old. Parents' determination to fight for their children has become one of the most important rallying points for such an effort. As the head of one Brazilian NGO explains:

We find that if we talk about police violence in the communities, the people will listen and say nothing. But when you start to talk about violence in the community and children – they really open up and you can mobilise every group, the theatre group, the church, the neighbours' association – everybody is concerned.[26]

Children can enable otherwise divided communities to overcome their differences. Jamaica's Spanish Town is riven by warfare between rival gangs affiliated to the country's two main political parties. One of the few places where parents from both parties can meet and talk is at the parenting groups organized by local child welfare workers to discuss how to ensure that children attend school. The group organizes fundraising and other activities to support its children's education, as well as getting parents directly involved in school.[27]

One of the most effective self-help efforts is Peru's network of 'Glass of Milk' committees. Set up in 1984 to provide feeding supplements to pregnant and nursing mothers, and children under six, the committees now feed over a million people.[28] With support from local and national government, the committees' aim, according to one of their founders, is to reverse the process through which 'milk for the impoverished majority of our country, has become a memory, a mythical food', to be replaced by tea, with minimal nutritional value.[29] The committees took off with astonishing speed, rapidly turning into vocal defenders of children's right to adequate nutrition, fending off guerrilla attacks and government attempts to cut back their budgets. The committees also became a catalyst for women's organization in the shanty towns – by 1994, there were over 12,000 Glass of Milk committees in Lima alone, almost exclusively run by 200,000 shanty town women.[30] Once the women got organized, the role of the committees rapidly broadened, as one activist from the Andean city of Huancayo recalls:

We soon saw the other problems. When the children were standing in line waiting for their glass of milk, we could see the nutritional problems, the problems at home. So we started to meet and talk about problems, like how to get hold of kerosene. We got everyone to come to talks about health, hygiene, nutrition. We started to organise activities so we could broaden the programme to food other than milk. We started to think of organising a soup kitchen.[31]

The Glass of Milk committees and other similar initiatives are transforming the face of both community life and politics across Latin America and the Caribbean. Increasingly, the poor are looking to transform their lives at the grassroots. Through their own organizations, Latin Americans are fighting the faceless forces of exclusion and social disintegration which are breaking up families and sending children out onto the streets.

Conclusion

Anyone seeking to understand the lives of children in Latin America and the Caribbean, be they street children, working children, school pupils or peasant children, must start with the family. Understanding the Latin American family means jettisoning ideas of what is 'normal', ideas which usually entail passing judgement on other family structures as aberrant and undesirable. Across the region, the 'normal' nuclear family is more common on the Europeanized billboards and television commercials of the continent than in the real lives of the poor. Instead, it means trying to grasp the extraordinary variety of the region's family structures, their fluidity and their emotional complexity.

It also means studying how the processes which are changing the face of Latin America and the Caribbean affect its families and, through them, its children. Poverty, inequality, the pace of economic change, and discrimination on the grounds of race or sex, all affect a child's life chances, as well as other, more positive, factors, such as the rise in community organization and the growing recognition of children's rights and the importance of child participation in any plan or project aiming to improve their lives. All these influences combine with the innate talents and energy of each child to forge the next generation, and with it the region's future.

Notes

1 Judith Ennew and Pansy Young, *Child Labour in Jamaica* (London, 1981), p. 21.

2 Lewis Aptekar, *Street Children of Cali* (Durham NC, 1988), p. 40.

3 CEPAL, *Cambios en el Perfil de las Familias* (Santiago, 1993), p. 35.

4 *Ibid.*, p. 65.

5 Jo Boyden, *Children of the Cities* (London, 1991), p. 19.

6 CBCA-Casa de Passagem, *Meninas de Rua do Recife* (Recife, 1992), p. 30.

7 Carolina Maria de Jesus, *Beyond All Pity: The Diary of Carolina Maria de Jesus* (London, 1990).

8 Mercedes González de la Rocha, *The Resources of Poverty: Women and Survival in a Mexican City* (Oxford, 1994), p. 32., and UNRISD, *States of Disarray: The Social*

Effects of Globalization (Geneva, 1995), p. 145.

9 Elisabeth Burgos-Debray (ed.), *I Rigoberta Menchú: An Indian Woman in Guatemala* (London, 1984).

10 *Ibid.*, p. 48.

11 *Ibid.*, p. 14.

12 Jo Fisher, *Out of the Shadows: Women, Resistance and Politics in South America* (London, 1993), p. 78.

13 This section is based on Minnesota Lawyers International Human Rights Committee, *Restavek: Child Domestic Labor in Haiti* (Minneapolis, August 1990).

14 Oscar Lewis, *The Children of Sánchez: Autobiography of a Mexican Family* (Harmondsworth, 1961), p. 153.

15 UNICEF, *Children of the Americas* (Bogotá, 1992), p. 7.

16 Tobias Hecht, *At Home in the Street: Street Children of Recife, Brazil* (Recife, 1995), p. 116 (draft).

17 *Ibid.*, p. 118.

18 Lewis Aptekar, *op cit.*, p. 160.

19 UN Convention on the Rights of the Child (Geneva, 1989), Article 19.

20 Tobias Hecht, *op cit.*, p. 121.

21 SCF UK, *Peru Draft Country Situation Analysis* (Lima, 1994), p. 16.

22 Annie Allsebrook and Anthony Swift, *Broken Promise: The World of Endangered Children* (Sevenoaks, 1989), p. 28.

23 Save the Children Británica, *Pininos* (Tegucigalpa, August 1996), p. 23.

24 *Ibid.*, p. 17.

25 Recife favela development worker, quoted in Annie Allsebrook and Anthony Swift, *op. cit.*, p. 53.

26 *Ibid.*, p. 214.

27 SCF UK, *Spanish Town Marginalised Youth Programme* (mimeo) (Kingston, February 1994).

28 Aida García Naranjo Morales, *Nosotras, las Mujeres del Vaso de Leche 1984–1994* (Lima, 1994), p. 113.

29 *Ibid.*, p. 96.

30 *Ibid.*, p. 109.

31 *Ibid.*, p. 180.

CHAPTER 2

All Work and No Play?

Working Children

By 6 a.m. in the market of San Pedro Sula, Honduras, horses are hauling carts loaded with pineapples, bananas and vegetables to the market stalls, sending up sweet smells of pineapple, coriander and rain (from last night's thunderstorm). When not sweating under their loads, horses munch cabbage leaves from the road. At this hour the market is largely a male preserve, as men load and unload the wagons and handcarts. The boxes of fruit display the logos of Chiquita and Dole, two of the banana multinationals that have dominated Honduras for over a century. A barefoot street child throws rotten fruit at the head of a younger one, perched on a cart. Both look tired and resentful.

As the traffic builds up, smog starts to clog the dawn sky. The first school uniforms appear. On the corner two small girls, aged perhaps five or six, are collating the newspaper supplements ready for sale. Everyone is chewing on mangoes. A group of teenage girls lounge around a table, each turning out tortillas from a huge ball of dough. Their bored, indolent faces contrast with the speed of their hands, mechanically but expertly slapping and patting the dough.

At 13, Marina is already part of Central America's tortilla production line. A diminutive, blonde girl with a prominent nose, she sports the ubiquitous market woman's apron, as she struggles back to her stall – a rickety table covered in blue plastic – with a large bucket of water. A charcoal brazier under a griddle stands ready for the tortillas. Marina's father comes past, face hidden under the obligatory straw cowboy hat, pushing hard on a handcart with wobbly wheels.

> *At 4 am I leave home with my dad. He's a porter in the market, so we come to work together – it's an hour's bus ride. I prepare the dough for the tortillas before the patrona arrives – she takes care of the selling. I finish around 10am, then I go home to eat. At 2pm, I change and go to the Academy – I'm learning dress-making (I've finished primary school). Academy finishes at 4, then I go home and help mum with the housework.*

I get about $2.70 a day, and give about $1.60 to my mum. I keep the rest for the Academy and all my materials. Some of the regulars buy me a drink or an avocado – today I even got sixty cents extra in tips.

My boss is a friend of my dad's. She asked me to come and wash her plates once, then she decided to give me work. Before then, I worked for another señora washing plates, but she bossed me about a lot, so I left after a month.

I like working. We were always bored at home. Here in the market I see lots of people, not just my mother and brothers. At home there was nothing much to eat – here I eat all the time!

Marina is typical of millions of child workers all over Latin America and the Caribbean. From as young as five or six, poor children start their working lives, either on the street or in the home. From then on, they must juggle the conflicting demands of school, work and home as best they can. Discussion of their work is complicated by the lack of reliable statistics. Much of the work performed by children, particularly domestic labour either in the home or as maids, as well as much agricultural work on the family farm, is invisible and fails to figure in surveys or statistics on child labour. Furthermore, neat definitions of what is and is not work are impossible when there is no clear dividing line between chores in the home and work which contributes to family income, or releases older relatives to go out to work.

Although they are probably underestimates, UN figures give a hint of the extent of child work, with one in five 10–14-year-olds working in Brazil, Honduras and Haiti, and more than one in 10 in most Latin American and Caribbean countries. The International Labour Organization (ILO) puts the figure for the total number of working children in Latin America and the Caribbean between 5 and 14 years of age at 17.5 million.[1] The proportions are many times higher among boys than girls, underlining the invisibility of much of girls' labour in the home.[2]

The reasons why children work are complex. Not all poor children work, and nor are all working children poor, but poverty is clearly an important factor. A child's gender also plays a role, as does the quality of schooling, the availability of paid jobs, and the need to care for younger children, animals or the house. On top of these factors, there are important cultural issues – many children want to go out to work, while many parents think work is at least as useful as Latin America's decrepit education system in giving their children a good start in life.

For any child, going out to work brings both benefits and costs. Many working children do not feel coerced, but are proud of their contribution to the family income, while usually having plenty to say about how their

Boys cleaning windscreens at the traffic lights in Kingston, Jamaica. Most working children are employed in such 'informal sector' jobs.

lives as child workers could be improved. By working, children gain self-esteem, skills and respect from their elders. On the other hand, working long hours can rob them of the chance of a decent education, since even if they manage to go to school, they are often too tired to concentrate in class. There are also more direct costs, in jobs where children run serious risks of damage to their health from poisonous chemicals, dust or workplace accidents, or simply by placing too much strain on growing bodies.

Adults concerned about the impact of children's work, however, often fail to weigh both the pros and cons of child labour, and rarely consult the children themselves. This can lead to counterproductive attempts to ban child labour through legislation, often making matters worse for the children involved.

Working on the streets

Like Marina, most child workers earn their income in the 'informal sector', a catch-all category that includes all those working on their own account, rather than for a regular wage. In many Latin American and Caribbean countries more people work in the informal sector than in 'regular' jobs. Children are especially likely to be found there, since the informal sector needs no prior qualifications, start-up capital or papers. Furthermore, it functions largely outside government control, making any existing child labour laws irrelevant. The hours are flexible, and can be fitted around school or other commitments, and often it can take place under the supervision of a parent, relative or friend, which on Latin America's perilous streets is a reassurance to both family and child. As one Lima market woman explains, 'I don't want my daughter to go out to work. The temptation of the devil is on all sides. I prefer her to sell potatoes here, where I can keep an eye on her.'[3]

In recent years the informal sector has been booming, as government austerity programmes have driven millions out of regular work, while firms have cut costs by adopting the new fashion of 'casualization', farming out production to home-workers and sweat shops in trades such as textiles and shoe-making. Nearly nine out of every 10 of the new jobs created in the first five years of the 1990s were in the informal sector.[4] In this brave new world of 'flexible working patterns', children are often perfect employees – the cheapest to hire, the easiest to fire and the least likely to protest. The informal sector's most visible child members are the street workers, described in lyrical terms by one Peruvian working children's organization:

> Working children swarm through the streets of Lima, they spring up
> at each corner, they are on the move day and night across the city,
> children, big and little, young boys and girls, alone, in twos, in small

35

groups, near their relatives or on their own, winter and summer, rain or shine, in the Ciudad or La Parada markets, in the inner city squares, opposite supermarkets, in car parks, in discotheques, at traffic lights, in bus stations, train stations, at the airport, in parks, at the seaside. Doing one, a hundred, a thousand jobs: taking fares on buses, singing on buses, selling on the street on their own patch or on the move, selling biscuits, sweets, chocolates, toilet paper, detergent, shampoo, food, trinkets, watering flowers in cemeteries, washing cars, keeping an eye on cars, selling newspapers, selling hot herbal drinks, pushing barrows, selling ice-cream, plucking chickens, collecting rubbish, buying bottles and paper, helping in carpenters' workshops, washing up, crushing sea-snails, cleaning shellfish, selling plastic covers for identity papers, hawking lottery tickets, mending shoes in the street, carrying luggage, wrapping goods, knitting, gardening, looking after children, clearing away guts from market stalls …[5]

Maids and housewives

Most children working in the street are boys, both because families are more fearful of letting girls work there, and because girls typically do housework, either at home, releasing their mothers to go out to work, or as maids in the houses of relatives or, more often, strangers.

The ILO believes that unpaid work performed for their families, particularly by girls, makes up 80 per cent of all child work.[6] Most children are given chores as soon as they can walk, and girls rapidly acquire enormous responsibilities within the home, as this 11-year-old Jamaican girl's school essay shows:

It was on a Friday when I was absent from school, because my mother wasn't going to be at home, and I had to stay home.

On that particular day, I had to stay with my little baby sister which is approximately two months, above all things I had to tidy the house, and give an eye to the shop, because I was the only person at home, except for my smaller brother and sister. They too help me by staying out front and telling me when someone needs to be served. When I'm not in the shop, I'm in the house tidying or nursing the baby.

After I had finished tidying the house I had another problem, and the problem was the baby. Although I had given her a bath and had fed her she didn't want to sleep so I locked the shop and took her up and sang her a rockaby song until she finally went to bed and my problem was solved. Then I opened the shop and as I opened the shop my mother arrived. She was very tired when she came, and I still had to stay in the shop while she went inside and rested awhile. Soon it was nightfall and I went to bed early because I was going out the next morning.[7]

Girls who begin by working in the home often progress to become domestic workers, earning meagre wages for long hours of toil in the houses of other families. The move is often encouraged by the girls' families, who farm them out to relatives or friends. Often, it involves a move from the countryside to the city, and parents hope that the child will get an education and a better start as a result. Children as young as five or six are given away – in Venezuela, one in four of child domestic workers are under 10 years old.[8] In Haiti, hundreds of thousands of children work in this way as *restaveks* (see p. 17), yet few are anything more than virtual slave labourers.

Life for maids is hard. According to the ILO, maids face 'serious psychological and social adjustment problems' when, as young children, they 'work very hard, among unloving adults and in almost total isolation from family and friends'.[9]

Maids are some of the invisible child workers of Latin America and the Caribbean, shut away behind millions of anonymous front doors, forced to work long hours, as Josefina, a 13-year-old Mexican, explains:

The señora is really good to me. I get up at 6.30 and make the breakfast, I help her dress the children for school. After everyone's gone – because she works too – I make the beds, sweep, dust, wash the dishes, put the washing machine on and make a soup for lunch. When the señora comes home she makes lunch, then the children and the señor arrive. Once the meal's over, I wash the dishes again and clean up the kitchen. The afternoon is quieter. On Tuesday and Thursday I iron and the other days I go with her and the children to the park or the supermarket. Sometimes the señora goes out with her friends and I look after the children while they do their homework, but she always comes back for dinner. I help her make it, then wash the dishes again and clean up the kitchen before going to bed, because I have to be up early the next day.

In the afternoons, when I'm not ironing, I watch TV with the children or watch them playing nintendo. It's great fun! I like work; I also used to like school, but when my Dad left I couldn't carry on. Let's hope he comes back![10]

Maids, particularly Indian girls, are often treated as barely human by their middle-class employers, as one 12-year-old Guatemalan girl found out. On her first night:

the mistress called me. The food they gave me was a few beans with some very hard tortillas. There was a dog in the house, a pretty, white, fat dog. When I saw the maid bring out the dog's food – bits of meat, rice, things that the family ate – that hurt me very much. I was lower than the animals in the house.[11]

The girl was Rigoberta Menchú, who later went on to win the Nobel Peace Prize for her work in promoting equal rights for Guatemala's impoverished Indian majority.

As well as the long hours, maids are often at the mercy of their male employers, with predictable consequences. One study of a hundred Peruvian families employing maids found that over half of the adolescent males in the household had their first sexual experience with a housegirl.[12] Often entering the house before their tenth birthday, suddenly bereft of their family ties, maids can easily become emotionally dependent on their employers, exposing them to more subtle forms of abuse, as in this example from Bolivia:

I was still a girl and I wanted to play with their toys. I wanted a doll, everything that they had, but I had to resign myself. My masters forgot that I was also a girl and even younger than some of their children. For them I was just a servant …

Children have the right to play, the right to be children. That's what they say all over the world, but the bosses think it only applies to their own children. I have wondered how it was possible for them to have treated me so differently from their own children. I think it comes from their contempt, because from the cradle, they learn discrimination and racism against the campesinos, who. are also the miners, the maids, the workers.

The old lady explained everything to me, and little by little she made me aware of my class, using words like 'Indians' and 'Yokels' and saying 'You shouldn't be like that, you're going to get civilised here.' When you hear it that often you end up being ashamed and uncomfortable about your own class and finally you find yourself supporting the class of your boss. I thought she loved me because she told me: 'I love you like a daughter; here you have everything.' And I accepted it all.

The truth is that the bosses use us even through love. Without realising, we end up loving them and so we say, 'Ay, my señora is good, she loves me a lot.' We look after her things as though they were our own, and after a while you start identifying totally with her mentality.[13]

Two boys carrying buckets of sand for building work in San Pedro Sula, Honduras.

Agriculture

Most child workers work in agriculture, whether on family plots or large commercial farms. Work on the farm starts even earlier than work in the cities, as Rigoberta Menchú found out:

> I was five and I looked after my little brother [while her mother was cooking for the coffee pickers]. Watching her made me feel useless and weak because I couldn't do anything to help her. I wanted to work, more than anything to help her, both economically and physically. When I turned eight, I started to earn money on the plantation. I set myself the task of picking 35 pounds of coffee a day. Sometimes I picked barely 28 pounds because I got tired, especially when it was very hot. I'd fall asleep under a coffee bush, when suddenly I'd hear my brothers and sisters coming to look for me ... . When I began earning, I felt like an adult, as if I was making a direct contribution to our subsistence. I now felt I was part of the life my parents lived.[14]

Until recently, eight-year-olds were also a regular sight on the sugar plantations of northeast Brazil. South of the regional capital of Recife, the rolling hills are cloaked in sugar, a blanket of spiky leaves. Unseasonal rain is falling, sending up rich wet smells of tarmac and vegetation. Dawn sunlight slants in under the cloud, lighting up the cane lime green against a slate grey sky. The harvest is just beginning and will go on for six months. Cleared patches are just starting to appear; dark brown burnt earth dotted with leftover cane leaves, bleached rapidly by the sun. From the road, numerous tiny figures can be seen chipping away at the green wall of cane, machetes flashing silver in the sun. Some of the figures are smaller than others; boys, working like men. Brazilian law forbids any kind of work by any child under 14 years old, yet even according to official figures, the country has 3.8 million working children between 5 and 14.[15] The ILO singled Brazil out as a priority problem country when it launched its programme for the elimination of child labour in 1990.

By 8 a.m., trucks are already rumbling along, laden with fresh-cut cane for the sugar mills. Lucas, 17, has the prematurely wrinkled feet of an old man. His legs bear the scars of numerous machete wounds. He started work in the fields at 14 but is now back at school, having lost his job after a campaign against child labour by a local trade union centre. The campaign was based on a study which revealed that the child cane-cutters of Recife have a life-expectancy of just 46 years, and work an average 44-hour week; over half have had at least one workplace accident. Six out of 10 cannot read or write (the proportion of illiterate parents is even higher). The study concluded that child labour in the sugar industry was 'a cycle of lost opportunity, irreversible in character, which has afflicted many generations'.[16] The report received widespread coverage in the Brazilian press and seems to have had a remarkable impact – a year ago, cane-cutters of seven and eight were a common sight. Now there is no-one under 13, although aid agency workers claim they are still to be found working on the more remote plantations further away from the road and the prying eyes of outsiders.

Lucas, like many of his friends, has conflicting views on cane-cutting, encapsulating the dilemmas facing child workers:

> *Work on the cane field is bad – I want to study instead. Really, I'd like to leave here and go to São Paulo. But it was better when we were working – now the boss has stopped employing kids and things have got worse. At least then we were earning, and had a bit of cash. Now my family's got very little coming in.*

Parents, too, face a harrowing decision over whether to send their child to work, according to a group of women sitting outside the local evangelical church:

> *It's hard out here – hard to put your kids through school, hard to buy uniforms and books when you've got a lot of kids. Sure, I think kids should only start work when they're 12 or 15, but my daughter's seven and she's already working – washing clothes and plates, cooking.*

Another parent confronts a visiting trade union official with barely concealed hostility: 'why shouldn't my children help me in the fields? We need the money!'

The fields smell of burnt sugar – the leaves are burnt off to make it easier to bring in the cane. Covered in ash, sweating in the rising heat, the cane-cutters can look up and see the plantation owner's whitewashed mansion disfigured by an enormous satellite dish. Brazil's phenomenal social inequality is at its most stark in the northeast.

A dozen barefoot, ash-covered boys come along, sucking on chunks of cane, idly sharpening their machetes with whetstones. They all like working, and are proud of their prowess with the machete. Only one has ever been to the big city of Recife, less than sixty miles away, but they all agree that life in the city is better.

All of them started work by the time they were eight. Now in their early teens, they are cutting from half a ton to a ton a day, and earning about $3. School is not an attractive option: 'I don't want to go to school with a bunch of little kids – I'm big now,' says one 15-year-old, loftily.

In many poor homes, children are expected to work from an early age to increase family incomes. Girls making straw hats in Honduras.

Severino is 13 and has been cutting cane for seven years. He smiles, revealing blackened stumps of teeth already eaten away by the cane, as he explains that he'd rather be working in a shop, selling shoes:

It's better than cane – you don't have accidents and there are no snakes. This life isn't good for kids, you have to be strong to cut properly and you can really hurt yourself. If I can make a better life for myself, I won't want my kids to cut cane.

The mixed local reactions to the impact of the anti-child labour campaign have prompted a rethink on the best way to approach the issue of child labour: 'People in NGOs and at the government level are becoming more aware that abolition is not enough, and can even make matters worse by reducing family incomes still further,' says Isa Ferreira, the Brazilian programme co-ordinator for Save the Children: 'We have to look at broader issues such as how to compensate families for the income they lose when a child stops working.'[17]

Impact on children

When children perform such a vast range of jobs, from near-slavery in the charcoal ovens of the Brazilian rainforest to a couple of hours after school serving in their parents' shop, it is futile to expect a simple answer to the question 'should children work?' Any job inevitably brings a child a combination of costs and benefits, some immediate, some longer term. The same can be said for the impact of a child's work on his or her family, or on society as a whole.

At a busy traffic intersection in the Honduran capital of Tegucigalpa, Don Alfonso shows how children's work can benefit the whole family. Now a grizzled patriarch of 68, Don Alfonso has spent 15 years steering his family through the rapids of the Central American economy. He sits on the pavement next to stacks of today's newspapers, as six of his sons and daughters weave through the choking traffic. When the lights turn to red, the children move up and down the lines of cars in search of customers. Periodically they return to Don Alfonso to exchange their haul of grubby notes for a new supply of papers. The family makes a profit of about eight cents on each paper sold, and business is brisk.

When the time comes, Don Alfonso packs his various children off to school, scattered across the morning and afternoon shifts of the creaking Honduran education system. Franklin, 15, goes to night school from 6 p.m. to 8.30 p.m., even though he has to be up and on the streets by 5.30 the next morning for another seven-hour stint at the traffic lights.

Fifteen years ago, Don Alfonso abandoned his barren farm and headed for the city. By working together with his family, he can keep a firm eye on his children, and he has succeeded in keeping the family united when many others have collapsed. With the proceeds of 15 years at the traffic lights, he has steadily upgraded his shanty town hut into a solid house, with a new tin roof, cement floor and electricity. The walls are hung with family photos and their children's diplomas. Don Alfonso is proudest of his eldest son, who trained as a mechanic and now has a prized regular job in a factory.

Across Central America, adult incomes are so low that children's work plays a vital role in putting food in children's mouths, even though, on average, children earn only half the wage of an adult with the same educational level.[18] One study showed that, of the Central American families with children of working age which have enough to eat and access to basic services such as housing, half rely on children's work. If this was taken away, they would fall below the poverty line.[19] Feeding themselves is not just an immediate need for children, but carries long-term benefits for society, since well-nourished children perform better at school and make more effective future citizens. Research in other countries, however, clouds the issues, suggesting that children's income only marginally affects the wellbeing of the family.

Work can improve a child's treatment within the family, as Juanito, a nine-year-old Mexican street seller, explains:

> Since I was little I've run away from home. I didn't like it because they beat me a lot. I started selling papers and cleaning car windows at the corner. I earned good money and took it to my mother; that's why, when they wanted to hit me, she would defend me. She used to tell my stepfather that I wasn't bad or lazy, that he shouldn't hit me because I was bringing a few pennies into the house.[20]

Across Latin America and the Caribbean, parents frequently see work as good for children, a form of education, and something which keeps them from misbehaving or joining the street gangs. As a father in a Brazilian shoe sweatshop told one journalist, 'I think they should legalise child work, because they learn a lot. I started work at seven.'[21]

In the best cases, the right kind of work, either at home or for money, allows children to grow gradually from dependants into capable adults, renegotiating family relationships along the way as they learn to cook, keep house, care for children and earn money. It is surely no accident that working children are at the forefront of the child rights movement in Latin America and the Caribbean, with dynamic organizations operating in countries such as Peru and Nicaragua. By contrast, it is hard to insist on the innate superiority of the childhood of the bored, disaffected European or middle-class Latin American child, slumped in front of the television waiting for life to begin.

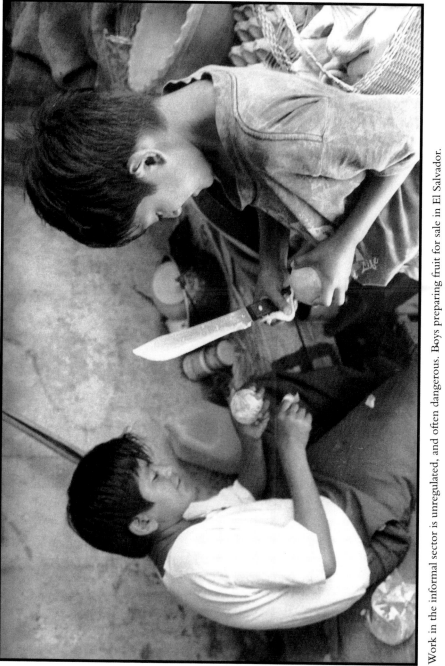

Work in the informal sector is unregulated, and often dangerous. Boys preparing fruit for sale in El Salvador.

Children's work and health

Some kinds of children's work take a horrendous toll on children's health. Growing bodies are especially vulnerable to long hours or bad workplace conditions such as dust, heat, or exposure to dangerous chemicals. In addition, children are more likely to suffer workplace accidents, because they are more tired, do not understand the tools, or are using machinery designed for adults. In domestic work, children run risks from carrying heavy loads, exhaustion and household accidents, as well as the psychological damage caused by the emotional deprivation and isolation of life as a servant.[22]

In the charcoal ovens which feed the giant steelmills of the Brazilian Amazon, inspectors found children as young as nine working a 12-hour day collecting and burning wood. Infectious diseases were rampant, made worse by the dust. 'People have just charcoal inside their chests,' one charcoal burner told an Anti-Slavery International researcher.[23] The meagre wages paid for piece-work exert inexorable pressure on children to work. One charcoal burner explains how hunger drove her to flout both the law and her child's interests in sending her 11-year-old into the ovens:

[The boss] says he doesn't want kids in the ovens and tells us to get them out when the inspectors are coming. But earning piece-work and with all the things he docks wages for, everyone works or we don't eat.[24]

Beauty has a poisonous edge for the hundreds of teenagers who work in the Colombian flower industry, producing thousands of delicate blooms for air shipment to the USA and Europe. One 14-year-old describes conditions in the greenhouses which dot the plain around Bogotá:

I think the flowers are beautiful – especially the roses. We buy the damaged ones to take home. But I hate the work. When you put on the plastic protective clothes you really sweat, and the pesticides are really fierce. They don't tell you which ones are dangerous, just send us off to spray. We get headaches, fevers and the patron won't let us go to hospital. If we don't go to work because we're ill, they take off three days wages. We have no contract – they can just tell us to go home at any time, if they see you standing up, or having a drink of water. But if they banned it we'd have to go and find work somewhere else – I'd like to study but we need the money.

In the sweatshops of Franca, near São Paulo, Brazil's booming shoe exports (the USA imported $1.4 billion of Brazilian shoes in 1993[25]) rely on the work of children like Pedro, 12, who inhales glue from dawn to dusk as he repairs shoes for $30 a month. There are over a thousand family workshops in Franca, and 7 out of every 10 of their workers are children, according to the Franca shoe-makers' union.[26]

Children's work and education

The connection between children's work and education is complicated. In the North, the conventional view, based largely on the experience of Victorian England, is that introducing compulsory education plays a key role in ending child labour. UNICEF holds that the same is true in Latin America,[27] but the key difference between Latin America today and England over a century ago is that most working children already go to school. One survey of 379,000 children aged from 7 to 14 in public and private primary schools in Bogotá found that 87 per cent worked, including those engaged in domestic activities. Over 40 per cent were doing paid work outside the home as well as domestic work within.[28] Surveys suggest that some jobs are easier to combine with school than others. The hardest are mobile street trades such as car washing. In general, girls seem to find it easier to combine school and work.[29]

Merely providing almost universal primary education has not stopped children going out to work, so there must be other factors involved. Save the Children sees poverty as the most significant cause of child work, and believes that structural economic change is required before children stop working.[30]

Although working children often go to school, many do badly. Most Latin American and Caribbean governments have responded to rising enrolment figures by operating a system of two or three different shifts per day. Working children typically study in the evening where, exhausted after a day on the streets, many perform poorly or drop out altogether. Given that working children who still attend school were found to work an average 35-hour week on top of studying, perhaps the surprising fact is that even more do not drop out.[31]

Paradoxically, the inadequacies of the education systems in Latin America and the Caribbean also play a part in forcing children to work. The cost of going to school, in terms of textbooks and uniforms and, increasingly, payments to teachers, can add to the pressure on children to work, as this quote from a Peruvian secondary student reveals:

I work in Lima during the summer months. But I come from Huancayo, a large town in the sierra. I work to put myself through school. Many kids like myself do the same. It is very hard to get jobs in the sierra ... I have already saved 2,000 soles. With this money, I'll buy my uniform, shoes and books. I need more money to pay for my room and board at a family's home near the school which is in the sierra.[32]

The rigidity and boredom of classroom routines also drive children out to work. Children trying to combine work and school find it particularly hard to move from a world in which they are treated as independents and given some level of respect, to the passive conformity of classroom dependence. Many, especially boys, who are more likely to have a hustling job on the streets, reject the role of pupil altogether and give up on school. This could explain why in many Latin American communities, girls' enrolment is higher than boys', in contrast to most of the Third World. Often, children reject the enforced 'infantilism' of the classroom and drop out, only to rue their lost educational opportunities as teenagers, by which time it is extremely hard to make up the lost ground.[33]

Nearly all children in Latin America and the Caribbean start school. The problem lies in the numbers who end up repeating years, or dropping out before completing even their primary education (see Chapter 7). Starting work increases the likelihood of dropping out or falling behind. One UN study showed that Latin American boys who start work between the ages of 13 and 17 accumulate an educational backlog of more than two years compared to those who start work from 18 to 24, although the impact on girls is not so great. Two years less education translates into about 20 per cent less wages for the rest of their working lives – in the end, they lose six times more money than they gain by starting work early.

However, such long-term considerations are a luxury for many families. The study also showed that if they did not work, the incidence of poverty among households with children of working age would go up by 10–20 per cent.[34] Short-term relief is bought only at the cost of future poverty.

Attitudes to children's work

The debates over child labour are often heated, exposing profound differences of opinion over the nature of childhood itself. In the North, even among the most well-intentioned activists and organizations, attitudes to children's work are often tinged with a Eurocentrism which sees it as 'abnormal' for children to work. 'Normal' childhood is seen as a safe haven of play and study, free from the pain and responsibilities of adult life. Yet child work has always been the norm in most of the world, barring the last century of European history. The result can be an inability to grasp the reality of children's lives in most of the world: 'The conventional view is that childhood and work are intrinsically incompatible. As a result, working children are seen as a schizophrenic barbarism: as children they are not real workers, and as workers they are not real children.'[35]

Some jobs are undoubtedly harmful to children, either to their long-term development, or to their immediate health and emotional wellbeing. The first challenge in curbing the damage to children is to distinguish good from bad in the world of children's work. This is sometimes characterized as the difference between 'child labour' and 'child work'. Child *labour* is seen as taking place outside the home, often paid, but with very low wages. It can threaten children's physical, psychological, emotional and social development because they are too young or small for the kind of work, the hours are too long, they are paid too little, and the work is too hard for a small growing body, because it is too dull and repetitive, or simply because it is too dangerous.[36] In contrast, child *work* is seen as a potentially healthy part of a child's development, perhaps learning the ropes on a family farm, or helping out on the family market stall, as long as it does not exclude other important aspects of child development such as play or education.

A further crucial factor is age – operating a lathe may be harmful and dangerous for a seven-year-old, but not for a youth of 14. Campaigners and policy-makers argue over whether there is a cut-off point below which no child should work – UNICEF argues that for children below the age of 12, *all* work should be classified as dangerous.[37] Others disagree, believing that the kind of work matters more than the age of the child. The UN Convention on the Rights of the Child commits signatory states to 'provide for a minimum age or minimum ages for admissions to employment', but does not specify what the age should be.[38]

In general terms, there are three broad currents of opinion on the issue of children's work,[39] as follows.

Abolition

This view holds that children should not work, except for light duties within the family. The proper place for children is in school or at play. Work and education are seen as antithetical. Campaigners for abolition believe that, through employers paying lower wages to children, children's work exerts downward pressure on wages for adults, forcing more families into poverty. As a result, they too must send their children out to work, and so on. Proponents of this view generally downplay the positive side to children's work, along with the detrimental impact on them and their families of ending it. The focus is on abolishing child work, usually through legislation, rather than on dealing with underlying causes such as poverty, social attitudes or the failings of the education system.

Working children's own views are rarely canvassed. Perhaps this is just as well, since children themselves usually oppose abolition. When Paraguayan child workers were asked what they most liked about their lives, their work was the most popular response, well ahead of school, family and playing

Young sugar cane cutters in northeast Brazil. Many working children are proud of the money they take home and prize the status that work brings.

ball (the next best things, apparently).[40] When 1500 Central American child workers were consulted, they came up with a list of their main grievances: they felt they were discriminated against in the workplace simply for being children; street workers and maids feared violence; working conditions and long hours were criticized; and children also resented being deprived of their income (by having to give it to their parents, for example) and freedom.

All of them, however, opposed legislation to outlaw children's work – instead they wanted protection and support. 'If we don't make any money, we can't get better or fix our teeth and goodbye to any chance of studying,' explained one. In the views of those who carried out the survey, such results amounted to a new view of childhood 'very distinct from the "infantilism" that is proposed to them by a paternalistic, adult-oriented society'.[41]

One of the strongest arguments against abolition is that it does not work in practice, and may even make matters worse for the children it seeks to help. Once children's work has been made illegal, it becomes impossible for the state to regulate (since that would be tantamount to sanctioning a crime). Once the work has been pushed underground, wages fall and conditions worsen, but poverty continues to drive families to send their children out to work, deprived of even the minimal protection or rights that existed before abolition. In other cases, as in the sugar fields of northeast Brazil, employers react to campaigns by sacking child workers in a region where no other jobs are available. The result is less food on family tables in communities already blighted by malnutrition and poverty.

One recent trend has been a campaign to include anti-child labour clauses in international trade treaties, often backed up by consumer boycotts in the North aimed at Third World exports which involve child labour. Many organizations in the Third World are deeply suspicious of such trade sanctions. Noting that they most often apply to textiles, an area where First World industries are being undercut by Third World imports, they believe protectionism is at least as much involved as philanthropy.

When they are introduced, such measures are often counterproductive, demonstrating the dangers of trying to help children without addressing the wider causes of child work, or consulting or involving the children in question before acting on their behalf. When the USA threatened to pass legislation preventing the import of products from Bangladesh made by children under 14, garment factory owners sacked thousands of girls, who were forced to exchange their jobs in relatively clean, hygienic textile factories for lower-paid jobs breaking bricks or collecting garbage. Many turned to prostitution.[42]

In Central America, US consumer pressure has also forced clothing factories significantly to reduce their use of child workers. Again, however, the focus has been purely on getting children out of the factories, not on ensuring they are any better off as a result. In late 1996, researchers for the US government's child labour office triumphantly reported that Honduran trade union representatives had told them that pressure from their US buyers had persuaded local factory owners to dismiss 2000 under-age workers, but failed to investigate what had happened to them subsequently.[43] Guatemalan labour leaders told the researchers that the larger factories which are now subject to scrutiny on child labour are increasingly subcontracting work out to smaller firms and family sweatshops, where children work in even worse conditions. Welcoming a report on the issue, US labour secretary Robert Reich showed the superficial and Eurocentric grasp of Third World children's lives which often underlies such measures, saying, 'Private industry recognises that it can take steps to make sure boys and girls are not robbed of their childhood.'[44] For most Central American children, whether working or not, it is a childhood that exists only on television.

Some corporations have attempted to take such criticisms into account. In Bangladesh, Levi-Strauss is paying for the schooling of children under 14 formerly employed in factories from which they buy their clothes. The subcontractors guarantee employment for these children when they leave school.[45]

Children's right to work

At the other end of the spectrum, a number of organizations in Latin America, especially those involving working children, argue that children have a right to work and that 'despite the many questionable and negative elements [of child work], there is also a positive core, a rich potential for autonomy, responsibility, social participation and commitment'.[46] For them, the real problem is the lack of suitable jobs for children, not children's work itself:

> We must recognise work as an integral part of childhood, like play or study, and create conditions which allow it to be restored as an enriching element of the human development of the child ... We must legislate and establish for children, without any age limit, the right to work. Society and the state must guarantee them the same labour rights as adult workers have. On top of that, because of the specific needs of childhood, the state must guarantee the rights contained in the Convention [on the Rights of the Child].[47]

Critics fear that this view both romanticizes children's work and downplays its negative impact on children's development. The working children's organizations who most actively promote this view tend to be dominated by older children, especially boys, who work on the streets.[48] They therefore underestimate the impact of work such as domestic service on younger children and girls. It also appears unnecessarily defeatist – many children work because of the lack of alternatives, either economic or educational, and it seems perverse to codify that kind of deprivation as a 'right to work'. Child campaigners express private concerns that such organizations are sometimes manipulated by adults with their own agenda.

Combined protection and abolition

In practice, the differences between child labour experts and campaigners are usually less polarized, and often revolve around definitions of what is acceptable and unacceptable work for children of a certain age. The middle ground is home to the views of the majority of major children's agencies, such as SCF and UNICEF, along with the ILO. They accept that some children's work may be beneficial, or at least better than the alternative of *not* working. The focus should therefore be on improving children's working conditions while aiming for the elimination of the most exploitative forms of work and tackling the underlying reasons why children work, such as poverty and poor education systems. According to SCF, its:

> overall goal is that children should only work out of their own choice, in ways which assist them to develop educationally, socially and give them useful skills and experience for the future, and not in hazardous, exploitative or educationally limiting occupations. Action both to address the reasons why children work, and to improve their working conditions is necessary. Where working conditions do not compromise children's development, health or education and where children themselves want to work, the 'right to work' argument may be more compelling.[49]

The UN Convention also opts for the centre ground. Under Article 32, signatory states

> recognise the right of the child to be protected from economic exploitation and from performing any work that is likely to be hazardous or to interfere with the child's education, or to be harmful to the child's health or physical, mental, spiritual, moral or social development.

What is to be done?

Legislation is the major tool used by states to regulate child work, whether by passing their own laws, or signing up to international legislation, notably the ILO's Convention 138 Concerning Minimum Ages for Admission to

Employment, and Article 32 of the UN Convention on the Rights of the Child.

Legislation can seek to either regulate or abolish child work. As we have seen, attempts to abolish it often backfire, and attempts to regulate also have their drawbacks. Most laws only cover waged labour, not the informal sector where most children work. Although domestic service is often covered in labour legislation, it is rarely implemented. Children under 12 are often covered only by prohibitive legislation, and therefore have no legal rights, whereas older children may have some legal protection.

In any case, states in Latin America and the Caribbean are notoriously poor at enforcing their laws. Child labour legislation is often little more than an expression of good intentions without the political will or capacity to make them reality. Given the counterproductive impact of some legislation, this may be just as well. On the other hand, child laws have become an important tool for advocacy in the hands of NGOs and other child rights activists, who use them to raise awareness with the children themselves, the authorities that deal with children, and the public at large.

Perhaps most importantly, legislation usually fails to deal with the root of the problem. Laws do not deal with public attitudes to child work and do not attack root causes such as poverty or poor schools.

One of the greatest drawbacks in the way most legislation is drawn up and implemented is the lack of participation by the children who are supposed to benefit from it. Child participation is an issue not only of natural justice, but of common sense. If children had been consulted before US legislation on Bangladesh was proposed, they could have warned of the dangers of 'quick-fix' trade boycotts and much suffering could have been avoided. Instead, legislators often seem more interested in salving their own consciences than in taking on the real challenges facing Third World children.

Governments are not the only 'child-blind' institutions. A 1996 ILO document *Child Labour: What is to be Done?*[50] maps out a detailed international strategy for dealing with the issue, yet its view is quintessentially 'adultist'. The document recommends 'creating a broad social alliance against child labour, involving governments, trade unions, non-governmental organisations, employers, teachers, the media' – everyone except the children themselves.

SCF UK sees child work as a symptom of a much deeper problem and believes that 'addressing poverty and inequality is critical to ending the need for children to work'.[51] It also believes that a radical overhaul of the education system is required to make it relevant and effective for working and non-working children alike. This must involve reforms to the ways education is funded and structured and children are taught, as well as measures to reduce the costs to families of sending children to school, such as those being introduced in several Brazilian cities, guaranteeing a minimum income to poor families who keep their children in school. In the case of working children, educational reform must also involve experimenting with more non-formal, flexible methods which are better able to allow children to combine work and school. Working children have a valuable reservoir of knowledge and experience on which teachers can build, but all too often, this is ignored in favour of the passive rote-learning of irrelevant facts and figures which passes for education in much of Latin America and the Caribbean.

Conclusion

If any working children are asked, it rapidly becomes clear that they do not want immediate abolition, except of the most dangerous jobs. Instead, they want respect for the right to work, and protection in line with the special needs of childhood in terms of education, health and emotional support. By and large, children know what they want and need, and putting them at the centre of the process is the best way to avoid well-meaning but mistaken interventions, instead enabling the children of Latin America and the Caribbean to grow, learn and develop.

In the long term, whether children work or not is likely to depend much more on the way the Latin American economy develops than on debates over the merits of abolition. Lord Shaftesbury was able to abolish child labour in Britain largely because industry had advanced to a point where it needed qualified workers rather than malnourished child slaves. In Latin America and the Caribbean children will continue to go out to work as long as their labour is the only way for their family to survive and the causes of poverty have not been addressed.

Notes

1 ILO, *Child Labour: Targetting the intolerable* (Geneva, 1996) (Press Release).

2 CEPAL, *Anuario Estadístico de América Latina y el Caribe* (Santiago, 1995), p. 34.

3 Giangi Schibotto and Alejandro Cussianovich, *Working Children: Building an Identity* (Lima, 1990), p. 54.

4 Carlos M. Vilas, 'Economic restructuring, neoliberal reforms and the working class in Latin America', in Sandor Halebsky and Richard Harris (eds), *Capital, Power and Inequality in Latin America* (Boulder CO, 1995), pp. 137–163.

5 Giangi Schibotto and Alejandro Cussianovich, *op. cit.*, p. 54.

6 Quoted in Rachel Marcus and Caroline Harper, *Small Hands: Children in the Working World* (London, 1996), p. 9.

7 Judith Ennew and Pansy Young, *Child Labour in Jamaica* (London, 1981), p. 41.

8 ILO, *Child Labour: Targetting the Intolerable* (Geneva, 1996) (Press Release).

9 ILO, *Child Labour: What is to be Done?* (Geneva, 12 June 1996).

10 Sandra Arenal, *No Hay Tiempo para Jugar* (Mexico City, 1991), p. 23.

11 Elisabeth Burgos-Debray (ed.), *I Rigoberta Menchú: An Indian Woman in Guatemala* (London, 1984), p. 91.

12 ICCB Report to the UN Committee on the Rights of the Child (Geneva, 4 October 1993).

13 Ana María Condori, *Mi Despertar* (La Paz, 1988), p. 78 (author's translation).

14 Elisabeth Burgos-Debray, *op. cit.*, p. 34.

15 1995 Brazilian government household survey, cited in *Folha de São Paulo* (São Paulo, 27 October 1996).

16 Centro Josué de Castro, *Os Trabalhadores Invisiveis* (Recife, August 1993).

17 Author interview (London, November 1996).

18 CEPAL, *Panorama Social de América Latina 1995* (Santiago, 1995), p. 58.

19 ILO/UNICEF, *Centroamérica: Los Menores de Edad y El Trabajo* (Guatemala City, September 1993).

20 Sandra Arenal, *op. cit.*, p. 13.

21 'Quem lucra com o trabalho infantil', *Atenção* (São Paulo, December 1995), p. 14.

22 Rachel Marcus and Caroline Harper, *op. cit.*, p. 30.

23 Alison Sutton, *Slavery in Brazil* (London, 1995), p. 71.

24 'Quem lucra com a trabalho infantil', *Atenção* (São Paulo, December 1995), p. 12.

25 US Department of Labor, *By the Sweat and Toil of Children: The Use of Child Labor in American Imports* (Washington, 1994), p. 36.

26 Iolanda Juzak and Jo Azevedo, *Crianças de Fibra* (Rio de Janeiro, 1994), p. 116.

27 UNICEF, *Trabajo Infantil y Educación Básica en América Latina y el Caribe* (mimeo) (Bogotá, 25 October 1996).

28 Cited in Jo Boyden, *The Relationship Between Education and Work* (Florence, September 1994), p. 7.

29 *Ibid.*, p. 8.

30 Rachel Marcus and Martin Kelsey, Report of the Latin American Seminar 'Towards a new Century without Child Labour' (mimeo) (Bogotá, 1996).

31 CEPAL, *Panorama Social de América Latina 1995* (Santiago, 1995), pp. 49–54.

32 Cited in Boyden, *op. cit.*, p. 30.

33 *Ibid.*, p. 14.

34 CEPAL, *Panorama Social de América Latina 1995* (Santiago, 1995), pp. 49–54.

35 Giangi Schibotto and Alejandro Cussianovich, *op. cit.*, p. 93.

36 Judith Ennew, *Street and Working Children: A Guide to Planning* (London, 1994), p. 29.

37 UNICEF, *Trabajo Infantil y Educación Básica en América Latina y el Caribe* (mimeo) (Bogotá, 25 October 1996).

38 UN Convention on the Rights of the Child (Geneva, 1989), Article 32.

39 Rachel Marcus and Caroline Harper, *op. cit.*, p. 13/14.

40 William E. Myers, *Characteristics of Some Urban Working Children: A Comparison of Four Surveys from South America* (mimeo) (1990), p. 19.

41 Manfred Liebel, 'What do working children want?' *Envio* (Managua, Feb./March 1996), p. 36.

42 Rachel Marcus and Caroline Harper, *op. cit.*, p. 50.

43 Child Labour Office, US Department of Labour, *The Apparel Industry and Codes of Conduct: A Solution to the International Child Labour Problem?* (Washington, October 1996), [www.dol.gov.].

44 *Financial Times* (London, 22 October 1996).

45 Rachel Marcus and Caroline Harper, *op. cit.*, p. 51.

46 Giangi Schibotto and Alejandro Cussianovich, *op. cit.*, p. 73.

47 Manfred Liebel, *Ninos Quieren Trabajar, Nueva Tierra Nuestra* (Managua, April/May 1995).

48 Rachel Marcus and Caroline Harper, *op. cit.*, p. 41.

49 *Ibid.*, p. 14.

50 ILO, *Child Labour: What is to be done?* (Geneva, 12 June 1996).

51 Rachel Marcus and Caroline Harper, *op. cit.*, p. 6.

CHAPTER 3

Taking to the Streets

Street Children

Arturo, 11, is a street child, sleeping rough on the streets of the Honduran city of San Pedro Sula. Today he is visiting his family, in the settlement of Casa Quemada (Burnt House) half an hour outside San Pedro, a community established 12 years ago when peasants migrating to the city invaded some land and built their homes. The house lies up a dirt track in fading light. Lush undergrowth hides the shacks. The track is gulleyed by rain and strewn with rubbish, plastic bags and tins. Even before the houses can be seen, the sounds of radios and cocks crowing betray their presence, accompanied by the slap of hands preparing the evening tortillas and a growing chorus of crickets. Woodsmoke mixes with the rich smells of earth in the foothills of the cordillera. Vultures wheel overhead on the evening thermals.

Arturo's parents are Mario, 53, and Ana Maria, 43. Their hut smells of urine and sweat. In contrast to the luxuriance outside, everything is brown and grey – the stamped earth floor, adobe walls, rusting tin roof. They sit on the bed with anxious expressions, explaining that they want to get their son off the streets but feel helpless. The father is grizzled, gap-toothed and lean-bodied; he has a regular job as a security guard in an autoparts distributor. They share the two-room hut with their six other children, and their eldest daughter's newborn baby. The walls are hung with the family's worldly goods – canvas bags, a machete, a plastic Christmas tree, a giant toy dog. Their spare clothes are slung over a rope – everything has to be kept off the ground. Outside, charcoal smokes in a mud oven under a tin lean-to.

Mario speaks softly:

He went away on Sunday. Said he was going to play and never came back. I can't stand it any more. I want to sell this house and move back to the mountains to farm. We'd rather work the land and keep the children with us, maybe grow beans and maize, but there's no land so I have to go into town and that's when they run off.

He never wanted to go to school. Someone even adopted him and bought him pens and paper, but he still didn't go.

Recently, Arturo's mother came home and found him sniffing glue with his friends:

They take no notice of anyone, they waste themselves because they want to. It's so sad to know some vehicle will run them down and we'll never know.

Both of them have given up hope of persuading Arturo to stay at home. Instead, they want him locked up in a secure centre run by the Catholic Church.

Arturo sees it all very differently. A plump, quietly spoken, lisping boy, in jeans and filthy T-shirt, he left home because he was scared:

There was enough to eat at home, but I left because my big sister beats me a lot with light flex. She beats me when she gets fed up with her baby daughter.

But the street is more than just a refuge from domestic violence:

I like being in the street — you have fun, jump cars, climb onto the horses and carts. It's more fun than being at home. I beg and find places to sleep. People give me a few centavos now and then. I hang out with the others. We buy food — rice and beans — and all sleep together.

Yet like almost all street children, Arturo has mixed feelings about his new life, and extremely conventional ambitions:

I suffer when I go to the city — my mummy cries when I leave, and I always tell her I'll come back. The worst thing on the street is the thieves — they've killed people, stabbed people, but I've never robbed anyone. When I'm big I want to work — any kind of work. I want a family.

Arturo also wants to get off glue:

I like glue because it makes me all dizzy, but it makes you puke if you use too much. My friends showed me how to use it, but some days I don't do it. I want to go to the [Catholic Church] Centre — if I stay on the street, I'll go back to glue again. The Centre has playing fields and beds. I'll come out a man, not a bum.

Street children strike a powerful human chord. For many people in Europe and North America, children in Latin America and the Caribbean are almost synonymous with street children and their suffering arouses enormous concern, yet numerous questions remain largely unanswered. Why are they on the streets? How do they spend their days? What are

Street child inhaling glue from a mineral water bottle, Recife, Brazil. Glue is the commonest drug among street children. Over long periods of time, glue-sniffing can cause brain damage and kidney failure.

their dreams? What kind of help do they want from adults? Where do street children end up when they leave the streets?

All too often, children are not listened to, taken seriously, or encouraged to participate in designing the policies and projects which are supposed to help them. As a result, many of these programmes are built on ignorance of children's real lives and aspirations. In the case of street children, the consequence has been a high level of failure rate among street children's projects, and, in some cases, results which have been completely opposite to those intended.

It is remarkable how few of the legion of books on street children actually give space to the words of street children themselves, because even the most superficial of conversations quickly dispels many of the misconceptions that surround them. Listening to the street children talk reveals the pressing need for a fundamental rethink on many of the questions listed above, not least of how sympathetic adults should try to help them improve their lives.

The numbers game

The first, and most basic, source of confusion is the bizarre nature of the numbers game, most clearly demonstrated in the case of Brazil, where journalists routinely quote UNICEF's estimate of seven to eight million street children. Yet when investigators actually tried to count them, setting out in the middle of the night to the places where street children habitually sleep, they were astonished to find that the numbers were in the hundreds, rather than the millions. Fewer than a thousand were found sleeping rough in Brazil's two major cities, Rio de Janeiro and São Paulo.[1] Similar studies suggested a total of 8,000–12,000 in the whole of Peru.[2]

Scaling up from the Brazilian results, and even assuming that only one in three sleeping children had actually been spotted, one researcher came to an estimate for the whole of Brazil of 38,000 children and concluded:

> 38,000, an enormous and frightening number in itself: 38,000 children sleeping, awakening, falling in love, crying, dancing and dying in the streets. The only consolation about this number is that it would suggest that 99.46% of UNICEF's seven million street children were a figment of this institution's distant imagination.[3]

Much of the disparity is caused by confusion over the definition of 'street child'. The common image is of the abandoned urchin without a family, sleeping, hustling and thieving on the streets. In fact, the vast majority of children on the streets of Latin America and the Caribbean have homes to go to, and most return there to sleep for at least some nights of the week. Counting 'street children' in the daytime produces figures many times higher than counting the hard core of homeless children in the middle of the night.[4]

UNICEF has attempted to clarify the issue by distinguishing between children who are 'on' and 'of' the streets. The former, the vast majority, are children who work on the streets but have a home to go to. For the rest, the street *is* home – they are the orphans, children who have left home, or children who have been abandoned by their families.

The logic of charitable fundraising also plays a role in distorting the figures. In recent years, donations have poured into street children's charities and projects, innumerable theses have been written and television documentaries made; the former UK prime minister John Major made the issue his special concern. A veritable street child industry has been created both within Latin America and the Caribbean and beyond. Perhaps unconsciously, that industry has acquired a vested interest in exaggerating the numbers, or blurring the distinctions between children who work on the streets and those who live there. When the numbers are questioned, so is the *raison d'être* of the projects and the livelihood of those that work for them.

But the international interest in Third World street children (often to the exclusion of all other children) stems from much more than exaggerated statistics. Considering their relatively small numbers, street children have aroused extraordinary levels of concern in the North. During the course of writing this book, the author would regularly tell friends and colleagues that he was writing a book on children in Latin America and the Caribbean, and invariably found that people would hear him saying he was writing a book on *street* children. In the eyes of the North, all Third World children have somehow become equated with street children, even though, according to the Brazilian calculation quoted above, they represent less than one in a thousand of Latin America's under-18s.

What can explain the extraordinary resonance of the issue? Street children strike at the heart of public perceptions of childhood, evoking powerful emotions, particularly among middle-class adults, because they see them as an aberration. First, they are in the wrong place. As one author wryly observed, children who play in fields or gardens are not called 'field children' or 'garden children'.[5] In the conventional scheme of things, children belong in the home, at school, or in the poor slums, not in the city centre, under the nose (and often with their hands in the pockets) of decent, adult citizens:

> A street child is, like our definition of dirt, soil that is out of place. Soil in the ground is clean, a potential garden; soil under the fingernails is filth. Likewise a poor, ragged kid running along an

unpaved road in a favela or playing in a field of sugar cane is just a kid. That same child, transposed to the main streets and plazas of town, is a threat, a potentially dangerous 'street kid' … . The very term 'street child' has no meaning in the shantytown.[6]

Furthermore, they are doing the wrong things. Conventional Western views of childhood see it as a protected time when children learn and play within the confines of the family home. Street children beg, sniff glue, steal, fight with bottles and knives, and have sex. They are dirty and dangerous.

The sight of such an 'unnatural' childhood provokes wildly differing emotions in adults. Outside Latin America and the Caribbean the commonest feeling is one of horrified pity, especially over the widely publicized attacks on street children by the police and 'death squads' in countries such as Brazil and Colombia. Such reactions have been encouraged by the numerous charities concentrating on the issue of street children, which have portrayed them as helpless victims of hunger and violence, creating, in the words of one respected expert on children's issues, a 'pornography of misery, which may unloose some brief charitable responses, but fails to change attitudes and policies towards children'.[7]

Paradoxically, street children can also evoke admiration, both in Latin America and the Caribbean and among foreigners who work with them, based on a romantic picture of their lives as 'urban pirates',[8] heroic rebels who have chosen freedom over the suffocation of family and social conformity. Comparisons are invariably made with Huck Finn, Tom Sawyer and the Artful Dodger of *Oliver Twist*.[9]

Sixty years ago, the Brazilian novelist Jorge Amado wrote *Captains of the Sands*, in which he created Latin America's own Artful Dodgers, in the shape of a gang of street kids roaming the docks of the port of Salvador:

> They stole, they fought in the streets, they cursed, they laid black girls on the sand, sometimes they wounded men or police with switchblades or knives. But they were good all the same, they were friends of one another. If they did all that it was because they had no home, no father or mother, their life had no regular meals and they slept in a building that almost had no roof.[10]

But within Latin America, a third stereotype is becoming ever more prevalent. As well as heroes and victims, evoking envy and pity, street children are increasingly seen as villains; dangerous vermin who arouse fear and anger among adults across the social spectrum. Amado's loveable urchins have become today's 'marginals'. The inhabitants of the shanty towns are often the first to defend the work of the death squads in 'cleaning up the streets', even though the filth in question may be their neighbour's children.

Hero, villain or victim; in practice, street children are all of these things. The stereotypes say more about the psychology of the adults involved than the lives of the children. In the chaotic, fast-moving world of Latin America's streets, the cheeky urchins of the morning can easily become the glue-sniffing muggers of the afternoon and the terrified children of the night, huddled together in fear of the dark.

Why go on the streets?

João, 13, is a skinny black boy, dressed only in a pair of tattered shorts. He is currently marking time in a street kids' shelter in the Brazilian city of Salvador:

> *I left home when I was ten because I was selling peanuts and someone stole them. I was too scared to go home because my mother always beat me when I lost stuff. But I still go home to visit – it's nice to see them, especially when there's a party. I'm sad when I think about my mother – I miss her.*

> *The street was good. We played, sniffing glue and we stole, mainly watches and wallets. We slept on a roof next to the river.*

> *I first had sex when I was 11, with another street girl. She never got pregnant – she used the pill. I don't use a condom – I know about AIDS but I don't think about it much. Having sex is when I'm happiest.*

> *When I'm sad I get drunk or sniff glue to get out of it, to feel good about myself. Every day we use glue and grass – I prefer glue. It makes me dizzy and a bit drunk, I sniff it with my friends.*

Street children's own accounts of why they left home differ strikingly from the conventional accounts of helplessness, abandonment and poverty. There are cases of orphans or abandoned children, but for the majority, leaving for the street is a conscious choice of one life over another. Often, for example, only one child from a large family will end up on the streets, while the brothers and sisters stay with their mothers back in the shanty town. For each child, the decision involves a different combination of 'push' factors, driving the child from home, and 'pull' factors, luring the child to the streets.

Home for most poor Latin American children is very far from media images of domestic harmony and comfort. Getting there frequently involves long, arduous journeys from their places of work in the city centres. When they arrive, there is often no food (unless they have brought it home with them), and bed is a mud floor, just as it would be if they stayed on the

Safety in numbers: street children huddle together at night for collective security in Recife, Brazil.

streets.[11] There is simply not that much difference in physical terms, between life on the streets and life at home. In fact, there is some evidence that street children, because they usually earn cash and can buy food, as well as scrounging it at all hours, are actually better nourished than their brothers and sisters who remain at home.[12] When researchers compared Honduran street children with other children working in markets they found that, although the street children had less regular meals, 'second- and third-degree malnutrition has so far been found only among the market children; no such cases have yet been seen among the children of the street'.[13]

As one investigator in Brazil recorded: 'Asked to tell me about all the things in her house, a five-year-old called Negona could only think to mention "mosquitoes and mud". Why then do so many children stay at home?'[14] Campaigners for street children stress the horrific levels of violence inflicted on street children, yet many of them are on the streets because they are fleeing even greater violence at home. In interview after interview, children like João cite domestic violence and sexual abuse (usually of girls) as their reason for leaving home.

In the Jamaican tourist resort of Montego Bay, a roomfull of 10–15-year-old street boys and one girl are talking about their lives on the streets and at home (most of them divide their days and nights between the two). As they talk, one boy is pulled out of the group by an uncle. He cursed his mother this morning and now the uncle has come with a large stick to beat him. As he goes, the others giggle nervously. The boys are loose-limbed and relaxed in shorts and trainers, sprawled around the plastic garden furniture. An electric fan barely stirs the hot, muggy air.

Violence drips off their conversation. Accounts of beatings are greeted with sombre laughs and a perverse sense of pride. There is endless talk of 'licking' [beating], hospitals and stitches:

My mother knocked me with a mop stick and was going to kill me with a stone, and another woman saved me.

My father bust my head with a shovel.

My father threw me sister in a plum tree. I didn't wash up the plate so he beat me with a tyre.

Everything they tell my mother, she believe. She beat me in front of other people to show she can still lick me.

Angriest of all is Derek:

If I had a gun, I'd shoot me father. He wicked and rude. My father tie me to a tree with a long piece of rope and lick me every day. In the end I had to jump in the sea to cool off.

Not only are children driven away from their homes, but the street seduces them, with its promise of excitement, food, money and friends. As Arturo from Casa Quemada in Honduras pointed out, for all its perils, the street can simply be more fun.

The transition from home to street is usually a gradual one. Typically, children who are already working on the streets test the waters, spending a night or two sleeping rough with friends. Slowly, they detach themselves from their families, returning less and less often to the home, although many street children still pay occasional visits to see their mothers or brothers and sisters. Often the move to the street is connected with a change in the family circumstances, as children are sent to live with relatives, parents move, or a new stepfather moves in.

Life on the streets

Life on the street is one of constant mobility. Every day, street children move through a vast panoply of characters, places, deals, threats and possibilities. To survive, they must navigate through the chaos, living on their wits. There is nowhere safe to store clothes or money, so street kids operate in a short-term world – clothes are often worn until dirty or ragged, then thrown away; money is spent before anyone else can steal it. In the 1980s, Lewis Aptekar, a US psychologist, spent a whole day trailing (with their permission) Antonio and Roberto, two 11-year-old Colombian street children, round the streets of Cali to produce a fascinating fly-on-the-street account of their daily voyage:

> They had made an arrangement with Pedro, a security guard, to spend the nights in a quiet corner of one of his buildings in exchange for bringing him cigarettes, food and, occasionally, liquor. Upon leaving 'home' they walked over to El Centro, where the early market was still open. On their way they passed through the park, where for a few minutes they stopped to watch a storyteller who, after talking about the mysteries of women in the Amazon, passed around his hat for money. By offering to do this for him they were able to earn a few pesos. Moving on, they stood very close to a fruit vendor, neither leaving nor asking for anything. They eventually were given a piece of pineapple, which they ate quickly, as they walked on. Seeing an old woman trying to move a heavy box across the street, they offered to help her and in exchange she gave them a few more pesos.
>
> A few blocks later they stopped at the El Paradiso restaurant where they went each morning to exchange washing the front sidewalk with a hose (which they also used for washing themselves) for leftover

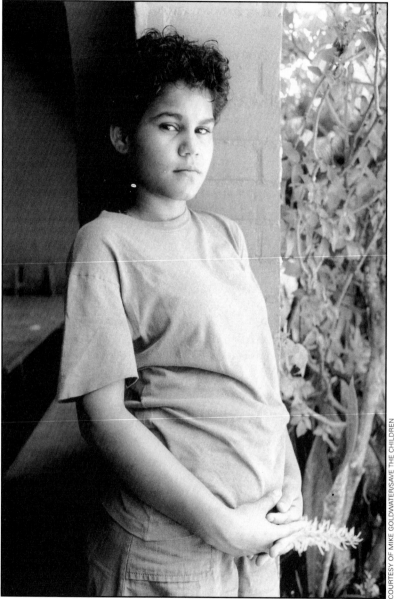

Street children become sexually active from an early age. This 13-year-old from Recife is four months pregnant.

food from the previous night. They went down a quiet side street and began separating the good from the chaff. They ate the few pieces of leftover meat, before throwing the bones as close to a tree as possible in a makeshift contest. Dessert was a conglomerate of sweets that was moulded together in an indiscriminate mass that they ate with their whole hands as they laughed loudly. They put the major part of the food, about two pounds of bread and yucca, back in the bag and took it a few blocks to where they knew a blind man begged. In exchange for their leftovers, they received a few pesos and a couple of cigarettes.

Walking past the movie house on their way to the bus stop, they saw that a new Mexican cowboy movie was playing. They got on the bus and Roberto put on a pitiful expression and began to sing soulfully about the difficulties of having a sick mother whom he was trying to support. He got a few pesos, enough to pay for their ride to the cemetery. Meanwhile, Antonio lodged himself in the exit well, standing in the way of exiting passengers, offering them his hand so that they might climb down more easily. Some passengers were indignant, but a few found his scheme amusing and gave him a peso.

At the cemetery, the two boys met a few older friends and gave them some of the bus money in exchange for a ladder, which they carried over to an area where relatives were visiting a loved one's grave. As it was nearly impossible to place wreaths on the higher grave sites, Roberto and Antonio rented out the use of the ladder. In the early afternoon the boys headed back to the centre and got off the bus when it became bogged down in congestion. They spotted a car with a single passenger and an open window. One of the older boys pounded his fist on the passenger side of the car. The loud noise startled the woman driver and while her attention was distracted the other older boy slipped over to the driver's side, reached into her car and grabbed her shopping bag. Then all four of them ran under a bridge, where they discovered that what they had stolen was only a few pieces of cloth. On their way to Bosconia (a street children's project) for the four o'clock afternoon lunch, they passed a street vendor and exchanged the material for a dozen cigarettes and a few pesos.

After lunch they went to the cowboy movie and took seats in the first row. During the movie they made loud catcalls of appreciation, laughing, clapping their hands and whistling each time someone was killed or when a disadvantaged person gained back his land from the government. After the show they searched the place for cigarette butts.

By now it was evening and they walked down the fashionable sixth avenue, where they were looked upon with disdain by the middle-class shoppers. They stopped in a side street where a young, affluent couple was dining. When the boys asked for food the couple tried to ignore them until finally, the man told them in a loud voice to leave. While Roberto approached the woman from one side and asked once again for something to eat, Antonio came from the other direction and grabbed a piece of meat from the man's plate. Running and laughing, they receded into the darkened street, and returned to Pedro, the vigilante (security guard). They gave him part of it as they tiredly entered their vacant corner, which they called their 'home'. Putting their blankets over themselves, they spent the few minutes before falling asleep planning, not much differently than other eleven year olds, what they would do tomorrow.[15]

Roberto and Antonio survive in large part thanks to their assiduous efforts to build up networks of adults and institutions who can provide food, money, shelter, or free rides on the buses. Each street child cultivates this network of contacts, some of whom help him out of altruism, while others swap food for services such as keeping an eye on their premises or running errands.

The children see the numerous well-intentioned projects intent on 'rescuing' them from the streets largely as just another contact. Their workers want to talk about condoms, jobs, AIDS and education, while children want somewhere to rest, wash their clothes and eat. The children are streetwise and play the field:

the institutions are viewed as one type of fish that falls into their nets. In the same way that kids ask for money in the street, they ask for clothing, food, money and other favours at the institutions. Generally, they are not surprised when they do not get what they request, but this by no means prevents them from insisting. And if there's no meat in the stew, they will complain.[16]

The problem with this arrangement is that it suggests the children have, at best, a limited interest in the longer-term purposes of the projects: health and education and their eventual removal from the street. If they are only interested in the immediate help the institutions can offer, this leaves many of the projects without a viable underlying strategy, reducing them instead to a subsidiary role, albeit greatly appreciated, in the street children's wider support network.

A Colombian child neatly summarized the rival attractions of home, street and institution:

At times you get bored – you get bored anywhere. For me, I always have this circle – I go to an institution, I go to the streets and I return home. That is street life. What I like about the institutions is that they dress you, the worst is that they are very small. The best of life on the streets is that you can stay with the gang; that's brilliant, but the worst is that there are people who beat you up. What is bad about home is that your parents beat you up. What is good about home is the food and the place to sleep. The food is better in the institution where a person has a bed; at home there are many to a bed and you hardly fit. I don't know where I will end up.[17]

Aptekar paints an optimistic picture of courageous, almost heroic figures who clearly fit into the Artful Dodger portrait of the street urchin. His account of Roberto and Antonio's day omits much of the darker side of life on the street, with its insecurity, violence and manifold dangers.

The most tangible threat is violence. Most attention outside Latin America has focused on the 'social cleansing' carried out by death squads, often made up of off-duty policemen, intent on cleaning up the streets (see Chapter 4). But even when on duty, the police routinely beat and brutalize street children. In Guatemala, police regularly punish glue-sniffers by pouring the glue over the heads and in the eyes of the children, while in 1990, a police car happened to be passing when Marvin Oswaldo de la Cruz Almengor, a 12-year-old street boy, stole a tourist's sunglasses. The two policemen grabbed him, put a revolver to his head and fired. A judge subsequently demonstrated the value put on a street child's life when he found them guilty of murder and sentenced them to a three and one year suspended sentence. The police were then allowed to pay off this sentence at $30 a year. The judge also ordered the policemen to pay Marvin's father $55 compensation.[18]

The police treat girls no better, according to one 17-year-old from Recife:

[The police] hit me in the back, in the belly, in my face, in the leg. Those truncheons they carry around, they use them to hit us. Sometimes when they don't hit you with the truncheons they hit you in the head with the butt of the revolver, or with the barrel. I got kicked in the face once. Sometimes the police beat up pregnant girls. Sometimes they hit them in the stomach because they don't know the girls are pregnant, but sometimes it's just to be evil.[19]

Besides beatings on the streets, back at the station the Brazilian police force has its quota of sadists who practise torture on a medieval scale on children and adults alike. Children, however, are less likely to protest. One of the favourites is the 'parrot's perch', in which the victims' arms are tied behind their legs, before they are hung upside down for long periods of time, and water and disinfectant poured into the nostrils. Other prisoners are often forced to carry out the tortures, leading to revenge killings between children once they are back on the street.[20]

Violence at the hands of the police produces shame and rage in the hearts of the children, as two 17-year-old Brazilian boys reveal:

> The worst thing in the world is for a person who's a thief to be beaten by someone he never saw before. That creates an enormous rebellion [revolta] in us. We start to rob ... to do so many things to people ... the police hitting us, we get even more rebellious [revoltados].
>
> When the police hit you and everyone stares, you feel embarrassed. When my mother comes to visit me [in the juvenile prison] the police yell at her and I feel like exploding. This business, man, of sticking us in here and keeping us prisoner doesn't do any good because it fills us with even more rebellion [revolta]. When you get out of here you leave with even more rage [raiva] and start stealing again.[21]

Yet violence at the hands of the police is just part of a much wider climate of violence in which children's lives are immersed. Many are fleeing the brutalities of domestic violence at home, while far more street children die at the hands of their peers than from death squad pistols. Girls in Brazil's streets carry razor blades in the roofs of their mouths, or rolled up in a piece of paper in their underwear. Fights with bottles, rocks and knives are routine. As one perturbed American commented after spending 15 months with Brazilian street children:

> Just as in developed countries, children are normally expected not to work, they are likewise expected not to smash bricks over the heads of their companions, set them on fire, or murder them. Yet among street children in Recife, all of these things happen with frightening regularity.[22]

Fear comes to a head at night, when the bravado and excitement of the day gives way to fear of the dark, and of unknown assailants; the traumas that have driven the children from their homes resurface as nightmares. In Colombia, street children talk of 'lleca', translated as 'the heaviness and loneliness of being on the street':

> Lleca means passing the night on the streets, but is more like the day, with fear placed on top of it. I worry that the police are coming. I

wrap myself with papers but it doesn't stop the cold, which is terrible. We make our beds like the soldiers, pressing against each other in order to keep warm. Almost without breathing, we pass the night this way while we help each other guard against the panic we all have.[23]

To fend off their fear, children sleep together for mutual reassurance and defence, many sniff glue to get them through the night, and they usually try to find sleeping places in the busiest (and therefore safest) parts of the city, such as next to all-night food stalls. Even so, sleep is elusive – one of the commonest sights in street children's institutions is of children catnapping at all hours of the day.

Drugs

Most street children use drugs, usually glue and other inhalants. As they get older, many graduate to using marijuana, crack or alcohol.[24] Although journalists usually claim that glue is sniffed to counter hunger and cold, the children themselves give other reasons, not least that they like the effects! Many sniff glue as a gang pastime, or in order to psyche themselves up for difficult tasks such as sleeping rough or stealing, as with this Brazilian child from Recife:

> I wake up on Dantas Barreto [busy city centre street]. I go to a public bathroom. I take a bath, wash my face. Then I go over to Seu Zé's stall, grab some toothpaste, brush my teeth. He gives me a roll and some juice. I eat. Then I go out to rustle up some money. I go around and say 'got any change?' Anyone who's eating, I ask 'em. Around noon when I've got some money I buy a huge lunch in the Bar do Gordo. Then I get up and say 'I'm gonna sniff glue now.' I go up to a kid, snatch his glue, the glue's almost dead [hard and with barely any smell] you know just so I can sniff a little. When my head is sort of feeling good I say 'time to steal'. I go around and 'bam', got a watch, I run, sell the watch and buy glue. I keep on sniffing glue and stealing watches to buy food at night.[25]

Whatever the motives, the effects on health are disastrous. In Central America street children sniff Resistol, the brand name of a glue manufactured by the multinational company HB Fullers of St Paul, Minnesota. Resistol's active agent is toluene, a neurotoxin which destroys the brain. It is so poisonous that an Environmental Protection Agency permit would be required to sell it in the USA, yet it can be bought over the counter in most parts of Central America.[26] It can cause birth defects (when the glue is used by pregnant girls), uncontrollable trembling, the loss of the ability to walk properly, temporary paralysis and kidney failure.

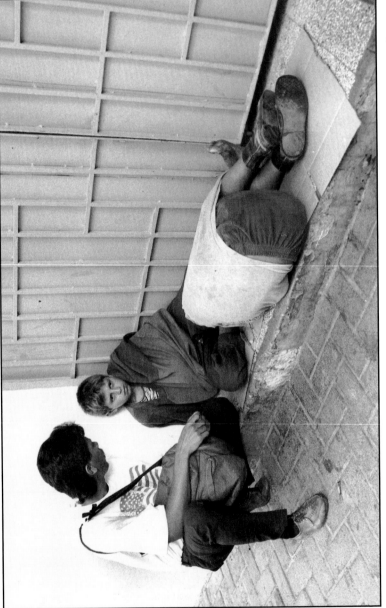

Projects working with street children must first send out educators and counsellors to befriend them on the streets. Project worker in Tegucigalpa, Honduras.

Critics say that Fullers could easily solve the problem by including oil of mustard in the product, a deterrent which stopped the 1960s craze among US children for sniffing model aeroplane glue. However, Fullers, which makes more than 20 per cent of its profits in Latin America, refuses and has lobbied against congressional legislation in Honduras and Guatemala. Tony Andersen, its chief executive officer, denies responsibility, saying 'The problem is not our produce, it is society.'[27]

Besides its physical effects, glue-sniffing turns the street child into the complete social pariah, easily identifiable as a 'resistolero' (the name varies according to the most popular brand in each country), whose glazed expression and stumbling gait are the hallmark of years with his or her mouth pressed to the telltale crumpled plastic bag or bottle. Glue-sniffers are seen as the dregs, suitable prey for a beating or summary execution by the death squads.

Sex and love

Like drugs, sex offers both solace and danger. Street children usually start having sex well before the onset of puberty and are very active. A study in Guatemala revealed that 101 out of a sample of 143 street children claimed to be having one or two sexual partners a day, while 36 (3 boys and 33 girls) claimed to have sex with more than four partners each day. Three-quarters slept with both sexes[28] – at least partially the result of the largely male world of the street child, reminiscent of same-sex relations in prisons or the British private school. While these figures may be distorted by braggadocio or prostitution, they give a sense of the level of sexual activity on the street. Whether through drugs or sex, physical pleasure is all that is available to children with nothing more than the clothes they wake up in.

Children's sexual relationships with other children are often their only source of love and self-esteem. Girls in particular often internalize the lessons of *machista* society, seeing themselves as little more than sexual objects and placing enormous importance on their sex lives. In Brazil, street girls dote on their boyfriends and smuggle drugs and cigarettes into them when they are in prison, raising the money from prostitution or petty crime.[29] Children also have sex with adults, but here the power relation is very different. In Recife, girls call it 'selling meat',[30] a cold-blooded, commercial and often dangerous transaction.

For street girls, sex is often their chief source of income. As one meeting of girls discussed, prostitution for them is not a 'profession', but more an occasional, chaotic response to the need for money, food, warmth or a bed.[31] Street girls are much more vulnerable than adult prostitutes. They are usually on their own, without even the limited protection provided by brothels or agencies. Street children are often largely ignorant of sexually transmitted diseases, cannot afford condoms, and are more powerless in their relations with men (who sometimes mistakenly see sex with a young girl as a way of avoiding AIDS). Girls are seldom jailed for prostitution – they know what the policemen's price is for turning a blind eye or releasing them once arrested.

Yet for all their toughness, street girls dream of love, indulging in adolescent fantasies of the white knight who will gallop up to their door and transform their lives. Their longing is given an extra edge by the grimness and violence of their daily experience, and extra improbability by the actual nature of their relationships with men. At the centre of their dreams, there is usually a house of their own, freeing them from street and favela alike.[32]

Boys, too, are highly vulnerable to exploitation at the hands of police, pimps and paedophiles alike. Augusto is a 12-year-old Honduran boy, eager to please and full of nervous energy. Disturbingly innocent and trusting, he is currently fleeing his usual place in the market:

> *El Chino the homosexual took me to his room various times. He never even paid me. Afterwards I felt bad. One day, he came at me with a knife – put a knife to my throat to make me, so what could I do? They put him in prison for a while, but when he got out he came looking for me and wanted to hit me because I wouldn't let him – I was worried about AIDS. We buried a friend once who died of AIDS – he said his whole body ached. Enrique was his name. Then there was Marvin. He died too. There was another homosexual who took photos of kids naked. He works in the international school. The first time my mum got sick I went to him, and he helped me.*

Augusto's mother seems oblivious to her son's life, proudly saying, 'He has some good friends – Watts and the Chinaman (El Chino).' When she is told that Chino raped Augusto she looks absolutely shocked, eyes glued to the social worker's face. She swallows nervously, and gives up sifting the beans in the blue washing-up bowl on her lap. So far Augusto has not had an AIDS test, but Honduras has the highest proportion of AIDS carriers in Latin America, estimated at 1 in 50 of the population, and his chances are not good. Girls are even more at risk, as AIDS in Latin America and the Caribbean (as elsewhere in the Third World) is increasingly transmitted by heterosexual sex, and female infection rates are higher for both physiological and cultural reasons (see Chapter 7).

Health and education

AIDS and other sexually transmitted diseases, along with brain damage from glue-sniffing, are just some of the health risks faced by street children. They also suffer from respiratory problems, skin infections, injuries from fights and other daily dangers, parasites, diarrhoea, kidney and bladder infections, bad teeth and eye infections.[33] The sheer physical toll of life on the Colombian streets led one author to describe the dozens of children in one institution, resting or tending innumerable cases of cuts, wounds, injured ankles and feet, as looking like 'soldiers barely old enough to have facial hair, already wounded in battle'.[34] To this physical onslaught must be added a range of psychological problems, including anxiety, depression and suicidal feelings. One researcher concluded, 'All in all, there is scarcely any aspect of a street existence that does not imperil the physical and emotional well-being of children.'[35]

One of the key obstacles to dealing with such problems is the lifestyle of the street. Children have little understanding of their own bodies, nowhere to store medicines, and a shifting, day-to-day lifestyle which makes preventive work very difficult. When death could lurk round any corner and daily survival is of the essence, it is extremely hard to make street children take seriously long-term threats such as AIDS. When they are sick, street children show a great reluctance to see a doctor, or go to hospital, often due to the kind of welcome that awaits them there. One survey of Colombian street children found that:

> Both boys and girls had been through numerous situations where they were badly treated or had been insulted [at the hospital/clinic]. One girl recalled a doctor who had tried to abuse her during a visit, while another boy had been left unattended in the hospital because he was dirty.[36]

Similar obstacles apply in education. Street children face enormous difficulties in going to school. Besides the stigma of their appearance, their constantly shifting, unpredictable, adrenaline-charged lifestyle makes it almost impossible for them to sit motionless in the standard 'chalk and talk' Latin American classroom, where they are expected to rote-learn facts entirely irrelevant to their lives.

For this reason, many projects working with street children employ 'street educators', part of whose job is to help the children to learn in their own environment, facilitating rather than force-feeding information. Children are free to come and go, and class times are geared to the children's needs – for example, breaking for the peak rush hour periods, when children may have to sell newspapers or wash windscreens at the traffic lights. Classes are built around the children's daily experiences, for example basing mathematics on their needs in the market, or literacy on the local shop signs.

This type of learning seldom takes place with children sitting quietly in rows, behind desks. It is often noisy and messy. It uses drama, song, puppets, mime, discussion, drawing, painting, modelling. It is fun. It is serious fun. It can lead to moments of intense concentration, quiet and reflection. The lessons learned are seldom forgotten.[37]

Street girls

Camila, 17, is a skinny mixed-race girl, with short curly hair and a skin complaint that has left her covered in blotchy marks. She wears one small crucifix earring and cut-off jeans. Her arms are covered in scars. For the last two weeks she has been staying at a refuge for street children in Recife, capital of Brazil's impoverished northeast.

I've been on the street off and on since I was seven, when my mother went off and left me with another woman. I don't know why she went away. I left because the husband of the woman was abusing me – he raped me when I was nine. There are always rapes on the street – any man can do it to you.

I've been pregnant three times. The first two, I had abortions by taking Citotec (an anti-ulcer drug used for inducing miscarriages). The last time, I loved the guy, a married man, and decided to have the baby. She's a year and five months old now, and the father's bringing her up with his wife – I only get to see her on Saturdays. I want her back, but I have no job or place to go with her.

The first time I got pregnant was with an Italian tourist. I met him on the sea-front and he promised to take me to Disneyland. I was 12 when I got pregnant with him – he paid me. I dreamed about Disneyland, but he never came back. The second time was a policeman. I liked him, but I knew he wouldn't take care of the kid.

My dream is to find a family where I can work in the house and have my kid with me. What I like most is working with kids. I tried to work at that once, but the woman didn't like the way I washed the clothes and beat me.

I'll be back on the streets soon – I'll have to leave here when I'm 18. I'm afraid, especially of sleeping out. The boys are all thieves and I've seen so many killers – I know their names, but I'll never tell the police.

Many studies show there are at least eight or nine street boys for every street girl,[38] and Camila's account partly explains why. Street girls face extra levels of threats and vulnerability. While boys usually leave home from a combination of physical violence, boredom and a desire for early independence, girls like Camila are likely to leave after traumatic experiences of sexual abuse at the hands of fathers, other male relatives or stepfathers. The girls may run away out of fear, because of feelings of shame or self-blame, or even, as in the case of this 13-year-old from Brazil, because their mothers refuse (or cannot bring themselves) to believe them:

> My mother chucked me out of the house. I told her that my stepfather had been doing bad things with me. She hit me, told me I was lying. Lady, she didn't believe me and now I'm pregnant. My mother said it was just men on the street. I swear to you I didn't want to, but he [the stepfather] beat me a lot, he got a knife and said if I told anyone he would kill me. I couldn't stand it any more.[39]

Becoming a street girl violates the social conventions of poor households far more than when boys leave for the streets. Boys are expected to be independent and cope with life on the streets, while girls are expected (and expect) to stay closer to home. Some girls even flee the home (as happens in Europe and the USA) out of a need to escape overprotective parents. In consequence, their mood can swing rapidly between rebellion and self-loathing. Street child workers in several countries report that girls are more prone to low self-esteem and often practice self-mutilation (probably the reason for the scars on Camila's arms), as one 14-year-old in Recife's 'Passage House' project for street girls describes: 'I know that the street has nothing to give, only beatings. That's why I sniff glue, I don't feel anything. I steal and get beaten up, I cut myself, but this has nothing to do with me.'[40]

Girls also cut themselves to avoid arrest, since it obliges the police to take them to hospital. Street girls get pregnant all the time and often have little idea about how their bodies function, or how to avoid sexually transmitted diseases. As with Camila, many pregnancies are aborted using Citotec or other backstreet methods. At other times the babies are adopted by a relative, given away to local women, or passed to a state institution – it is very difficult for young girls to keep their babies with them on the street.

Even so, according to the girls themselves, pregnancy is not just bad news. It can bring status and self-esteem when both are chronically lacking. If the girl manages to keep the baby, she suddenly becomes someone important (to the baby) and is better treated by others, including other street children.[41]

Mother love
Ask any Latin American street child what they would do if they found a box full of money and their response never varies: 'give it to my mother'. Their relationship to their mothers remains a central part of street children's

identity, reflecting an emotional need which enables girls like Severina, a 16-year-old from Recife, to ignore the cruel truth that their mothers may well have abandoned them, given them away to relatives or even sold them to total strangers in their struggle to survive:

> My mother lives in São Paulo. She gave me to my aunt as soon as I was born. I lived with my aunt but she beat me so I left there for another aunt. I haven't seen my mother in 15 years. Can't even remember what she looks like. She was poor and didn't think she could care for me. I have one brother who lives with my mother, and a sister who lives with our grandmother.

> My dream is to work in a nursery and have a real job with legal documents. Then go to São Paulo and live with my mother. She stopped writing for a while – I don't know why. But last month she phoned and said this summer I could go to São Paulo. Going to São Paulo to see my mother is the most important thing in my life right now.

Street girls, in particular, often express a violent mixture of hatred and love towards their mothers, born of the conflicting emotions of identification, rejection, self-loathing and abandonment. One 16-year-old told a researcher:

> I wanted to wake up dead and stabbed all over. I wanted the newspaper to publish my picture very large. I wanted my mother to see me dead in the newspaper. I wanted her to feel embarrassed about not helping her daughter.[42]

Mothers' actions concerning their errant children cover the spectrum from resignation or indifference to fruitlessly combing the bus stations and main squares. Women see the street as a seducer, stealing their children from them, after they have lost their emotional grip on the child. Many blame their failure to keep the children on having to go out to work, as in the case of Augusto's mother from Honduras, who seems baffled, buffeted by the winds of the city that are stripping her children away from her:

> I thought it was all going to be fine. I was 15 when I got pregnant. My mother died when Augusto was 10 months so I went to work in a gentleman's house, before I went to live with Noel, the father of the other boys. After four or five years, he started to ruin himself, drinking more all the time, out with friends or other women. In the end he stopped giving me money and I had to go out to work again.

> Now I'm hardly ever here. Augusto says he doesn't like being here because his brother fights with him too much. If I didn't have to work, I could keep them in hand, but once I go to work, that's it. If I had been stricter, maybe

it wouldn't have happened, but I'm not like that and now they won't let me touch them.

The importance of their relationship to their mothers is the key to understanding how street children see themselves, according to US anthropologist Tobias Hecht.

Being at home is being with one's mother, even if the physical space called 'home' is nothing more than a few makeshift walls under a bridge, the same type of physical space where a group of children might sleep on their own without their mothers. But 'home' is far more than physical proximity to one's mother: it implies foremost 'helping' one's mother, doing things in the home that she wants done, accepting her advice and discipline and augmenting the family income. Home also frequently implies attending school. In a general sense, home means sticking to what the children refer to as the 'vida boa', the good life, or the right track.[43]

Street children call their world 'essa vida', short for 'essa vida de malandragem' – 'that life as a vagabond/urchin/thief'. They see sleeping in the street itself as an addictive vice – from which flow other vices (glue, thieving, etc.). In the words of one 16-year-old, 'I am of the street. When I'm at home, I can't stop thinking about the street. I can't stop! Then this urge hits me to get the hell out and steal.'

Many children blame themselves for becoming street children: 'Children can sometimes be heard speaking about themselves in terms akin to those used by supporters of the death squad murders of street children.'[44] Children see themselves as 'bad', lost to their mothers, who represent everything 'good'. They see themselves as very different from favela kids, who mock them as 'glue-sniffers'. Street children who are genuinely *of* the street are outcasts everywhere, even in their own minds.

Growing up

As boys grow up on the street they change from cute kids to burly adolescents, and see fear and hostility grow in the faces of the adults around them. Begging becomes both more difficult and more humiliating for older children, forcing them to find new ways of earning money, through either work or thieving. Sometimes older children live off the younger ones, offering protection (or threats) in return for a cut of the proceeds from their begging.[45]

But how and when do they leave the streets, or do street children just become street adults, homeless drifters in the cities? For such a high-profile issue, and one in which such large amounts of money are raised and spent on 'rescuing' the children, there is remarkably little information. According to street child expert, Brian Milne:

> Children come and go and numbers fluctuate. Very few have long street careers, but some of them do stay on the street. Those who are mentally ill in the first place or become so may account for a fairly large proportion of those, as too the ones whose substance addictions causes permanent brain damage.
>
> So where do they go? Of the lower number with long street careers there are several possibilities. Firstly, permanent relationships, especially when children are born, change their status – there are certain ages at which it becomes acceptable for people to begin to squat a bit of land on the edge of a shanty town. Secondly, health and death drive them off the street one way or another. Third, in countries with obligatory military service, street boys are usually not exempted. Fourth, girls 'marry' off the streets.[46]

Through his work in Recife, Tobias Hecht came to more pessimistic conclusions:

> Those who do manage somehow to get older often find themselves taken to adult jails. Others end up in the mental hospital. A few become adult street people, and a few settle into cardboard shacks in the favelas, trying their best to blend in with the wretched poor of the shanty towns.[47]

When Hecht returned to Recife after an absence of two years, he found some of the children he had got to know still on the same street corners, others dead or in prison or mental hospital, but 'I heard no reports of children "returning home". Not one.' As he left again, one young woman told him she would be dead by the time he returned, adding, 'street children only have three futures – prison, insanity or death.'[48]

Other evidence confirms his gloomy view of the prospects for Brazil's street children. In September 1990, photojournalist Lalo de Almeida photographed 17 street children aged from 8 to 21. Almost six years later the Brazilian daily, *Folha de São Paulo,* tried to track them down, with the help of other street children. Of the 17, eight were in prison, two at the state home for young offenders, four still lived on the street and two were dead. Only one, now 18, had changed her lifestyle and worked as a maid, earning $80 a month.[49]

Others are more optimistic. On the basis of his work in Cali, Lewis Aptekar concluded that their ability to make the transition to adulthood depended on street children 'making connections', much as for other adults in Colombia, where getting a job often depends more on *palanca* –

connections – than on qualifications or merit. Aptekar calculated that a quarter of the children he worked with became *desamparados* (helpless). They 'were often physically and emotionally in crisis and barely able to care for themselves'.[50] Their future held little beyond mental hospital, alcohol, skid row or death. He identified a further third of the children as 'survivors', coping, but only just. They experienced bouts of depression and/or aggression when things went wrong, but with help they could 'maintain their shaky stake in adulthood'.[51]

The remainder, which he put at nearly half of all the children he met, were the 'fortunate ones'. They grew up, using their streetwise skills to build a network of clients and seizing opportunities to gain a firm foot in the door to adulthood in the barrio. With their greater experience and contacts, they often did better than their siblings who had stayed at home.

The projects

What of the role of street children's projects in this process? When Hecht added up the numbers of adults working exclusively on street children in Recife, he came to a total of at least 330, roughly one for every street child, yet he found no evidence of the children being able to fight their way back into a stable adulthood.[52] Are the projects a waste of time and money?

The projects' workers and supporters think not, showing enormous dedication to the children and a crusader's fervour in their work. For them, the work 'is a kind of alchemy, which offers to transform deprivation into an advantage, despair into hope and the role of victim into that of activist against injustice'.[53] Their role often resembles that of missionaries, giving up their former lives to devote themselves to 'saving' children. One such woman was Sarah de Carvalho, whose experiences were published as *The Street Children of Brazil: One Woman's Remarkable Story*. The back cover blurb gushes:

> Her glittering career in film promotion and TV production took her to California, Sydney and London … . Sarah left her career and joined a missionary organisation in Brazil. This is the remarkable true story of a life transformed. It tells of the incredible work that Sarah de Carvalho and her husband have founded in the Happy Child Mission. It is a story of immense faith, suffering and love.[54]

But is it a story of success, in terms of the children? Street kids undoubtedly find the projects useful, incorporating them into their support networks of adults who provide food, shelter and clothing. But such short-term help is rarely the final goal of the projects, most of which want to get the child off the streets for good. Yet by making life on the streets more palatable and failing to address the root issues in the home, projects may even make it easier for more children to leave impoverished or abusive homes, thereby increasing the numbers of street children!

Most coverage of street children's projects concentrates on the mechanics: the use of street educators, vocational training for the children, health advice and so on. Usually they point to a handful of success stories, children who have left the street and often end up working for the project itself.

Yet there is very little hard statistical evidence on where most street children go after leaving projects and institutions. Very few projects monitor the impact of their work on the children they help, let alone look at what happens to them after they have left the streets. This is partly because of the difficulty of tracking individuals after they lose touch with the project, and because the resources used are less easily justified than feeding schemes and education programmes. As a result, many people are effectively working in the dark, substituting compassion for a more hard-headed approach based on research and analysis.

One of the commonest problems is that projects are concerned exclusively with helping street children or committing them to institutions (often referred to as 'rescuing' the children). Very few go to the heart of the matter – the reasons why children are on the street in the first place, a complex amalgam of the need to work, domestic violence and boredom. Rescue projects try to persuade the children to move to shelters, often farms located outside the city. Often linked to religious missionary organizations, they typically stress the urgency of their task. Children are dying all the time, so there is no time to waste on studies and questionnaires. They often quote the poem by Chile's Nobel Prize-winning poet, Gabriela Mistral: 'Many things can wait. Children cannot. To them we cannot say tomorrow, their name is today.'[55]

Such projects use street educators to befriend children in the street and offer them a place in a shelter. Yet as we have seen, many children reject shelters as a long-term option, preferring to come and go. Part of the reason for the emphasis on shelters, according to one expert, lies with the funders who are:

> hooked on the idea of rescue. Charity is rarely free. Donors want something back, whether this is their name on a plaque or minibus, a photograph of a building or of smiling children for the office wall. Donors like to be able to visit, and to show other people round. They want visible results from their charitable investment. It is far more difficult to get them to invest in something intangible.[56]

Rescue projects and others see vocational training as a key means of getting children off the street. Typically, they teach children tailoring, silkscreening, baking or other manual trades. Critics say, however, that many projects fail to research the jobs market before deciding what to teach (how many silk-screen printers does a Third World city need?), and ignore the skills that street children already possess, which are those of experienced hustlers and traders, rather than artisans.[57]

Other projects concentrate on trying to persuade the children to return to their families. 'At the beginning the emphasis was on the children, but we soon saw the need to work with the family as well,' says Eliane Rodrigues of Projeto Axé, a project in the Brazilian city of Salvador which has pioneered many innovative techniques of working with street children.[58] 'The family needs help too' explains Eliane, 'to find ways out of the problems it's going through.' Axé sees jobs and housing as the two main problems leading children onto the street, highlighting the difficulties of reintegrating children with their families – projects are usually powerless to change the original situation, be it poverty, domestic violence, sexual abuse or boredom, which made children leave home in the first place.

In response to the poor record (and high expense in terms of spending per child) of such projects, new experiments are taking place in prevention – trying to stop children leaving home. In Bogotá, one project works with families where one child has already run away, trying to prevent the rest following suit.[59] Similar approaches are being adopted in Mexico.

Some of the most interesting work is taking place where projects abandon the whole idea of 'saving' the children (who, after all, often see the street not as a prison, but as an escape from worse conditions at home). Here, 'the emphasis should not be on making children leave the streets or stop work, but on increasing the range of choices available to them and helping them to make their own decisions.'[60] In Honduras, one project works with shoeshine boys and other working children, as project worker Jesús Pérez Espinoza explains:

> We started a child bank, to give out loans and help them save money. Now we have 185 accounts ranging from fifty cents to two hundred dollars. At first they didn't trust it, but now they understand how it works – for example they save up to buy Christmas presents. It's been going three or four years now. We give classes – sewing, how to look after their clothes and we try and teach them to read and write.

The project shows how different the approach becomes when it starts from the children's lives and seeks ways of helping them within their everyday struggle to survive. If done well, this can enable the child gradually to move from unplanned (or unwanted) work tantamount to begging, such as wiping car windscreens, to something approaching a trade, bringing higher income, self-respect and education.

More generally, critics argue that most street children projects are failing because they are addressing the wrong issue. The existence of street children is a symptom of the broader malaise in Latin American society, and it is that malaise that must be addressed if children are to stop taking to the streets. That means concentrating on community development, strengthening grassroots organization, helping families, reintegrating street children where possible, and preventing the next generation from having to join them. It also involves changing public attitudes to domestic violence and putting pressure on governments to reduce poverty and improve dilapidated housing and education services.

Such an approach eschews the tendency to concentrate solely on street children to the exclusion of all other children. Street children are working children; poor children work and can easily end up on the streets. In Brazil, the National Movement of Street Boys and Girls (MNMMR) has led the way both in involving street and working children in a common organization, and being an organization of, rather than for, the children.

The MNMMR talks not of 'rescuing' street children, but of making Brazil a fit society for them to live in, turning the tables on those who prefer to define street children as 'the problem'. It organizes children together in *núcleos* (cells) of children engaged in the same work – kids who shine shoes, kids who watch cars and so on – or children who hang out in the same square or bus station. The city of Recife alone has over thirty núcleos. Representatives from the various núcleos meet together weekly, and every three years the MNMMR organizes a national meeting in the capital, Brasília, when street children usually succeed in grabbing the national headlines by occupying the national Congress or through other well-organized stunts.[61]

As a national movement, the MNMMR has had extraordinary success in raising the public profile of issues like child rights and death squad assassinations of street children, yet its name is a misnomer. It is a movement of poor children, not street children (who make up relatively few of its activists). Its name itself is an implicit criticism of the public's exclusive interest in street children, at the expense of the far more numerous, forgotten masses of poor and working children. As one MNMMR activist remarked: 'It is called the National Movement of Street Boys and Girls for reasons of marketing. If it were called the National Movement of Children, no-one would listen.'[62]

Conclusion

Street children undoubtedly face a harsh life, full of fear and insecurity. But so do a far greater number of poor children. Many street children are on the streets not because they have been abandoned, but out of an admittedly unpalatable choice, because conditions at home were even worse than those on the street, in terms of poverty, violence or hunger.

Yet despite their small numbers and the difficulties faced by millions of other poor, working, disabled or indigenous children, street children continue to command enormous attention and a disproportionate share of the resources devoted to improving children's lives in the Third World.

Does this matter? The danger is that money and political pressure will be misdirected away from the most needy, or the place where they can be most effective. Street children are not the 'problem', but a symptom of the wider social crisis in Latin America and the Caribbean. Improving street children's lives or reducing their numbers in any sustainable way cannot be achieved without improving living conditions in the homes and communities from which they have fled.

Finding solutions to this wider crisis of growing social exclusion, poverty and inequality requires a different approach, emphasizing the need for community development, involving increased participation by children and poor families in the choices that affect their lives. It means pressing for a shift in political and economic priorities within Latin America to give greater weight to the needs of the poor.

If the international public's sometimes over-exclusive concern at the plight of street children can bring it to understand and support this wider agenda, then it will end up benefiting not just the street children themselves, but *all* the poor children of Latin America and the Caribbean.

Notes

1 SCF UK, *Brazil Draft Country Situation Analysis* (mimeo) (Recife, 1995), p. 34.

2 SCF UK, *Peru Draft Country Situation Analysis* (mimeo) (Lima, 1994), p. 23.

3 Tobias Hecht, *At Home in the Street: Street Children of Recife, Brazil* (Recife, 1995) (draft), p. 134.

4 Projeto Axé, *Meninos que vivem nas ruas de Salvador* (Salvador, 1993), p. 17.

5 Benno Glauser, 'Street children: deconstructing a construct', in Allison James and Alan Prout (eds), *Constructing and Reconstructing Childhood* (Basingstoke, Hants, 1990), p. 145.

6 Nancy Scheper-Hughes and Daniel Hoffman, 'Kids out of place', in *Nacla Report on the Americas* (May/June 1994), p. 17.

7 Judith Ennew, *Street and Working Children: A Guide to Planning* (London, 1994), p. 122.

8 Anthony Swift, *Brazil: The Fight for Childhood in the City* (Florence, 1991), p. 37.

9 Lewis Aptekar, *Street Children of Cali* (Durham NC, 1988), p. 13.

10 Jorge Amado, *Captains of the Sands* (New York, 1988), p. 94.

11 Hecht, *op. cit.*, p. 139.

12 Ennew, *op. cit.*, p. 20.

13 Wright, Kaminsky and Wittig, 'Health and social conditions of street children in Honduras', in *American Journal of Diseases of Children* (March 1993), Vol. 147, p. 282.

14 Hecht, *op. cit.*, p. 239.

15 Aptekar, *op. cit.*, pp. 62–6, © 1988, Duke University Press. All rights reserved. Reprinted with permission.

16 Hecht, *op. cit.*, p. 224.

17 V.C. Muñoz and X.C. Pachón, *Gamines Testimonios* (Bogotá, 1980), p. 95.

18 Casa Alianza, *Report to the UN Committee Against Torture on the Torture of Guatemalan Street Children* (Guatemala City, 1995), p. 10.

19 Hecht, *op. cit.*, p. 48.

20 *Ibid.*, p. 161.

21 *Ibid.*, p. 175.

22 *Ibid.*, p. 165.

23 J. Gutiérrez, *Gamin: Un Ser Olvidado* (Mexico City, 1972), p. 12.

24 Riccardo Lucchini, *Street-Child and Drug Consumption in Brazil. Thoughts about Addiction*, (Institute for Economic and Social Sciences, University of Freiburg, Switzerland, 1993), Working Paper 231, p. 22.

25 Hecht, *op. cit.*, p. 40.

26 *Sticky Business – An Overview*, http://www.casa-alianza.org/sticky2.html#glu4 (31 October 1996), p. 4.

27 Bonnie Hayskar, 'Sticking with addiction in Latin America', in *Multinational Monitor* (Washington, April 1994), p. 26.

28 'Crece prostitución infantil en Guatemala', in *Barricada* (Managua, 8 March 1994).

29 Kate Ewart-Biggs, *The Freedom Trap: The Dreams and Realities of the Street Girls of Recife* (mimeo) (Brazil, 1990), p. 16.

30 *Ibid.*, p. 10.

31 'As meninas e a rua', *Revista CEAP*, #3 (Rio de Janeiro, March 1993), p. 10.

32 Ewart-Biggs, *op. cit.*, p. 57.

33 Ennew, *op. cit.*, p. 97.

34 Aptekar, *op. cit.*, p. 85.

35 Wright, Kaminsky and Wittig, *op. cit.*, p. 282.

36 Childhope, La Bergerie, and Programa Nueva Vida, *SOS, Jovenes de la Calle de Bogotá* (Derecho a la Salud y Prevención del VIH/SIDA, Bogotá, 1992), p. 30.

37 Ennew, *op. cit.*, p. 107.

38 For example, Projeto Axé, *Meninos que vivem nas ruas de Salvador* (Salvador, 1993), gives a figure of 86 per cent in Salvador, Brazil; *Street Children in Jamaica, 1987*, Survey by the Council of Voluntary Social Services in Jamaica, gives 97 per cent for Jamaica, while SCF UK, *Peru Draft Country Situation Analysis* (Lima, 1994) gives at least three-quarters for Peru.

39 'As meninas e a rua', *Revista CEAP*, #3 (Rio de Janeiro, March 1993), p. 42.

40 Gilberto Dimenstein, *Brazil: War on Children* (London, 1991), p. 37.

41 'As meninas e a rua', *Revista CEAP*, #3 (Rio de Janeiro, March 1993), p. 35.

42 Quoted in Ewart-Biggs, *op. cit.*, p. 89.

43 Hecht, *op. cit.*, pp. 144–6.

44 *Ibid.*, p. 146.

45 Aptekar, *op. cit.*, p. 47.

46 Brian Milne, private communication (9 January 1997).

47 Hecht, *op. cit.*, p. 99.

48 *Ibid.*, p. 243.

49 *Latinamerica Press* (Lima, 16 May 1996), p. 5.

50 Aptekar, *op. cit.*, p. 82.

51 *Ibid.*, p. 83.

52 Hecht, *op. cit.*, p. 196.

53 Swift, *op. cit.*, p. 10.

54 Sarah de Carvalho, *The Street Children of Brazil: One Woman's Remarkable Story* (London, 1996).

55 Cited in Ennew, *op. cit.*, p. 50.

56 Ennew, *op. cit.*, p. 89.

57 *Ibid.*, p. 108.

58 *Folha de São Paulo* (São Paulo, 13 October 1996).

59 Ennew, *op. cit.*, p. 120.

60 *Ibid.*, p. 83.

61 Scheper-Hughes and Hoffman, *op. cit.*, p. 21.

62 Cited in Hecht, *op. cit.*, p. 148.

CHAPTER 4

Culprits or Victims?

Child Criminals and Social Cleansing

Pelourinho, the former slave quarter in Salvador, capital of black Brazil, is a tourist's delight of cobbled alleyways and ornate churches. In a busy square, four or five skinny boys, perhaps 10–12 years old, are working the crowd, picking pockets like something out of *Oliver Twist*. But unlike the Artful Dodger, they are not very good at it, stumbling through a fog of hunger and glue. One boy with glazed eyes is sniffing from a plastic bottle half-concealed up a ragged T-shirt, as he searches blearily for victims. He tries to pickpocket a tall, white-haired man but his clumsiness makes him easily detected. The man half-heartedly gives chase and the child retreats out of range, but not very far. The man gives up. No-one takes any interest. Having your pocket picked by street kids is just part of the daily stresses of city life in Brazil.

The people crossing the square want the children dealt with. Since Brazil's hopelessly inefficient and corrupt police force is unable to do the job, a large slice of the public supports far more drastic measures. A few years ago in the centre of Brazil's largest city, São Paulo, a lawyer kicked and stamped a 13-year-old boy called Jesus to death when he grabbed a woman's gold necklace. A crowd stood round watching and egging him on.[1] In Colombia, the down-and-out children, with their glue bottles, rags and matted hair, are known as the 'disposables', legitimate targets for the self-appointed hit-men who practise 'social cleansing'.

Such actions can, of course, never be justified, but many street children and even adolescents from more stable backgrounds are involved in crime. The excluded millions of Latin America's children survive on the street by using their wits in a world of danger, insecurity and brutality. No-one else plays fair, and, often, neither do they. Boys are drawn into petty thieving and gang life, ranging across the spectrum from the inept pickpockets of Salvador, to the Uzi-toting teenage gangsters of Medellín, the cocaine capital of Colombia. Girls (and some boys) also join the ranks of Latin America's child prostitutes.

Child criminals are a part of the broader wave of rising crime which is causing panic through much of Latin America and the Caribbean: muggings, violent crime and burglary affect shanty town and middle-class suburb alike, while kidnapping for ransom and car theft are increasingly alarming the better-off. The crime wave's roots are complex and controversial, a mixture of social breakdown in the cities, rising poverty and inequality, and, more generally, a growing sense of exclusion among millions of Latin Americans, locked out of the consumer society they see flaunted on their television screens and in the lifestyles of the better-off.

Anger and fear at the crime wave have been compounded by the continent's moribund and corrupt criminal justice system. Criminals, whether on the streets or in the police force, are rarely brought to justice. Instead, the region has witnessed an alarming rise in vigilante justice, often known as 'social cleansing', where off-duty police, security guards and other self-appointed executioners clean the streets of 'undesirables', many of them children. That same anger and fear has seen the public increasingly stigmatize street children and child criminals as barely human vermin, best exterminated – death squads have a significant level of public support.

Yet there are growing calls for an end to the activities of the death squads. Seeking to break the vicious circle of juvenile crime and vigilante revenge, the ever-more vocal movement for child rights is using a combination of legislative change, public information campaigns and grassroots activism (with some notable successes) to end impunity for the killers and to change public perceptions so that people 'revalue' the continent's children.

Gang life

Besides the prospect of making some easy money, youth gangs across the continent provide safety in numbers, accomplices, large doses of danger and excitement and, in many cases, a substitute family far more loving and supportive than the violent, broken homes from which the children are fleeing. Gangs give their members an outlet for youthful rebellion and a sense of belonging: 'through gang membership, the children replace the work ethic with an adventure ethic through which they have a sense of themselves as urban pirates who are aiming not at citizenship, but to conquer the city.'[2] Gangs also provide potent identity symbols such as distinctive tattoos, haircuts, clothes and even drug habits, along with a love of rap music and impenetrable slang. Loyalty is central to gang life, a modern-day version of the three musketeers' creed of 'all for one and one for all'. As one study of Colombian gangs concludes:

Their families neglect them, the gangs don't. Their families impose rules and timetables, the gangs don't. The school is authoritarian, the gang isn't. Family and school maltreat them, the gang doesn't. Family and school give them no love, the gang does.[3]

For all their violence, gang members often long for the kind of family stability they never had. Andrés is a rangy black youth from Cali, with a bead necklace, bracelets and strikingly long fingernails. He is 17, and has a one-month-old baby with his girlfriend of the same age. Last month the boys from a rival gang called the Retiros shot him through the hip. A shopkeeper pays the Retiros US$500 per head. Andrés smiles guiltily as he admits in a deep lazy voice, 'Yes, I've had to kill some of them [the Retiros] in the past.' Andrés is used to danger:

They've been trying to kill me ever since I was on the street. I've been shot, macheted, by the Retiros, by hooded men, including two policemen. I survive because I'm always thinking what could happen next.

He pulls up his T-shirt to show broad, short machete scars on his back and shoulders and explains, 'I got that from Richard, from another gang.' But having a child has changed him:

I don't know if I'll live to be old – life brings many surprises. Now I've got a kid, I'd like to change, to find a job, maybe have more kids. I get a week's work now and then, helping on building sites, as a mechanic or selling on the streets. I haven't stolen anything for some time – a month, maybe. I don't want to take the risks now I've got a kid. I like to see him every day.

This is not the three musketeers, Robin Hood, or any other romantic myth: violence, including rape, is a commonplace feature of the pecking order within many gangs. Members may love their fellows and weep over their deaths, but they can rapidly become hardened killers, as Antonio, a teenage gang leader, recalls in *Born to Die in Medellín*, Alonso Salazar's best-selling account of Colombia's gang underworld:

I'll never forget the first time I had to kill someone. We were breaking into a farmhouse one morning when the watchman suddenly appeared out of nowhere. I was behind a wall, he ran in front of me, I looked up and was so startled I emptied my revolver into him. He was stone dead. That was tough, I won't lie. For two weeks I couldn't eat a thing because I saw his face even in my food … but after that it got easy. You learn to kill without it disturbing your sleep.[4]

Each succeeding generation grows up worshipping the 'hard men' of the gangs. One Medellín 12-year-old wrote in an essay in his first year at secondary school:

> I'd like to be a killer. I want me and my family to be respected. Just like Raton, who has been shot now, but who was a guy who said nothing but killed anyone that stepped out of line. He would stand there with his 9mm pistol and if anyone stared at him he'd say 'What are you staring at?' And if they got cheeky he'd kill them, spit on them and walk off laughing. That's how I'd like to be.[5]

Compared to the excitement and immediacy of gang life, the stuffy traditionalist school systems of Latin America and the Caribbean have little to offer:

> They teach you things that are no use. Things are really difficult here, and you end up with no notebooks, no textbooks, often with no breakfast inside you, with other things on your mind ... and when you get to school, the teachers only ask for the same old things: presentation, that you wear school uniform, the right shirt, the right trousers, even the right haircut. The moment you get to school, you start feeling you're in trouble. Another thing the teachers worry about is shutting the doors at a certain time. Sometimes we end up trying to get in over the walls if we arrive late![6]

In Colombia, where the state is either absent, ineffective or corrupt, and violence is used as a matter of routine by the army, police, guerrillas, drug barons and others, joining gangs is seen as a legitimate step by many of those 'excluded' from the wealth and opportunities enjoyed by the few. In the words of one gang leader:

> In this country, everybody has to look out for themselves. There's nobody straight or honest. Look at all the politicians: what we do is kids stuff compared to them. They clean up millions just with a signature. The police are just crooks in uniform. You can't trust anybody else to help you. No chance! It's everyone for themselves.[7]

Interviews with gangs in Guatemala suggest that they are rather more socially aware than their Colombian counterparts: 'Look, the only ones I rob are the people with money. It wouldn't be cool to rob someone the same as me.'[8]

In Colombia, the gang phenomenon has been exacerbated by the combined influences of the country's drug mafias and widespread political violence. In Medellín, drug barons such as Pablo Escobar recruited 'sicarios', or hired gunmen, to wipe out opponents, while in the mid-

1980s, several guerrilla organizations established military training camps for youngsters, many of whom had more interest in handling weapons than learning about revolutionary politics. After the camps were broken up by the government, their pupils went on to found some of the most notorious gangs.

Politicians and businessmen are among those who hire teenage killers to wipe out their opponents. Their readiness to kill in pursuit of fleeting fame, and perhaps a pay-off to their families, often defies logic: in April 1990, a 16-year-old boy shot dead left-wing presidential candidate Carlos Pizarro on a plane. He had no chance of escape and was immediately gunned down.[9]

'We were all born to die,' Antonio, a mortally wounded gang leader, told Alonso Salazar from his hospital bed.[10] Antonio first killed a man when he was 11 years old, after his father gave him a revolver and told him to sort out a family feud. Death and violence surrounds gang life, blurring the neat distinctions between political and criminal violence. Death can come in a shoot-out with the police, on a street corner at the hands of a 'social cleansing' squad, or in a war with a rival gang.

Within Colombia, gangs vary enormously. Some are despised as parasites, preying on their own communities, often to feed drug habits which are out of control. Others stick closer to the Robin Hood image, taking care to keep the public on their side, according to one former gangster:

> they've done a lot for the neighbourhood. Whenever they could, they'd hand out 200 maybe 300 bags of groceries down at the church. At Christmas they'd buy 15 or 20 pigs, close off the streets, then hold parties for everyone. They helped kids who were studying: 'Oh, so you haven't got any running shoes, look here's 30,000 pesos, go buy yourself a pair.' That's why everybody's on their side.[11]

Gangs in Colombia are an extreme case, with higher rewards and higher death-rates than in the rest of Latin America and the Caribbean, but gang culture is on the rise throughout the region, part of the crime wave which has become a feature of the 1990s. In Brazil, it is linked to the spread of crack in the favelas; in Jamaica, a combination of the drug trade and political rivalry has stoked a gang culture which has spread to New York and London;[12] after the end of the civil war in El Salvador, refugees returned from the USA, bringing children who had grown up among the Chicano gangs of Los Angeles – they rapidly reproduced them on the streets of Central America.

Gangs, violence and street crime attract girls too. Miriam is a dark-haired 15-year-old Honduran with curly hair and a sullen expression, occasionally banished by a sudden childish smile. Traces of nail varnish cling to her nails, bitten back to the quick. With her pronounced cheekbones and black, flashing eyes, she looks like a Central American Carmen, full of bravado in her black leather jacket and white miniskirt. Miriam talks of fights, of beating up other girls and men – tough-girl street talk:

> *My father went off with another woman when I was two. My granny brought me up – my mum's in the women's prison for drug-trafficking. A man gave her money to carry drugs and she's been inside for three years. My mother always loved me – she's got problems, but she still loves me.*

> *Prison's an ugly place – I've been inside three times, for being on the street. There's a lot of trouble there – if you're not aggressive they beat you up, but I know how to look after myself.*

> *I left my granny's place when my mother went to prison. I felt disillusioned, lost my friends. It was hard, so I went on the street. I was 12 and it frightened me at first, then I started to like it, especially the glue – you can see things that aren't there! When we were doing a lot of drugs we'd buy glue around 6am, then go out thieving. Then I got cut up and I didn't like it any more, so I stopped. Now I'm living with a good friend who doesn't let me go out thieving.*

> *My stepfather raped me last year. I think it was to get his own back on my mother – he put a knife to my throat and knew how to use it. A drug dealer called Miguel Angel raped me as well. Another man did this to me.*

Miriam pulls up her sleeves to reveal vicious scars on both arms from a man in a bar who pulled a knife on her and stabbed her in the arms and stomach:

> *This year I want to study and work, maybe in the market. I'm pregnant and it'll be good for me, it'll help me quit the street and drugs. It's logical for a woman to want kids, even if you're not with the father. My mother will help me – she's getting out in a month or so.*

But Miriam is deluding herself with her dreams for the future. She is HIV positive, and there is a high probability that her child will be born seropositive too. 'I wouldn't want my daughter to have a life like mine,' she says, but the odds are against her. Lightning flashes over the city, carving out the cathedral dome in silhouette. It is 11 p.m. and the streets are full of people. A block away from Miriam's hostel, a man's body is lying in the road. The car headlights light up the blood drenching his clothes from a stab wound. The man is dead.

Violence is ever-present on the streets, especially at night. A street child lies in pain in the road, having been shot in the leg.

Punishment

Prisons are 'ugly places' throughout Latin America and the Caribbean, seemingly designed to criminalize and brutalize the inmates rather than rehabilitate them. Dusk is falling at the Provisional Collection Centre for Minors, a remand centre at Paratibe, set in tropical undergrowth half an hour's drive outside the Brazilian city of Recife. The place is a mess, following a riot by inmates the previous week. Piles of wreckage stand outside the building, whose walls are smashed and pockmarked. The corridors are covered in hieroglyphs, 'tags' and badly crayoned cartoon characters. Each rebellion uses the rubble and building material from the previous riot as ammunition.

'Be happy – speak less, listen more' exhorts a notice on the abandoned arts room. It hardly applies to the prison authorities – since the riot last Thursday, all the inmates have had their privileges withdrawn; everyone is cooped up and frustrated, the caged, corrupted energy of the adolescent boys eating into itself. The riot started when some were prevented from having visits from their families.

'It's bad here and getting worse,' whispers one inmate. 'Yesterday the military police came in and started beating the kids, broke some guys' arms.' They show off wounds which they say are from police boots. The police threatened a bloodbath if there are any more rebellions.

If the inmates are not hardened when they arrive, they probably will be by the time they leave. In cell 53, two friends of 14 and 15 are nursing their bruises. When they refused to join in the rebellion, the leaders put them in the middle of a circle of boys who beat them with sticks. These two say they are in for possession of grass, but are locked up with others who are in for attempted murder.

Feeding time is like the zoo. Guards slide containers through the bars, as a school-meal smell briefly overcomes the smell of urine. Outside, guns poke out of slits in the watch-towers as night falls, pink and clean, the crisp white lines of concrete in the floodlights contrasting with the messy human chaos within.

It is hard to believe that Brazil is a signatory to the UN Convention on the Rights of the Child, in which it promises to treat children convicted of an offence 'in a manner consistent with the promotion of the child's sense of dignity and worth, which reinforces the child's respect for the human rights and fundamental freedoms of others'.[13]

Yet the Convention has improved the situation. Brazil's new Child and Adolescent Statute, passed in 1990 to make Brazilian law conform with the Convention, abolished the notorious FEBEMs, the misnamed state institutions for the 'wellbeing of minors', which at that time held almost 700,000 Brazilian children and adolescents.[14] Despite the riots, the new centres are considered a great improvement on the FEBEMs. Now, however, this progress is under threat. In response to the increasing incidence of youth crime, right-wing politicians in Brazil are calling for a reduction in the age of legal impunity. So far, the government has refused.

Article 37 of the Convention says that 'every child deprived of liberty shall be separated from adults', but is widely ignored in much of the region. In the Caribbean, Haitian children under 13 are routinely beaten up during arrest and then are frequently held with adults,[15] while in a report on Jamaica's 'lockups', the US-based organization Human Rights Watch says:

> Every day in Jamaica, children as young as ten years of age are locked in dark, overcrowded, filthy cells which they share with rodents and insects. Sometimes they are held with adults charged with serious crimes. While in the cells the children are subjected to physical and mental abuse from police and other inmates.[16]

Many of the children are not even suspected of any crime, having been placed there because they have been abused, neglected or abandoned by their guardians – the police fail to move them to the right places because there is no room, or they are too far away.

Prostitution

While criminal activity for boys mostly revolves around gang life and petty thieving, girls have a different option: prostitution. There are thought to be 27,000 sex workers in Peru between the ages of 12 and 18.[17] In Colombia, the number of child prostitutes has doubled in the last three years and over a third of them are under 14. Some are already on the streets by their tenth birthday. Most already have a child and regularly use glue and *bazuco* (a highly addictive by-product from the manufacture of cocaine).[18] Peru and Colombia have both signed the UN Convention on the Rights of the Child, committing them to end 'the exploitative use of children in prostitution'.[19]

The commonest reason for leaving home is sexual abuse at the hands of a father, other male relative or stepfather. Sexual innocence does not last long. Luiza, now a scrawny 20-year-old, always carries a razor blade with her on the streets of Recife in northeast Brazil. Her body is peppered with scars from knife fights, bullet wounds, and bites from police dogs, and she has a burn from an iron which a former lover forced onto her leg. Although she was raped by her stepfather when she was seven, that was not her first sexual experience:

> *When I was six, a policeman caught me. He said I had to have sex with him – jerk him off. He said if I told his chief, he'd kill my family – he knew where*

we lived. I did what he said. The next day he came back with five other guys and I had to do the same thing to all of them.

After that came five years living on the street, before entering a brothel. Now she is at the Casa de Passagem, a centre for former girl prostitutes in the Brazilian city of Recife.

Although prostitution in clubs and brothels at least avoids the dangers of living on the streets, it has its own risks: a third of Colombia's child prostitutes have no understanding of contraception, leading to unwanted pregnancies and a significant risk of contracting HIV/AIDS and other sexually transmitted diseases.[20]

Turning to prostitution is often a last resort for girls who have left abusive homes and have no other options. It can also involve an element of choice, albeit between limited alternatives. In the words of one young runaway from the northeast, who preferred the streets of São Paulo to working as a maid back in Pernambuco, 'the first time I sold my body was the first time I felt that it belonged to me'.[21]

In other cases girls are simply tricked into prostitution under conditions of near-slavery. In Brazil, under-age girls are lured away from their families in the north with promises of work as waitresses and cooks in the lawless mining towns of Amazonia, described by one investigator as 'a no-man's land where traffic in coca-paste, gold, girls and arms are intertwined'.[22] Agents pay up to US$500 to the fathers of virgins under 15. Instead of being given the promised jobs, they are told on arrival that they have to work as prostitutes in order to pay off the debts incurred for transport and medicines.[23] Every time they get sick (a frequent occurrence in a malaria zone such as the Amazon) or need to buy clothes, the debt rises, calculated in grams of gold dust in such a way that the girls can never pay it off. Meanwhile the conditions in the mining camps where they work are sub-human, according to one of the estimated 3000 under-age prostitutes in the state of Rondônia:

> We were going to be waitresses. They were always beating us. One girl's throat was slit when she wouldn't go with one of the men and others were killed when they got sick, fooled around or tried to run away. Some of the girls who tried to get out were locked up in a small room ... . We never saw any police at the mines.[24]

By the time they are 18, the girls' 'career' is over, according to the president of the Prostitutes' Association of Belém:

> Virgins draw a higher value, and young girls are in greater demand. By the time a woman is 18, she is no longer in demand. The brothels rotate girls to different mines and small towns to create the impression

of variety by bringing in fresh young faces, which they call 'renewing the harvest'.[25]

Adolescent boys also work as prostitutes, and they start young. In Bogotá, one in six male prostitutes starts turning tricks before he is 10.[26] A tradition of transvestite sexuality is one of the Andean nations' better kept secrets. At 17, Johnny is a slighter, more beautiful version of William Hurt in the film *Kiss of the Spider Woman*, an outrageously camp raconteur with shoulder-length wavy dark hair, full red lips and a permanent pout. For Johnny, every day is lived on the edge in a high drama of tragedy, love, instability and violence:

> *I'm from Medellín, the eldest of six. I left home when my mother died of cancer 15 months ago, but I'd started working before I left home, as a boy, when I was 14. Then I got to Pereira and switched to being a woman – you earn more that way. Anyway, I loved dressing as a woman. I loved standing on the street corner, with the cars going past, men whistling at me. I had lots of boyfriends. I realized I was gay when I was eight.*

> *We work in groups of four or five – there are so many dangers in the street: the police, sicarios (hit-men), men who come to beat you up and kill you. I carry tear gas and a knife, and I use them almost every night. The worst are the gangs of 18-year-olds who go round on their motorbikes to hassle the travestis (transvestites).*

> *Most of the customers are nice people: we get all types, but mainly the upper class – businessmen, professionals, police. They're people with a weakness for travestis, then they go back to their wives and important jobs. With the rich ones, you can charge US$100. You can make good money if you're pretty, and so can the ugly ones if they steal!*

Johnny's world is full of grisly knife fights, feuds, police shootings and arguments with the older travestis, who are jealous of the younger ones' success and try to 'tax' them:

> *They killed my husband six months ago – on 3 June 1995 – he was the first man in my life. I was like a wife to him. His name was Ricardo. The sicarios killed him because he was stealing. I felt terrible, even though we'd split up. One day we wanted to live together. I wanted to get really hormoned up and be a real woman for him, so we could walk down the street together hand in hand, like man and wife. When they told me he was dead, I was terrible – cut my wrists and everything. My mother died in August 94; my auntie died of a heart attack in October, then in June they killed Ricardo. I went crazy.*

Miraculously, Johnny has so far avoided the AIDS virus, and so can still dream of a different future:

> *By the time I'm 27, I want to be rich. I want to travel, go to Italy, to Rome and be a travesti prostitute there. Get a handsome husband and see my brothers and sisters right. Or I want to be a famous designer. If I get AIDS, I'll try and leave something in the world, some way people can learn from my life.*

Social cleansing

Travestis like Johnny, along with down-and-outs, petty thieves, drug addicts and drunks, make up Colombia's 'disposables', reviled by the public and targeted by police and death squads intent on 'cleaning up the streets'.

Brazil has the worst extremes of what goes by the horribly clinical name of 'social cleansing'. In the entrance hall of a centre for street children run by the Catholic Church in a Rio shanty town stands a two-metre high plaque with the names of dead children written in large red letters. They have been killed by death squads. Even the act of recording their names is dangerous, according to Wolmer do Nascimento, a worker at the centre: 'I have stopped counting. I found that each time we protested at the death of a child, more children were killed. It seemed like they were taking revenge.'[27]

Social cleansing in Brazil is carried out both by uniformed police officers and by death squads, shadowy organizations with names like 'Black Hand' and 'Final Justice'. The police are particularly trigger happy in São Paulo, Brazil's largest city. There, according to its own figures, the military police killed 1470 civilians in 1992. By comparison, the notorious Los Angeles Police Department in the USA notched up 69 killings in that year. Although the Brazilian police routinely claim that the deaths occur in shoot-outs with criminal gangs, not a single officer was killed in the first six months of that bloody year.[28]

Statements by the few survivors of police attacks tell of the widespread use of torture, planting weapons on the body, intimidation of witnesses and the destruction of evidence. When a special commission investigated 761 police homicides in the state of Espirito Santo in 1991, they found that 334 cases had disappeared from police files.[29]

One of the main reasons for police brutality is the impunity that lies at the heart of Brazil's criminal justice system. Police wrongdoers are rarely tried and almost never convicted, giving them effective *carte blanche* to break the law. But as well as police impunity, child impunity feeds the problem. In Recife, one study showed that of 555 criminal cases involving minors, 97 per cent did not result in sentences.[30]

Frustration at the impotence of the legal system lies behind the rise of the death squads, which are often formed when local merchants hire security firms to 'eliminate' suspected criminals and street children who are either stealing from the businesses or driving customers away. According to one newspaper report, they pay from US$10 to US$40 per dead child.[31] The businessmen who order such killings feel little compunction. The president of Rio's Club of Store Directors told a national newspaper in 1991, 'when a street kid is killed, they are performing a service to society'.[32]

Such 'services' accounted for a large number of the 5644 children between the ages of 5 and 17 who fell victim to violent deaths from 1988 to 1991.[33] Most of them were boys from 14 to 17, and three-quarters were black, perhaps because poverty is highest among black Brazilians, but also suggesting an additional racist motive behind the killings. Street children were the most likely victims, both because they are more likely to be involved in crime, and because they have nowhere to hide.

According to Human Rights Watch, the death squads 'are often composed of off-duty policemen and sometimes operate with the acquiescence, if not active support, of local police officials'.[34] In July 1989, a chance police patrol in Rio caught a death squad red-handed as it was about to shoot a local thief in a Rio shanty town. The six-man squad comprised four off-duty policemen and two employees of the Justice Department.

Death squads often take a macabre pleasure in their task. In Recife, the killers routinely torture and castrate their victims before killing them. The trademark of one notorious killer in the Brazilian city of São Bernardo was to shoot his victims five times in the head. By a cruel irony, he was himself merely 17 when he became leader of the death squad.[35] In Rio, nine-year-old Patricio Hilario da Silva was found on the beach, strangled, with a note left on his body saying 'I killed you because you didn't go to school and had no future.'[36]

In Colombia the situation is more confused. Death squads target street children and other 'disposables', but their members may be otherwise 'respectable' local businessmen or the committees of the neighbourhood association, desperately trying to save their barrio from anarchy and fear. Other killers are more indiscriminate – Bogotá has seen a rise in street-corner shootings where any youths 'hanging out' after dark are considered fair game by the gunmen.

Some political groups have also got involved, operating as a substitute police force with high levels of public support and participation. At night, Moravia, a shanty town built on an old rubbish dump in the centre of Medellín, breaths a new-found freedom. Families mingle in the ill-lit cobbled streets; the night air is full of mouth-watering cooking smells. A

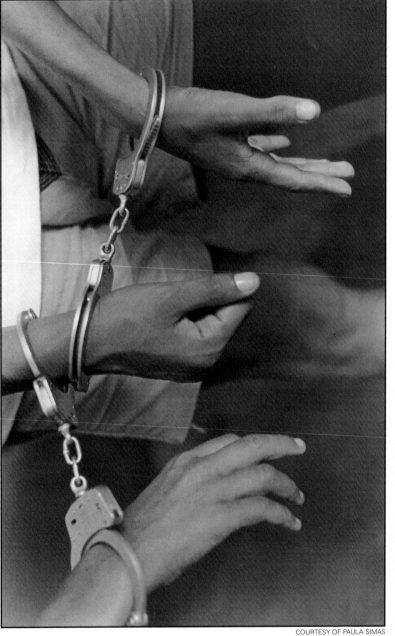

Suspected child offenders are held for long periods without trial, often in harsh conditions. Youth detention centre, Brazil.

few years ago, people would have been shut up in their houses after dark, in terror of the nine different gangs engaged in permanent warfare in the barrio. Now the main threat to life and limb is posed by the kids who whizz up and down at murderous speeds on their treasured bikes.

The cause of the change is a group of ex-guerrillas who took on and killed or drove out the gangs in the early 1990s, to the acclaim of the local people. 'The community came and told you where a thief was,' says the leader of the 'militia', as they are known in the nuanced lexicon of Colombian violence. 'We tried to talk to them, but they didn't want to dialogue, so we had to *ajusticiar* [kill] them.' Now, two years since the last shoot-out, the militia have evolved into the *de facto* authority in the community. Some have even received government training as community policemen. 'So far the people love us, and we're a better alternative than the state,' he explains.

Elsewhere in Colombia, these kind of self-defence groups began by targeting gangs but, without the discipline of the guerrillas, have rapidly acquired a taste for blood, becoming little more than gangsters themselves. As one previously law-abiding citizen who joined a group of hooded 'avengers' explained, 'When you pull on a hood, it's as if you take on another identity. You're no longer yourself, you only think of terror, of spreading fear in your enemy.'[37]

Perhaps the most disturbing aspect of social cleansing is its popularity. Ana Maria, 34, lives in a shanty town on the abandoned edge of the Colombian capital of Bogotá. She has a rubbery, drinker's face, and shares a two-room shack with her father and her four children. As she talks, Madonna is gyrating about on a black and white television, singing *Get Into the Groove*.

> I'm very strict with the kids. I beat them if they go on the street. I try to show them it's not the way for them to live, and they accept it. The worst problem about being a mother here is that you're worried all the time for your kids. When we were young, there was not so much evil, it was healthier. Now there are bad things everywhere.

> Should you kill delinquents? What can I say? If there's no other way to clean up the world, even though it's cruel, I agree with social cleansing – and I think most people support it.

Support for killing criminals, including children, is widespread, driven by the drug and crime wave that has hit the continent in recent years, the inefficiency and corruption of the police and the criminal justice system, and the resulting sense of helplessness felt by many shanty town residents. According to Human Rights Watch, 'only three per cent of the crimes in

Colombia ever reach a judicial verdict, an astonishing two verdicts per month for the entire country'.[38]

Once started, social cleansing acquires a momentum of its own, developing a growing appetite for victims, as even the Colombian government recognized in 1992 in a statement condemning two police agents for murdering a petty thief while in custody:

> 'cleaning' a country ... begins with those called, by these new righteous people, human waste (homosexuals, vagrants, thieves, drug addicts, prostitutes) but later includes peasant leaders, community activists, trade unionists or those who profess an ideology that goes against the system and make [those righteous people] uncomfortable.

However, the official support and impunity enjoyed by the killers was made blatantly clear when the Defence Ministry refused to pay reparations to the thief's family, saying '[the] individual ... was not useful or productive to society or his family, but instead was a vagrant who no one in the municipality wanted'.[39] Of the 2190 child murders recorded by the government in 1993, only 12 cases resulted in a trial.[40]

Justice at the hands of vigilantes or lynch mobs does not only violate the victims' basic human rights. By ignoring the need to prove anyone guilty, this kind of vengeance leads to tragic mistakes. In July 1993, three teenage boys were chased by a mob who accused them of robbing a bus in Rio de Janeiro. The boys were caught, beaten with sticks and clubs, doused with alcohol, and set on fire and killed. A subsequent police investigation showed they had no connection with the robbery and no prior criminal record. They had just been going home on the bus after playing football on the beach.[41]

Ironically, progressive legislation in recent years to guarantee the rights of children has sometimes made matters worse. In Colombia, the government failed to commit the money required to build the rehabilitation centres required by the Children's Charter (Codigo del Menor) of 1989. The Charter also decrees that children can no longer be locked up in adult prisons for their offences, but should be sent to special rehabilitation centres. Since such centres have not yet been built, even child murderers are often released within days of arrest, creating further public support for the death squads as the only viable means of dealing with them.

Ending the massacre

Although there is still a good deal of public support for the killings, the tide of opinion seems to be changing in Brazil, where a network of child rights organizations, along with street children's own organizations, like the MNMMR, have campaigned on the issue with some effect. They have received crucial backing from international human rights and children's organizations which have put pressure on the government to clean up the cleansers.

The battle for the hearts and minds of the public has seen a growing awareness of the importance of child rights, reflected in the new Child and Adolescent Statute (1990). The focus of a number of human rights and children's organizations has been to 'revalue' the child in the public eye, enabling their opinions to be heard and their participation sought in finding lasting solutions to the crime wave and other problems afflicting Brazil's towns and cities.

The campaigns have succeeded in changing public opinion – child rights activists claim it is highly unlikely that the São Paulo lawyer mentioned at the start of this chapter would be allowed to stamp a child to death in the 1990s.[42] The death toll has fallen somewhat, and there are signs of cracks appearing in the system of impunity which lies behind the death squads. A policeman was jailed in 1996 for 30 years for his part in the killing three years earlier of eight Rio de Janeiro children in the notorious Candelária massacre.[43] However, two other officers implicated in the massacre were acquitted in December 1996, after a bizarre 10-hour trial in which the state prosecution had recommended acquittal, while the convicted policeman was reported to be receiving a salary from the state and working within a Rio military police barracks.[44] The one prison sentence handed out was only achieved following an unprecedented national and international campaign. Amnesty International cautiously greeted the sentence as 'an encouraging but small wedge in the fortress of impunity for human rights violations in Brazil'.[45]

In the rest of Latin America, however vigilante justice seems to be spreading. In early 1996, mobs lynched at least a dozen suspected criminals in Guatemala and burned them alive, while in neighbouring El Salvador, homicides were running at 21 a day, higher than during that country's bloody civil war in the 1980s.[46]

In the short term, ending the reign of the death squads and the police killers requires a radical overhaul of the region's criminal justice systems, ending impunity for the police and vigilantes, as well as ensuring that criminals go to jail, and children convicted of crimes are given adequate rehabilitation or other treatment. Overcoming a history of corruption and inefficiency in order to rebuild public confidence in the rule of law will not be easy.

In the longer term, ending the fear that stalks the streets of Brazil and Colombia means removing the forces which drive children onto the streets and into crime. It means ending the exclusion of millions of young people who feel abandoned by a society in which they see the rich growing richer and more powerful, while the poor languish in the shanty towns and hungry villages of the countryside.

It also means changing public perceptions; the millions of excluded young Latin Americans who have become mere 'disposables', 'delinquents' and 'marginals' to its voters, media, governments and police must be given back their rightful identity as children. Their rights must be respected and voices heard if Latin America is to emerge from its current social crisis into a brighter future.

Notes

1 Introduction by Jan Rocha to Gilberto Dimenstein, *Brazil: War on Children* (London, 1991), p. 4.

2 Anthony Swift, *Brazil: The Fight for Childhood in the City* (Florence, 1991), p. 37.

3 Amparo Ardila Pedraza *et al.*, *Pandillas Juveniles: Una Historia de Amor y Desamor* (Bogotá, 1995), p. 42.

4 Alonso Salazar, *Born to Die in Medellín* (London, 1992), p. 13.

5 Quoted in Salazar, *op. cit.*, p. 126.

6 Amparo Ardila Pedraza *et al.*, *op. cit.*, p. 129.

7 Salazar, *op. cit.*, p. 68.

8 AVANCSO, *Por si Mismos, Un estudio preliminar de las 'maras' en la ciudad de Guatemala* (Guatemala City, 1988), p. 23.

9 Human Rights Watch, *Generation Under Fire: Children and Violence in Colombia* (New York, 1994), p. xii.

10 Salazar, *op. cit.*, p. 32.

11 *Ibid.*, p. 64.

12 Laurie Gunst, *Born Fi' Dead* (New York, 1995).

13 UN Convention on the Rights of the Child (Geneva, 1989), Article 40.

14 Nancy Scheper-Hughes and Daniel Hoffman, 'Kids out of place', in *Nacla Report on the Americas* (New York, May/June 1994), p. 20.

15 Aide à l'Enfance-Canada et Enfants du Monde/Droits de l'Homme, *Enfance et Violence* (Port-au-Prince, 1996), p. 39.

16 Human Rights Watch Children's Rights Project, Jamaica, *Children Improperly Detained in Police Lockups* (Washington, October 1994), p. 2.

17 SCF UK, *Peru Draft Country Situation Analysis* (Lima, 1994), p. 24.

18 *La prostitución infantil en el centro de Santafé de Bogotá*, Cámara de Comercio de Bogotá (Bogotá, 1993), pp. 39, 81.

19 UN Convention on the Rights of the Child (Geneva, 1989), Article 34.

20 Cámara de Comercio de Bogotá, *op. cit.*, p. 60.

21 Scheper-Hughes and Hoffman, *op. cit.*, p. 19.

22 Rebecca Reichmann, *Traffic in Girls in Brazil's Amazon and Northeast* (mimeo) (Rio de Janeiro, 1994), p. 1.

23 Alison Sutton, *Slavery in Brazil* (London, 1994), p. 94.

24 Reichmann, *op. cit.*, p. 32.

25 *Ibid.*, p. 31.

26 Cámara de Comercio de Bogotá, *'Pirobos': Trabajadores sexuales en el centro de Santafé de Bogotá* (Bogotá, 1995), p. 32.

27 Dimenstein, *op. cit.*, p. 19.

28 Human Rights Watch, *Final Justice: Police and Death Squad Homicides of Adolescents in Brazil* (New York, 1994), p. 49.

29 *Ibid.*, p. 86.

30 Hecht, *op. cit.*, p. 163.

31 Human Rights Watch, *Final Justice, op. cit.*, p. 82.

32 *Diario do Brasil* (12 January 1991).

33 Human Rights Watch, *Final Justice, op. cit.*

34 *Ibid.*, p. 83.

35 Dimenstein, *op. cit.*, p. 47.

36 *Ibid.*, p. 31.

37 Salazar, *op. cit.*, p. 47.

38 Human Rights Watch, *Generation Under Fire, op. cit.*, p. 8.

39 *Ibid.*, p. 27.

40 *Ibid.*, p. xi.

41 Human Rights Watch, *Final Justice, op. cit.*, p. 32.

42 Sylvia Beales, SCF UK (London, 1996), author interview.

43 'Candelária massacre: still much to be done', in *Brazil Network Newsletter* (London, Sept./Oct. 1996).

44 *The Independent* (London, 11 December 1996).

45 Cited in 'Candelária massacre: still much to be done', *op. cit.*

46 *Inforpress Centroamericana* (Guatemala City, 28 March 1996), p. 8.

CHAPTER 5

Political Violence

That's maize, an apple tree – we had all sorts of fruit. That's a garden. That's a golero – a bird that eats the dead. There were lots of goleros where we lived.

Half a dozen black vultures darken the sky in Ursula's drawing of her old house in the Colombian countryside. A toothy nine-year-old, she wears red stud earrings, an array of cheap plastic bangles, and traces of varnish on her nails. One battered sandal is broken and flaps lugubriously as she walks. Her dark Indian features grow solemn as she explains why she had to leave her farm.

We saw everything when they shot my papa. Everything. They made us go outside when they got there at 6am. When my mother tried to go back in they said 'get out or we'll shoot you'. My brother tried to escape and they shot him, then my Dad went crazy and attacked them with a machete and they shot him too.

My mother only cried a month or two after they buried him. She was pregnant with my little sister. She said she was going to come out all sick, but she was fat and big. She's five now and she's nearly as big as me! Lots of mothers in my barrio lose their babies.

Ursula thinks it was the guerrillas who killed her father, but she's not sure. In Colombia, everyone from peasant to president leads their lives immersed in a rich tapestry of fear. Death could come at the hands of the army, the police, drug gangs, paramilitary death squads, common criminals, guerrilla fighters or street gangs. Colombia's murder rate is one of the highest in the world, over nine times that of the USA. According to the national police, 26,700 Colombians met violent deaths in 1996, amounting to a killing every 20 minutes.[1]

Colombia may be the most violent country, but across Latin America and the Caribbean, political violence has exacted an enormous human toll in recent decades, and children have often been at the sharp end. Under both military and civilian governments, children have witnessed innumerable atrocities by soldiers, death squads and guerrillas. Many have themselves been caught up in the fray, becoming child combatants for the guerrillas, teenage executioners, or gunmen for the region's political godfathers. The scars that such events leave on young minds may never heal, creating a legacy of vengeance and violence deeply ingrained in Latin American society.

According to Amnesty International, one in seven Colombian murders has a political motive:

> For the past five years, a daily average of 10 people have been killed in politically motivated violence. Of these five are assassinated, four die in armed conflict (including guerrillas, members of the security forces and unarmed civilians), and one is killed in 'social cleansing' operations.[2]

Amnesty goes on to apportion blame for the killings, saying 'by far the greatest number of political killings are the work of the Colombian armed forces and the paramilitary groups they have created'.[3]

Next to Ursula, sitting hunched over his drawing, Carlos paints, and then describes, the reality behind Amnesty's conclusions, speaking in spare, factual sentences devoid of emotion. In his painting, a blue helicopter stands by, as black stick-figures clutching recognizable rifles lurk either side of the neat green door of a peasant hut. Once again, vultures hang overhead:

> *This is the helicopter they came in. We were sleeping here in the house. These are the men who came with their faces covered. They came on 2 May 1994. Two of them came in with rifles, the others went off to the village to kill more people. They took my cousin out and kicked him around. My grandfather told them to leave him alone, that he was innocent. They took my grandfather out, tied him to a post and shot him twice here.*

Carlos points to his neck. A skinny, manic boy who boasts he is 'almost nine', he does not remember the father who disappeared six years ago, after leaving the family farm to sort out his papers in a nearby town. Two men called him across to their car and he was never seen again.

After the threats, and the attack, comes flight to the safety of the city, in this case Montería, sweltering near Colombia's Caribbean coast. For the survivors, the problems are only beginning.

'Call me Susana. I'd rather you invented a name.' Susana has a sorrowful, sombre face which melts into a smile as she talks. She is 35 but looks older, her body swollen by poverty and childbirth. The gaps which serve as windows in her plank shack are strung with barbed wire against thieves. Beyond the wire, dugout canoes and fishermen ply the brown, badly polluted waters of the river Sinú.

Children have been involved in all aspects of guerrilla conflicts. In Guatemala, they formed part of the Civil Defence Patrols – anti-guerrilla forces set up by the army, in which indigenous communities were forced to participate.

Home is a room two metres by three, where she shares her bed with the children. The shack is on the last remaining bit of free ground, on the river bank. When it rains the river rises and enters the house, but what most frightens the children are the snakes that seek refuge from the rain. The toilet is the river.

Susana's barrio of Casa Finca is a warren of tin and palm-roofed huts, separated by beaten-earth paths. Pigs sleep in the shade, flattened by the heat. Shanty towns are never quiet, even in the midday sun – radios blare; caged parrots scream; cocks crow. The sound of hammering never stops, as the barrio's residents put up new shacks or improve them little by little, as money allows. The women are doing the washing, pounding away in giant wooden washing bowls a yard wide, carved from a single trunk.

Susana is surrounded by her four remaining children – two twins of seven, a girl of four and a crying skinny baby, still breast-feeding at 18 months. The children are clearly malnourished, with pale hair, stick limbs and protruding navels. Susana has flu and coughs quietly but persistently, trying ineffectually to smother it:

> I had five, but they killed one. He was almost 14. I don't know why they killed him. I've been here three months so far. We lived in Urabá, working on a farm. When they killed my husband, they gave us 24 hours to get out. They came and killed him at night – people came and told me he was dead. There were 18 deaths that night. We had to leave everything.

> Since Sunday the kids have had diarrhoea, fevers and headaches. We haven't the money to go to a doctor so I'm just giving them aspirin. The last week has been hard – we've had nothing to eat [she smiles with embarrassment, as the baby tugs at her breast, moaning quietly as she sucks]. I've been having migraines, but I'm feeling better now and can start work taking in washing. We have water sometimes from the standpipe.

> I'll never go back to Urabá. My children are all I've got left. They killed my eldest son two weeks ago – he stayed in Urabá and now he's buried there.

Susana is 'displaced', a curiously anaemic word for something as traumatic as her experience. There are currently 700,000 displaced people in Colombia, according to government figures.[4]

The barrio is full of women and children, malnourished and yellowed by fever, displaced from the killing fields of Urabá, where paramilitaries linked to the armed forces are driving out peasants by the thousand – perhaps because they want their land, or because they think the peasants support the guerrillas. In Colombia, reasons are always elusive. The guerrillas, too, have caused displacement, by their own admission executing suspected informers.

Displaced families founded the barrio seven years ago by 'invading' unoccupied land and defending their new homes against bailiffs and police until they were left alone. Every year the local authorities promise to rehouse them. When new families arrive, the barrio does what it can. A local human rights committee finds them somewhere to sleep, helps them settle in, and tries to help them deal with the depression and trauma that follow. Everyone misses their farms back in Urabá, according to Susana:

> *When we were children life in the country was easy. We grew our rice, picked coconuts off the trees. Here, children have to think about prices all the time, where they can get coconuts a hundred pesos cheaper. We only went to the market every few months – we had every kind of fruit on the farm. When my kids are sick, sometimes we wish we could go back, sow some papaya, eat well again.*

If such a rural idyll ever existed, it is long gone now, according to Susana's 46-year-old neighbour, Berta:

> *In the countryside you live without confidence, with fear. You never know where death will come from. I feel calmer here – it's a refuge. The kids were afraid too. You asked them to fetch the water and they'd start crying and say 'mama, don't make me go alone'. Here in the city they feel safer.*

The army adds to the climate of suspicion and fear in the countryside, by using children as informers, as in this example from a nine-year-old girl living in a Colombian conflict zone:

> A while ago – maybe more than two years – the army came and asked the teacher for permission to come into the classroom. They showed us their weapons, gave them to us so we could touch them, and asked us if anyone in the village had the same kind of guns. Two first year boys said that Don Mario, the one who owned the shop, had one just like it. So they said Don Mario was a guerrilla and took him away. We never saw him again.[5]

Despite the danger, some of the displaced, especially the older men, cannot adjust to life in the city and prefer to risk going home, often with predictable consequences, as in Berta's case:

> *My husband couldn't find work – he was 61, too old to change to the city. He went back to our village because we were in a real crisis here – nothing to eat. The kids all sell in the market, and he hated to see them walking all the way there. So he went back, but visited us every two weeks. It was harvest time. The maize was ready – nice and dry. I hadn't heard from him and was*

worried, so I went to find him. They killed him on a Sunday, stole his whole crop – we never got a grain of maize.

That was four months ago, on 9 July. I have good days and bad days. Today I've had a few visitors and I feel OK. Other days, I don't even want to open the door.

Impact on children

Displacement damages every aspect of children's lives. Local teachers in Montería say new arrivals are either silent, closed-in children, or aggressive, continually getting into fights. They never talk about what has happened to them. Terror returns whenever anyone in uniform passes the school, and they are always sick with headaches, stomach-aches or eating problems. At a nearby crèche, a worker agrees: 'Displaced kids get scared easily – if I put on a mask they scream and cry. We don't let them play guns here. They're very malnourished at first, but we feed them up.'

A Kermit the Frog growth chart hangs on the crèche wall, showing most of the children with heights in the red zone, corresponding to stunting caused by malnutrition, but all are catching up, thanks to the crèche feeding programme.

Children who have seen their parents and siblings killed experience profound trauma, including bed-wetting, anxiety when left by the remaining parent and depression, sometimes resulting in permanent mental disability.[6] Attention span, memory and sleep are all affected, with knock-on effects at school. Children become listless and apathetic; one 10-year-old boy told an interviewer, 'Why bother studying, when they could kill me at any moment?'[7]

For many children, sleep brings little relief:

Sometimes I have nightmares. That they caught my uncle and cut off his body bit by bit and hung him up. Once I dreamt that a dead man came back in another body and followed us to Bogotá and stabbed us all. I cry a lot.[8]

On top of the trauma caused by the original act of violence, comes the shock of the flight to the city. Peasant families lose their livelihood and their profound ties to the land, and must find their way in a new and strange world of money, markets and crowded streets. Men who were local community leaders or political figures suddenly become unemployed city nobodies; if the attack was prompted by the man's political involvement, the ensuing suffering often leads to recriminations with his partner and even violence. As their family slides into poverty, they are taunted by the city's mirage of abundance, the shops crowded with glittering goods beyond their reach.

Still fearful of informers and the stigma attached to displaced families, parents pressure their children to tell no-one where they have come from, as one nine-year-old explains:

> We had to leave La Macarena because the army was going to kill us. There were spies everywhere. They killed a few people on the very day we left. Here we have many friends, but you have to be careful because there are many informers. It's better not to speak of the past, if we say anything everyone starts to ask questions. It's better to keep your mouth shut.[9]

Parents also avoid talking of the past, according to Berta from Montería: 'We never talk about what's happened – the kids just cry too much if we do.'

But for the children, this can be profoundly disorientating. With no-one to confide in or discuss their experiences with, they grow depressed and confused, unable to come to terms with their trauma or start new lives in the city.

At a broader social level, these personal horrors take place in a climate of impunity for the perpetrators. Almost no-one is ever brought to justice for the thousands of political murders committed every year. Between January 1985 and September 1992, 717 members of the left-wing UP party were assassinated. In only four cases were those responsible convicted of crimes.[10]

Families have nowhere to turn for justice, becoming filled with frustration and depression at the seemingly untouchable powers ranged against them. In such a climate, the Colombian tradition of seeking personal vengeance has flourished, a burden often passed from the mother to eldest son, when the father has been killed. This could explain why psychologists have found that displaced boys tend to show more severe mental problems than girls,[11] although it could also be because girls' problems command less attention, particularly when they do not show violent behaviour. When the perpetrators are beyond reach, this becomes fertile ground for the creation of a new generation of violence, as the depressed, alienated children of displaced families grow up into tomorrow's teenage gangsters.

Around them, the climate of fear and suspicion generated by impunity and the widespread use of informers is destroying the social bonds that tie families and individuals to the wider community. The social and cultural restraints against violent behaviour fall away, leaving a savage world of sudden death and the personal settling of scores. As Amnesty International reports, 'When the security forces literally get away with murder on a daily basis, impunity becomes part of a nation's life. The rule of law disintegrates, causing an epidemic of casual murder.'[12]

Violence in Colombia

Casual murder is no stranger to Colombia, where a whole period of its history is known simply as 'La Violencia'. During the years 1948–57 as many as 300,000 Colombians died in an orgy of blood-letting triggered by rivalries between the two main political parties.[13] Quite why Colombia should be so much more violent than its neighbours has baffled many writers, but some explanation seems to lie in the years following independence in 1830, when the ruling elites opted to prevent the state and the armed forces from acquiring too much power. In their absence, disputes were settled by ferocious conflicts between private armies of regional leaders, often linked to the main political parties. A cycle of violence and vengeance began which has been passed down through succeeding generations.[14]

Today, Colombia remains a paradox; a country which combines a long democratic tradition, a flourishing economy, and the worst human rights record in the continent. Its new constitution, approved in 1991, enshrines numerous rights for groups such as Indians and children; it says, 'The rights of children prevail over the rights of all others,'[15] words that must ring hollow to the traumatized children of the Montería slums.

Out of the years of La Violencia was born a resilient guerrilla movement which is now entering its third generation. While enjoying a degree of popular support in some regions of the country, above all for their stance against poverty and inequality, the guerrillas too have added to Colombia's human rights nightmare with the widespread use of kidnapping and death threats, as well as 'deliberate and arbitrary killings of civilians'.[16] The guerrillas have also spread the seeds of violence by providing arms and training to numerous teenagers in cities such as Medellín, many of whom subsequently went off to found criminal gangs.[17]

Estimates for the number of guerrilla fighters in Colombia range from 10,000 to 25,000, but everyone agrees that a sizeable proportion of them are children. The guerrilla leadership itself admits that about one in ten guerrilla fighters are children, while eye-witness accounts from former child combatants often put it at two or three times that figure.[18] As a representative from the guerrillas explained, 'The younger, the better. Boys are more intrepid, they are braver in war. And even though they are given almost no responsibility, when they are given it, they do it much better.'[19]

In a survey, one in five child combatants claimed to have killed at least one person, and more than half had seen people killed in front of them. Children's motives for joining are varied, but the commonest is the lure of uniforms and carrying weapons, conferring instant status on impoverished country children with little else in the way of prospects. Others join simply because life in the Colombian countryside has little else to offer. Only one in seven claim to have been forcibly recruited by the guerrillas. Guerrillas carry out active recruitment campaigns in schools and from house to house, often paying their families for several months when the children sign up.[20]

Colombia's civil war has been going on for generations, and guerrillas themselves have children, who are farmed out to other families to be reared, but often then rejoin the ranks of the fighters at 13 or 14. Vengeance also ensures that one generation's war becomes that of their children. Many guerrilla fighters say they joined up to avenge attacks on their families, as in the case of Juan Camilo:

My brother, captured; me, a deserter; my stepfather, in jail; some members of my family, dead ... almost all my family have been fighters. Maybe that's why I started so young. Since I was a kid I ran errands for them, worked for them since I was eleven or even younger.

I remember that before I went off to the front to fight, we were looking after some kidnapped politicians in our house, and one of them escaped. The next thing we knew, the army came in and burned down our house. That's when I decided to join the guerrillas – I wanted vengeance. I went to fight just after my twelfth birthday.

I only studied up to second year of primary school, but in the guerrillas you learn loads of things, about revolution, and how to avoid pregnancies. About human rights – they teach you that you shouldn't use torture, that it's very inhumane.

What I learned has stayed in my mind and I pretty much understand why they are fighting: for a more equal society, so that the gringos won't stick their noses in so much, so that they stop controlling our oil, our mines.

I had twenty days of training. At the beginning I was with the urban militias. There the main job was to sort out problems, gather intelligence, shoot down the soldiers' lead guys, place bombs. When we weren't in combat, I carried a 38mm revolver and three grenades.

Once we were at the front [in the countryside], I had to place anti-personnel mines (that was my speciality), fight, ambush the paramilitaries and soldiers, gather intelligence, look after kidnapped people, although it depends – at other times you just have to read the newspaper, do the accounts, listen to the radio, stand watch or help people sow their crops and stuff like that.

COURTESY OF JOSEPH CASTRO

The conflict between the Peruvian army and the guerrillas of the Shining Path movement has led to numerous human rights abuses, and traumatized a generation of Peruvian children.

To calm our nerves we used to drink milk mixed with gunpowder. The gunpowder makes you energetic, as if you really wanted soldiers to walk past, to kill them. You say to yourself, I hope they come from over there, you pop another cartridge and you feel more able, more determined.

The guerrilla presence across large tracts of the countryside provides the Colombian army with the pretext for most of its attacks on civilians. 'Draining the sea from the fish', in counter-insurgency parlance, means treating civilians suspected of supporting the enemy as legitimate military targets. The twisted logic of national security thus makes it legitimate for the army to bomb and machine-gun peasant families on their farms.

In Colombia, the army has gone further, helping establish a network of paramilitary gangs, including the private armies of some of the country's drug barons, creating a 'terrifying alliance of the forces of the state, and those of private individuals and organised crime'.[21]

One such 'private individual' is the notorious Fidel Castaño, alias 'Rambo'. Castaño, a cattle rancher and known drug trafficker, has driven thousands of peasant families out of northwest Colombia over the past 15 years. According to Amnesty International, these peasants are 'the target of "fumigation" campaigns' and are usually 'civilians suspected of sympathising with guerrillas, and smallholders in the way of expanding ranches'.[22]

One such target is Paulino, a 10-year-old with a sweet, nervous face, from Pueblo Bello (beautiful village):

They came and took my father. They put him a long way away. They kicked my door down, told mum not to cry, that they'd let him go if he wasn't up to anything, so she calmed down.

But they took him, and my mum went on a horse to warn the rest of her family. I stayed in the house with my sister and three little brothers.

Everyone was crying when they were taken away. We still get sad, especially at bed time. Many people recognized the ones without masks and said they were from …

Paulino catches himself just in time, remembering his mother's strictures to keep silent. Blame the guerrillas and you sound like a paramilitary supporter, blame the paramilitaries and they will mark you down as a guerrilla.

The attack on Pueblo Bello was news, even by Colombian standards, and was described in a subsequent Amnesty International report:

On the evening of 14 January 1990, 43 people 'disappeared' from the village of Pueblo Bello. According to witnesses, a squad of armed men, some in military uniform, others hooded and in plain clothes, raided the village and seized forty men from their houses. They were then forced onto two trucks which had earlier been hijacked by the armed squad. Eye witnesses saw the trucks passing through two army check points. Official investigations confirmed that the men had been abducted by a paramilitary group headed by Fidel Castaño.[23]

A subsequent investigation found nine unmarked graves, containing 24 bodies showing signs of torture; 20 of these were believed to be the men of Pueblo Bello, but only six were positively identified. The remains of the others were reburied in plastic bags labelled 'NN' (No Name). An arrest warrant against Fidel Castaño was never carried out.

Paulino's mother is a wreck. Flat broke and relying on support from the community, she still maintains her husband will return. Paulino believes her. 'My dad will come back,' he says quietly. Disappearance is the cruellest of Latin America's catalogue of human rights abuses, condemning the victim's family to suffer in limbo, refusing to acknowledge the death, unable to start living again.

Later, when the balloons are handed out, Paulino is briefly transformed, his face shining as he clutches at his balloon. Seconds later, his face closes in again.

Political violence in Latin America and the Caribbean

Aspects of Colombia's nightmare can be found up and down Latin America and the Caribbean. In what has been called a 'plague of violence', starting in 1964 with the military coup in Brazil, most of the continent has suffered wave upon wave of repression and violence, most of it carried out by states, persecuting their own citizens.[24] Conflicts between, rather than within, countries have been rare.

Although military dictatorship has not been a problem in the English-speaking Caribbean, there too, political violence has touched the lives of children. In Jamaica in the 1960s, the two main political parties, the People's National Party and the Jamaica Labour Party, signed up, armed, protected and financed rival gangs in the ghettos of Kingston to fight a proxy war over turf and votes. Violence built through the 1970s, reaching a peak in the election of 1980, when 889 people died in street fighting.[25]

By then, however, the politicians were already losing control over the gangs they had turned into the kings of the street. The gunmen soon moved in on the growing cocaine trade. After the election bloodbath, the gangs headed for the USA, setting up the feared 'posses', often named after their home neighbourhood in Kingston. Known as the 'Yardies' when they spread to Britain, the Jamaican gangs gained a reputation for extraordinary brutality and an apparent *sang froid* in the face of death, rapidly coming to dominate the street trade in crack cocaine and other drugs, and fighting murderous turf wars with rival gangs.

For boys growing up in the violent slums of Kingston, the charismatic, fearless 'rankings' of the gangs proved seductive role models, and crime seemed to offer the only way to achieve the 'respect' so prized in Jamaican society. As one posse gunman explains:

> You see it all your life. Even before I killed somebody, I felt like I killed before ... . When I shot at people, it wasn't like I was trembling and asking, 'what is this I'm doing?' It was like I was into it all along. And I think that's just from the social settings, from growing up around all that violence, the way Jamaica was with politics. The way it was when I was just a youth comin' up. And once you get up to New York, you find that being affiliated with Jamaican politics, you get stronger because of the reputation it carries. People respect you more and don't mess with your territory.[26]

In Latin America, political violence has more often been linked to the military, paramilitary groups and their opponents in the continent's numerous guerrilla movements. After Brazil's military coup in 1964, military rule spread to much of Latin America, as the armed forces overthrew governments in the name of 'national security'. By the end of 1976, two-thirds of people on the Latin American mainland lived under military dictatorship.[27] National security was Latin America's version of Cold War McCarthyism, coming to dominate military thinking throughout the Americas. A rash of guerrilla movements which sprang up across the region in the wake of the guerrilla victory which brought Fidel Castro to power in Cuba in 1959 further justified the generals' new role.

The military came to see its job as defending order in the broadest sense, including economic development and internal political and social stability. The chief threat to these was communism. A leaked minute from a 1987 meeting of the armies of the Americas revealed the extraordinary extent of the paranoia: 'The International Communist Movement objective of Marxist-Leninist infiltration in South America is a fact in the Armed Forces, in the Church, in workers' and students organisations. All ... are part of the plans for subversion.'[28] Trade unionists, peasant leaders, and their families became targets in what the military saw as a third world war against the communist menace.

Children have been profoundly affected both by guerrilla wars in their areas, and by the military's new national security doctrine, which turns their communities and families into potential targets. The damage is often more serious than that of a conventional frontier war, fought between professional (and usually adult) armies. Children grow up surrounded by fear and violence, with profound psychological consequences, as in the case of Raulito, a four-year-old Peruvian boy whose father was killed in Peru's bloody civil war:

> The terrorists shoot bullets. They come from up in the mountains. They come in ponchos, make the men lie on the floor. They kill them with bullets. The soldiers come to our village in vehicles. They arrest people. Afterwards, no-one knows anything. They shoot everywhere. They scare us.
>
> The terrorists and the soldiers fight. They shoot a lot, like devils. The soldiers are bad. If you look at them, they shoot at you or they take you to the river like a terrorist, tied up, and throw you in the water.
>
> Everyone kills, the terrorists kill the soldiers and burst the tyres on the vehicles. The soldiers kill the terrorists and other people. When I grow up I want to buy a car with a siren and bullets to shoot soldiers and terrorists. I'm going to shoot![29]

Argentina was one of the worst hit by the military's new zeal for fighting the enemy within. Following a coup in 1976, anything from 9000 to 30,000 people 'disappeared',[30] dragged from their homes in the middle of the night by members of the security forces, who spirited them away in the unmarked Ford Falcons that came to be dreaded in Buenos Aires.

The psychological impact of disappearance was particularly bad, as one Argentine woman recalls:

> It's very difficult to explain how you feel when they take a child from you and you don't know what's happened to that child. It's like a terrible emptiness. No one would help us. At the police stations and the barracks we stood in queues for hours and they turned us away. As we began to recognise in the faces of other women the same despair and desperation we felt, we began to realise that we weren't alone, that there were hundreds of mothers like us, searching for their children.[31]

The disappearances galvanized a whole new human rights phenomenon in Latin America, the Mothers of the Disappeared. Women who had previously lived their whole lives in the home entered politics through their role as mothers. As repression spread to Central America and Peru, so did the mothers' organizations, becoming one of the most effective and courageous human rights movements in recent years.

As hope of finding their lost children faded amid stories of concentration camps and clandestine cemeteries, a new twist to the story unfolded. Many of the teenagers and young people taken by the Argentine military were

DRAWN FROM LIFE

An exhibition of drawings by refugee children from El Salvador

Drawing by Cidela Solozano, Fatima Refugee Camp, Costa Rica.

Organised by the El Salvador Committee for Human Rights, 21 Compton Terrace, London N1 2UN. Telephone 01-359 1836

Children are often witnesses to army atrocities in countries such as Peru, Colombia or Guatemala, and suffer severe psychological disturbance as a result. Drawing by a Salvadorean child in a refugee camp in Costa Rica in the 1980s.

either pregnant or had babies with them at the time of capture. Many were subsequently given away to childless army and police families. Some Mothers of the Disappeared became the Grandmothers, using photographs and genetic fingerprinting to search for their missing grandchildren. When success came, it was shattering, as in the case of Paula, who at 18 months had been kidnapped along with her parents and handed over to a policeman and his wife. In 1985 she became the first child to be restored to her rightful grandmother, Elsa, who recalls:

> I went to speak to her with my husband. She was crying a lot, she was very angry. I told her I was the mother of her mother. 'Lies!' she shouted, 'My mother is Raquel and my father is Ruben.' She began to scream, saying that the only thing I wanted was to destroy her family. I replied that the only thing I wanted was her, because she was my granddaughter. 'I don't believe you.' 'I've brought you some photos so you can see what you think, see if you remember your parents.'
>
> I'd made enlargements of photos of her parents with Paula in their arms. She looked at one photo of herself and said, 'yes, that's like one in my house'. She stood looking at the photo of her mother and said nothing. She looked at the photograph of her father and cried and cried, we couldn't stop her. So I said to her, 'Do you know what you used to call your father?' 'No', she said. 'You used to call him Calio.' When I said it she just looked at me and repeated it, in just the same way as she used to when she was little. Then she began to scream.[32]

Although some critics feared that the interests of the grandmother were being placed before those of the child in a second uprooting, Paula was reported to have settled in well in her new home.

As civilian rule returned to countries such as Argentina and Brazil in the 1980s, the centre of violence moved north, to Central America and the Andes. In the wake of the Nicaraguan revolution of 1979, the military in El Salvador and Guatemala tried to crush guerrilla wars by carrying out particularly barbaric attacks on their civilian supporters, real or imagined. Bombardments, massacres and more targeted disappearances, often at the hands of 'death squads' made up from off-duty members of the security forces, spread fear throughout the countryside.

The bloodiest conflict was in Guatemala, where the military went on the rampage against the country's majority Indian population – 100,000 people have been killed in the last thirty years, and in the worst of the killing during the early 1980s, 440 Indian villages were wiped off the map.[33] A further 200,000 people, mainly Indians, fled the countryside for refugee camps in Mexico, and a million more sought the relative safety of Guatemala's cities.[34] Intent on terrorizing the Indian population, the military specifically targeted children. Eye-witness accounts confirm that soldiers used machetes to kill children as young as two. When investigators later exhumed 74 skeletons from a 1982 massacre in Dos Erres, El Petén, 67 of them were of children under the age of 12.[35]

The impact on children was similar to that in Colombia, creating a scarred, disoriented, often angry generation, including 250,000 orphans.[36] As one 13-year-old daughter of a disappeared father told a Canadian author, 'I don't know who they were, or where to find them. But I am angry. Sometimes I feel angry at everybody.'[37] Indian children further suffered from the racial overtones of the army's assault, often abandoning their traditional ways as they fled to the cities, starting to speak Spanish and adopting anonymous Western dress.

In neighbouring El Salvador, the death toll was similar, although without the racial dimension, since the country's Indians were virtually wiped out in a previous army massacre in 1932. Under the UN Convention, governments are supposed to 'take all feasible measures to ensure protection and care of children who are affected by an armed conflict'.[38] The reality was altogether more horrific. In 1980, the feared Atlacatl battalion of the Salvadorean army massacred at least 800 people in an orgy of bloodletting at the peasant community of El Mozote. The killing lasted all day on 11 December, as the soldiers slaughtered first the men, then the women, and finally the children, according to the sole surviving eye-witness, Rufina Amaya, who managed to escape as darkness fell:

> By six o'clock night was falling. When they had finished killing the women, the soldiers set fire to the bodies. Some of the women had taken their children with them, while others had remained behind. Just by the bonfire of corpses a child cried out, and one of the soldiers said, 'Why don't you kill that one?' There was a burst of gunfire, and the child didn't cry out any more. I was desperate, because I'd left my four children who'd been locked up.
>
> At about eleven that night, I could hear cries from the children, calling for their mothers. The soldiers were killing them too. They were hanging them, cutting their throats. I couldn't hear any shots, just the children's screams. I was the only survivor of El Mozote. My four children and my husband were among those who were killed.[39]

Thousands of peasant families fled across the border to Honduras, or into the refugee camps of the capital, where one Belgian nun said of the incoming orphans, 'They come to me like angry wolves.'[40]

As in Argentina, Salvadorean children were seized by government soldiers intent on terrorizing the civilian population, even though, under the UN Convention, governments are committed to 'prevent the abduction of, the sale of or traffic in children'.[41] The stolen children were handed out to wealthy Salvadorean families and military officers. Others were sent to the so-called 'fattening houses' prior to being sold to foreign families (including the US military advisers training the army) in a lucrative adoption racket which brought in as much as £13,000 per child.[42]

According to Jon Cortina, a Jesuit priest who is campaigning for the return of the children, as many as 400 were taken. To date his 'Children's Search Association' has documented 280 cases; 29 children have been located as far afield as Italy and France. Three cases have been confirmed using DNA testing, including that of the long-lost daughter of José and Victoria Laínez, who was found living in Ohio. Her name had been changed from Imelda to Gina by her well-meaning American parents, who had been told that her real parents had been killed.

One difference with the case of the Argentine Grandmothers of the Disappeared is that in El Salvador relatives are not seeking the return of the children, accepting that the children will lead better lives with their adoptive parents than in their poverty-stricken home villages. Instead, the group is seeking access for the relatives and 'building a healthy relationship between the child and their natural family'.[43]

The greater strength of the guerrillas in El Salvador also meant more child combatants. In many cases, children as young as 11 sought revenge by joining up with the guerrillas, who accepted them, according to Human Rights Watch, claiming they were joining of their own free will, and with the consent of their parents.[44] Guerrilla armies everywhere use children as lookouts, messengers and fighters – it is not for nothing that the guerrillas in El Salvador were referred to by the general public as 'los muchachos', 'the boys'.

Long after the Central American wars ended in a series of peace agreements in the early 1990s, children continued to pay the price. In the words of two Nicaraguan market children, both of whom lost their fathers in that country's civil war in the 1980s, 'Adults go to war, but they don't realise what damage they are doing to children.' Ironically, the much-vaunted peace agreements in both El Salvador and Nicaragua have been followed by an epidemic of violent crime. In El Salvador, children who had fled the country to Los Angeles brought its gang culture back with them, and by 1996 the death-rate was substantially higher than during the war. In Nicaragua, most of the violent crime has come from ex-soldiers, thrown out of both the government and the guerrilla forces of the 'Contras'. Abandoned by the state, they have turned to the gun for survival. A further legacy of the wars are the minefields still dotted around former war zones in Central America and the Andes. Although not on the horrific scale of Angola or Afghanistan, they continue to claim young victims.

Further south, in Peru, a particularly bloodthirsty guerrilla movement, known as the Shining Path, matched the barbarity of the government soldiers. Both sides wiped out villages and massacred civilians they saw as supporting the enemy. Shining Path made widespread use of child fighters, recruiting them from secondary schools as young as 13. In one particularly barbarous practice, Shining Path used children to execute those deemed guilty in so-called 'popular trials'.[45]

Teenagers were attracted by the glamour of guerrilla life, as one young man told a Peruvian investigator, 'They were adolescent kids, and they were desperate to learn about arms, a submachine gun for example. For them, handling dynamite was a big thing.'[46] One priest recalls arriving to teach at a school in a Shining Path-dominated area and asking the pupils to sing. The children duly sang Shining Path's battle song, convinced it was Peru's national anthem.[47]

Violence and weaponry indelibly mark the imagination of children, as in the following story written in broken Spanish by a 12-year-old Indian girl from the Peruvian Andes.[48]

> Helicopters are like toys. In the United States everyone has them. Flying, they go. That's why they send them here. But they are useful for other things. So that the soldiers can travel.

> One day, everyone will fight with helicopters, boats and planes. I'm going to die. You too.

> They say the helicopter looks for people in the mountains, it is like an animal. But bigger. Inside its belly there are bombs. Boom! Boom! they go.

> That's why the pigeons get scared, the cows, the chickens run a long way away.

> No-one will be left after the battle.

In Peru, the vast majority of the victims of both guerrillas and army were Indians, adding new twists to the fate of the country's estimated 600,000 displaced.[49] In a desiccated, boulder-strewn barrio on the outskirts of Peru's capital city, Lima, a whole village set up home 10 years ago, after fleeing the violence in the interior. Initially, the village held together, but according to Rosa Maria, a community leader in the new village who herself has abandoned the long pony-tail and broad skirts of her mother's generation, parents have watched their children inexorably grow away from their roots, drawn by city life and the availability of better schooling, always in Spanish:

> *Most of us spoke Quechua back there, even the children. Now my daughters understand it, but don't speak it. I talk to them and they say 'Mum, you're an old lady! You're speaking Quechua!' Even the ones who have gone back to our village speak Spanish now. It's a shame to lose our ancestors' language – we are Peruvians.*

According to Rosa Maria, a wedge has been driven between the generations. Children who have grown up in the city hate the idea of returning to the countryside, while parents pine for their lost fields. Most parents seem to accept that the change is permanent, perhaps returning to plant and harvest their fields, but keeping their families in Lima for the children's sake.

Conclusion

Political violence often begins in obedience to short-term political logic, whether as a response to inequality or injustice, or as a consequence of the élite's determination to keep power in its hands. But whether by stoking gang warfare in Jamaica, recruiting child combatants in Colombia, or brutalizing civilians in Peru and Central America, it sets in train a process which rapidly escapes political control. Children and young people witness or take part in atrocities which scar them for ever, creating a new generation for whom violence is a legitimate way to settle conflicts, take revenge, or earn money. Violence is a genie that cannot be put back in the bottle. Political violence eats away at the social fabric, bequeathing a legacy of social violence, crime and brutality long after their political origins have been forgotten.

Across Latin America and the Caribbean, with the exception of Colombia, the levels of political repression have fallen in recent years, as military regimes have given way to elected governments. Yet violence has if anything increased, as the seeds of political violence have become a harvest of crime and social violence reaching epidemic proportions. The politicians, generals and *comandantes* who decided to turn the guns on their own population must bear a substantial part of the blame.

Notes

1 Reuters (14 January 1997).

2 Amnesty International, *Colombia: Political Violence: Myth and Reality* (London, 1994), p. 15.

3 *Ibid.*, p. 5.

4 SCF UK, private communication (Bogotá, September 1996).

5 Otros Niños, *Testimonios de la Infancia Colombiana* (Bogotá, 1993), p. 130.

6 Bertha Lucia Castaño, *Violencia Socio-Política en Colombia: Repercusión en la Salud Mental de las Víctimas* (Bogotá, 1994), p. 32.

7 Edgar Ardila, 'Infancia y conflicto armado en Colombia', in *Niños y Jovenes en la Colombia de Hoy* (Bogotá, 1995), p. 51.

8 Flor Edilma Osorio Pérez, *La Violencia del Silencio: Desplazados del Campo a la Ciudad* (Bogotá, 1993), p. 123.

9 Edgar Ardila, *op. cit.*, p. 56.

10 Amnesty International, *op. cit.*, p. 87.

11 Bertha Lucia Castaño, *op. cit.*, p. 49.

12 Amnesty International, *op. cit.*, p. 7.

13 Colin Harding, *Colombia in Focus* (London, 1995), p. 22.

14 Harvey F. Kline, *Colombia: Democracy Under Assault* (Boulder CO, 1995), p. 38.

15 Constitución Política de Colombia (Bogotá, 1992), Article 44, p. 22.

16 Amnesty International, *op. cit.*, p. 67.

17 Human Rights Watch, *Generation Under Fire: Children and Violence in Colombia* (New York, 1994), p. 38.

18 Defensoría del Pueblo, *La niñez y sus derechos*, Boletin No. 2 (Santafé de Bogotá, May 1996).

19 *Ibid.*

20 *Ibid.*

21 Amnesty International, *op. cit.*, p. 5.

22 *Ibid.*, p. 52.

23 *Ibid.*, p. 50.

24 Peter Oakley, *Working with Children in Situations of Violence: The Case of Latin America*, SCF Working Paper #12 (London, September 1995), p. 9.

25 Laurie Gunst, *Born Fi' Dead* (New York, 1995), p. 111.

26 *Ibid.*, p. 167.

27 Duncan Green, *Faces of Latin America* (London, 1991), p. 188.

28 *Total War Against the Poor* (New York, 1990).

29 Sonia Goldenberg, *Reportaje al Perú Anónimo* (Lima, 1990), p. 118.

30 Jo Fisher, *Out of the Shadows* (London, 1993), p. 102.

31 *Ibid.*, p. 105.

32 *Ibid.*, p. 127.

33 Duncan Green, *Guatemala: Burden of Paradise* (London, 1992), p. 33.

34 Ana Silvia Monzón, *The Impact of Armed Conflict on Maya Children in Guatemala* (mimeo) (London, 1996), p. 2.

35 *Ibid.*, p. 5.

36 *Ibid.*, p. 6.

37 Alison Acker, *Children of the Volcano* (London, 1986), p. 41.

38 UN Convention on the Rights of the Child (Geneva, 1989), Article 38.

39 Mandy Macdonald and Mike Gatehouse, *In the Mountains of Morazán: Portrait of a Returned Refugee Community in El Salvador* (London, 1995), p. 43.

40 Alison Acker, *op. cit.*, p. 80.

41 UN Convention on the Rights of the Child (Geneva, 1989), Article 38.

42 Steve Fainaru, 'El Salvador seeks its lost children', *Guardian* (London, 20 July 1996).

43 *Latin America Press* (Lima, 8 February 1996), p. 3.

44 Human Rights Watch Children's Project, *Children in Combat* (New York, January 1996), p. 7.

45 *Ibid.*, p. 13.

46 Deborah Poole and Gerardo Rénique, *Peru: Time of Fear* (London, 1992), p. 61.

47 Interview with author (Cusco, December 1995).

48 Los Helicópteros, in Juan Granda Oré, *Los Pequeños Zorros: Relatos Orales de Niños Ayacuchanos* (Lima, 1990), p. 50.

49 Representative of National Repopulation Support Programme, cited in *Diario la República* (Lima, 24 October 1996).

CHAPTER 6

Underdeveloping Children

The Price of Economic Change

The air over the main rubbish dump outside the Nicaraguan capital of Managua is heavy with the impending storm. Dust devils fling litter and flocks of scavenging vultures high into the air. A rainbow, broad and low, hangs incongruously over the scene as the storm approaches.

Vying with the famished dogs and phlegmatic cows, hundreds of huddled figures rake through the rubbish with long poles. 'Yesterday I found bottles and shoe soles, and sold them for 10 córdobas' (about 80p), says 14-year-old Cándida, a skinny girl with brown curly hair and two earrings in each ear.

Times are getting harder for the rubbish-pickers of Managua, according to Cándida, who explains with unconscious irony, 'The dump's changed – now it's just rubbish. Before, few people went – now it's full and there's nothing worth finding.' She remembers better days: 'Once, my father found a gold ring and gave it to my mum, but she had to sell it to buy medicine when my little brother got sick.'

Cándida lives with both parents and her five brothers and sisters in a one-room hut made of planks studded with cooking utensils and plates, hanging from nails banged into the walls. The air is acrid with woodsmoke as her mother Maria, a big slow-moving 35-year-old, cooks rice and beans over a fire in the yard. A radio hung from a nearby tree pumps out salsa music. A fence made of scrap iron marks the edge of their stamped-earth 'garden'. The woodsmoke helps keep the clouds of malarial mosquitoes at bay.

It may seem a long way from the dump at Acagualinca to the boardrooms of Washington, but the changes that Cándida has seen in her brief working life have been deeply influenced by the workings of international politics and economics. Nicaragua is but the latest example of the enormous social cost of the economic reforms demanded from Third World countries over recent years by such powerful bodies as the International Monetary Fund (IMF), World Bank and the governments of the wealthier nations. One way or another, these reforms, which go under the name of 'structural adjustment', have affected every man, woman and child in Latin America and the Caribbean.

Although structural adjustment programmes in Latin America and the Caribbean have achieved some success in terms of reducing inflation and rekindling economic growth, they have exacerbated inequality, increased poverty and damaged already meagre health and education services. Children have borne the brunt of many of these changes. Many Latin Americans also blame structural adjustment for the region's rising levels of crime and social breakdown, saying that the new economic model has effectively excluded a large proportion of the population from the limited benefits it has brought to the economy as a whole.

Nicaragua entered the 1990s in chaos. For just over a decade, the left-wing government of the Sandinista National Liberation Front had presided over a crumbling economy, largely the result of a merciless war of attrition by the US government, which saw in the Sandinistas a communist menace that could easily spread throughout Washington's 'back yard' in Central America. Presidents Reagan and Bush cut aid, imposed an embargo on trade between the two countries, and blocked loans to Nicaragua from international lenders.

In addition, the US government financed the creation of an army of disaffected 'Contras', who launched raids into Nicaragua from their bases in neighbouring countries, aiming both to damage morale and force a massive diversion of scarce government funds into defence. The result (compounded by Sandinista inexperience and misjudgement) was a nightmare of hyperinflation, falling living standards and rising poverty. Economic crisis rapidly reversed the early gains of the revolution, which had handed thousands of farms over to the peasants and greatly improved health and education services.

By 1990 the Nicaraguan population had had enough of war, hyperinflation and rising poverty, and elected the anti-Sandinista candidate, Violeta Chamorro, to the presidency. The voters' main hope was that, once the pro-US Chamorro took office, a flood of US and other aid would pull Nicaragua from the economic mire.

The aid duly poured in, in astonishing quantities for a country of Nicaragua's size. Between 1990 and 1993, the government received US$500 for every Nicaraguan man, woman and child.[1] But it has come with numerous strings attached. Within two months of the election, Nicaragua was obliged to sign the first of a series of agreements with the IMF, World Bank, InterAmerican Development Bank and USAID, under which the government has promised to implement painful economic reforms in exchange for aid.[2] These powerful economic institutions have used Nicaragua's desperation to shepherd (some might say frog-march) the country at high speed along the road to reform.

The main aims of the reforms were to end hyperinflation (running at 13,000 per cent in the year that Chamorro took office) and to shift Nicaragua from being a state-led economy, dominated by government-owned farms, state regulation and nationalized industries, towards a system where market forces decide the fate of the country.

In a series of 'stabilization programmes', the Chamorro government raised interest rates and cut spending to the bone, duly getting inflation down from 13,000 per cent to just 19 per cent in 1993.[3] It privatized hundreds of state-owned companies, removed regulations on trade and banks and other financial institutions, and pushed up interest rates to 'squeeze inflation out of the system'.

The social impact of such measures is felt throughout the country, not least in Acagualinca, where, in the shanty town next to the dump, most breadwinners have lost their jobs in recent years, driving entire families to swell the ranks of the rubbish-pickers. Early on in the recession, Cándida's father lost his job loading trucks and joined his neighbours on the dump.

Nationwide, the combination of rocketing interest rates and lay-offs among thousands of state employees precipitated yet further economic collapse, despite the huge dollar inflows. Unemployment surged from 25 per cent in 1988 to 52 per cent in 1993. By 1994, three out of every four Nicaraguans were living below the poverty line. The state has ended all food subsidies and cut most school feeding programmes, so children eat less – per capita consumption of the national staples of rice and beans fell by 15 per cent between 1990 and 1993.[4] Many of Nicaragua's social improvements, which won admiration around the world in the 1980s, are being swiftly reversed.

Education

The impact on the education system has been immediate, according to Ana Elizabeth Sandra Madrigal, the director of a primary school in the northern town of El Viejo:

In the end it all comes down to economics. People have always been poor here, but things are getting worse. The few people who had permanent jobs are losing them. Most of the people round here worked on the banana plantations and they've been shutting them down since they were privatized. I've seen parents stop sending their kids to school, because they hate sending them with nothing to eat. Drop-out rates have gone right up.

The basic teacher's wage is just US$60 a month, and that's after a pay rise! It's not enough to keep even one person, let alone a family. Three teachers *here give extra classes in a private school. In my old school, several of them took in washing and ironing to get through. And its getting worse. They freeze our wages, but prices carry on rising. Many of our teachers are leaving the country – two went to the US recently.*

This school has nothing. When it rains, we can't have classes because the rain pours through the roof. Everything is running out – there aren't enough desks, so the kids have to come in early if they want to grab one. If not, they have to go home and find a chair to bring in. The parents are supposed to buy the notebooks and pencils, but if they can't afford them we have to help – we get donations from private schools.

I don't think we are proud of our education system any more. All those things we did – literacy, adult education, it's all disappeared. Many people can't read or write – they've lost it. Kids used to get books, pencils, everything free, now you have to pay and teachers have to find their own books and materials. There's no training any more – the Ministry gives us nothing. My uncle's high up in the Ministry and he drives round in a brand new car – he loves the new system!

Health

As part of the adjustment programme, 'user fees' have been introduced into the health system, and many people have simply given up going to hospitals when they fall ill. As Cándida's mother explains, 'I'm sick, but what's the point of going to hospitals if you can't afford the medicines? These days you just go to hospital to die.'

The Chamorro government came to power in the same year as the UN Convention on the Rights of the Child, duly signed by Nicaragua, came into force. Article 24 of the Convention clearly says signatory states shall 'recognise the right of the child to the enjoyment of the highest attainable standard of health and to the facilities for the treatment of illness'. They 'shall strive to ensure that no child is deprived of his or her right of access to such health services'.

Yet such paper promises count for nothing in the face of the pressures to cut back on state spending. By 1993 government expenditure on health and education was only two-thirds of its mid-1980s figure.[5] Hospitals have been forced to open private wards to generate income, while health centres in the countryside are starved of cash and supplies. In one provincial town, a notice on a health centre's grimy wall reads: 'Anyone coming for an injection must bring their own syringe, elastoplast, gauze and bandages. Attention is free. Thank you.'

According to Maira Guzmán, the harassed head of the health centre:

Economic reforms in recent years have increased the gap between rich and poor. A well-off father and son shop in a supermarket in Tegucigalpa, Honduras.

Ninety per cent of the children we see are underweight, and of these about ten per cent are seriously malnourished. Before, we had a few medicines once in a while, and we had a bit of milk to give out. Now there's almost nothing – the ministry sends medicines once a month, but they barely last a week. People have to buy from private pharmacies and most can't afford it.

We see mothers coming back three times in one week with the same kid, worse each time, because they can't afford to buy any medicines at the pharmacy. So they come back in desperation to see if any medicines have arrived here. You see it in their faces. You say, 'but you brought this kid yesterday and now she's worse'. It's very frustrating, and in the countryside it's even worse – they never see medicines there.

Cuts in the health service, compounded by mismanagement, have had a devastating impact on children's welfare at just the time when poverty and malnutrition are increasing. Studies show that, after decades of steady decline, the number of children born underweight or dying before their first birthday is once again rising sharply.[6] While the poor see their precious health centres rot away, the better-off are turning to the burgeoning private health service, which is able to lure many of the best doctors away from the demoralized public system. As the public health service came under attack, private health spending rose by a quarter from 1988 to 1994.[7]

In Acagualinca, malnutrition is evident. Across the dirt street from Cándida's shack, a naked flaccid-skinned toddler plays alone, spinning round and round, gape-mouthed. His two-year-old brother died this morning, after a bout of diarrhoea. Their mother has to leave them alone in the house every day, as she goes off to scavenge on the dump. The father is an alcoholic.

As regular waged jobs disappear under the double blow of state lay-offs and recession, people have no choice but to swell the ranks of the so-called informal sector, the army of the self-employed that in much of Latin America and the Caribbean now outnumbers the ranks of those in 'regular' jobs. Rules on child labour are largely ignored and virtually impossible to enforce in the informal sector, and the growing number of these kind of jobs, allied to families' desperation to make ends meet, has led to a sharp increase in the number of children working in the streets, rubbish dumps and backstreet sweatshops of the region.

Recycling rubbish on the Managua dump is just one of many informal sector trades, most of them plagued by insecurity and pitiful wages. At one Managua crossroads, 30 people, most of them children, weave between the cars, begging or selling everything from chewing gum to superglue. The children are so small that their larger brothers and sisters have to hoist them onto the car bonnets before they can run a dirty rag over the windscreens in exchange for a few coins or a curse.

Ironically, the children at the traffic lights find their task made easier by another by-product of structural adjustment – traffic jams. Ten years ago, traffic congestion was unknown on the deserted streets. Since then, the unleashing of market forces has made the rich richer, sharply increasing inequality and filling the streets of Managua with shiny new cars and jeeps.

Adjustment in Latin America and the Caribbean[8]

Nicaragua is experiencing an accelerated version of a process which has been going on in most of the rest of Latin America and the Caribbean since 1982, when Mexico, like a mortgage-holder unable to keep up its repayments, announced it could no longer repay its debts, and was rapidly followed by most other governments in the region. Instead of being repossessed, Mexico was bailed out by the IMF and other institutions, but the price for such help was introducing the same brand of economic reforms as Nicaragua was to follow a decade later.

In retrospect, the Mexican crash was a watershed for development in Latin America and the Caribbean. For almost fifty years, since the shockwaves of the Great Depression in Europe and North America battered the Latin American economy in the 1930s, the region's governments used the state to try and kick-start development. In a southern variant of the New Deal in the USA, or Keynesianism in the UK, nationalized industries took over and developed crucial areas such as oil, iron and steel, and telecommunications, while the state regulated economies, invested in essential infrastructure such as water and electricity supplies, and protected new local industries against competition from cheap imports.

The drive for industrialization was known as 'import substitution', since it aimed to end Third World countries' reliance on imported machinery and other manufactured goods. For a time it was a great success. Much of the region, especially the larger economies such as Mexico and Brazil, entered a period of record growth. However, the state-led model eventually suffered much the same fate as the state-run economies in Eastern Europe. Protected industries had no need to invest or innovate, and fell behind the rest of the world in technology and productivity; political interference encouraged corruption and incompetence, as people were appointed to run state companies on the basis of political favouritism rather than merit. The ever-growing state sector began to outspend meagre revenues (rich Latin Americans have always been adept at avoiding taxes), generating growing inflation.

Import substitution also failed in social terms. Latin America and the Caribbean have always had hugely unequal societies, and import substitution further aggravated the situation. In order to keep wage costs down in industry, governments held down food prices, penalizing the peasant farmers who grew the food and creating growing poverty in the countryside. Millions of peasants gave up hope of earning a living from the land and drifted to the cities, where they joined the armies of hopeful job-seekers in the shanty towns that sprang up on the edges of the continent's cities. Some achieved their ambition of a steady, waged job, but most ended up as street sellers, as domestic servants or doing odd jobs. Even so, they generally fared better than those they left behind in the forgotten farms and villages of rural Latin America.

Latin America at the time of the Mexican crash was an economic basket case; the most unequal continent on earth, with economies unable to produce enough jobs for its rising population. Increasingly, the poor, who had been exploited ever since the Spanish conquest, were becoming surplus even to the requirements of the exploiters. As new generations of children grew up without hope of a steady job, social scientists and politicians began to talk of 'exclusion' from national political and economic processes, rather than exploitation, as the true obstacle to development in Latin America and the Caribbean.

The debt crisis which broke over the continent in August 1982 brought in its wake further recession and hardship for millions of Latin Americans. But for Sir William Ryrie, a top World Bank official, it was 'a blessing in disguise'.[9] The debt crisis forced Latin America into a constant round of debt negotiations, providing the Reagan government, along with the IMF and the other international financial institutions, with all the leverage it needed to overhaul the region's economy, in alliance with Northern commercial creditor banks and the region's home-grown free-marketeers. Latin America was ripe for a free market revolution.

Since then, almost all of Latin America and the Caribbean has followed a similar path to that of Nicaragua. In the initial stage of reform, known as 'stabilization', the IMF and banks pressured governments both to crack down on inflation by cutting spending, and to keep up their debt repayments. At the same time, commercial banks decided that Latin America had become a bad risk, and stopped lending. Throughout the 1980s, capital flowed out of Latin America, destined for the rich countries of the North. This perverse flow of wealth from the poor to the wealthy squeezed out US$218.6 billion, over US$500 for every man, woman and child in the region.[10]

With time, reforms have moved on to full structural adjustment, involving a relentless assault on the state's role in the economy, including cuts in social spending, privatization, and deregulation of everything from trade to banking to employers' abilities to hire and fire at will. The aim of such measures is to move Latin America and the Caribbean rapidly to a dynamic market-based economy, but up to now, the panorama has largely been one of recession and austerity.

Few countries in the region have escaped the structural adjustment steamroller. In the Caribbean, the most recent recruit is Haiti, where Father Jean-Bertrand Aristide, a radical priest, was elected president in 1991 but was then rapidly overthrown by the Haitian military. The US government agreed to back Aristide's restoration, and helped put through a $1.2 billion aid package in loans and grants, but in exchange he had to promise to sign up for the full structural adjustment treatment, including privatization of state companies, ending import tariffs, and cutting food subsidies and public spending.[11]

In 1994, US troops duly helped put Father Aristide back in the presidential palace, and the economic programme got under way. From the US and World Bank perspective, Haiti's only option is to trade its way out of poverty, attracting foreign investors with its low wages. In its cheap-labour assembly plants, owned by Haitian contractors, women sew Mickey Mouse and Pocahontas pyjamas for just seven cents a pair. After export to the USA, they go on sale in Wal-mart for $11.97 a pair. The Haitian workers' wages in some cases work out at just 12 cents per hour, far below even the minimum wage of 30 cents.[12]

Impact on children

Economists may argue over the economic costs and benefits of structural adjustment, but the human cost is plain to see. 'No gain without pain', goes the mantra, but to date most Latin Americans have seen plenty of pain, while the promised benefits, in the shape of steady growth and rising standards of living, have failed to materialize. Instead, the family has borne the brunt of austerity, causing permanent damage to the region's children.

The social cost of structural adjustment is particularly stark in the mining towns of Bolivia, held up by international lenders as a model adjuster. In one small mining community, a tiny adobe house is crammed with gnarled *pailliris* (mining women) in patched shawls and battered felt hats, whose calloused hands work breaking up rocks on the surface in search of scraps of tin ore. Outside, the scene is one of high-altitude poverty, all greys and browns in the thin air. The paths between the miners' huts are strewn with plastic bags and human excrement, dried black in the unforgiving *altiplano* sun. Rising beyond the squalid settlement, the barren hills and grey slagheaps of the tin mines complete the bleak panorama. The litany of poor women's woes begins, gathering momentum as it goes:

Before, it was not too bad, but now we never have a good month. We're mainly widows or abandoned. My husband left to look for work and never came back. Now I have to look after four kids – I can't pay for their schoolbooks and clothes. I've been doing this work for seven years now and my lungs are finished. I've vomited blood for weeks at a time and still had to keep working.

In the old days, women used to stay at home because the men had work. Now, with the recession, we've had to go out to work. Many of our children have been abandoned. Their fathers have left and there's no love left in us when we get home late from work. We leave food for them, they play in the streets – there are always accidents, and no doctors. I feel like a slave in my own country – we get up at 4am and at 11 at night we are still mending and patching.

The speaker, Josefina Muruchi, breaks down in a coughing fit. Suddenly, in a mixture of Spanish and Quechua, all the other women burst into speech, unleashing a torrent of pain and suffering. In the gloom, most of the women are sobbing.

This is doloroso for us. We have nothing. Nothing. Only coca [a stimulant leaf chewed to suppress hunger] to keep us going. It's the children, we want them to study, but they're so malnourished and the price of tin is so low. Our kids say 'mami, I want to help' and don't do their homework, but then they fail their exams and have to repeat the year and the teachers are always asking for money and we haven't got it and because our children are so ashamed they drop out of school. If I start vomiting blood again, what's going to happen to my children?

The pailliris' lament reveals the devastating effects of structural adjustment on women and children. Families have been hit from all sides: wages have fallen and jobs have become more insecure; men have been forced to migrate in search of work, often failing to return; children are forced out to work early, driven by poverty and the rising costs of schooling; women have increasingly found themselves forced to play the roles of both breadwinners and mothers, at a time when support structures such as social services and government food subsidies are being cut.

For many women, the burden becomes too much to bear. One study in a poor barrio of the Ecuadorean city of Guayaquil showed how economic adjustment over a 10-year period left one in seven women 'burnt out', as they simply gave up the unequal struggle.[13] The study also revealed how the impact on women has a knock-on effect on their children. Women with only very young children, forced out to work, have to lock them up while away, increasing the danger of accidents. In families with older children, the eldest daughter rapidly becomes a 'little mother', taking over the cooking, cleaning and childcare by the age of 10 or 11, wrecking her chances of getting a decent education. Children are also likely victims of increasing domestic violence, as arguments erupt between their mothers and angry, frustrated fathers, humiliated by their inability to fulfil the traditional role of breadwinner.

In the 1990s the region has returned to spasmodic economic growth, but the benefits show few signs of 'trickling down' to the poor. Instead, critics believe that a new kind of 'jobless growth' is taking place, where, even during economic booms, firms constantly cut their workforce and governments cut spending. As a result, unemployment remains high even in periods of high growth in economies such as Argentina's. In good times and in bad, exclusion appears to be an inevitable consequence of the new model, and an increasing range of academics, politicians and grass-roots groups have begun to call for a fundamental change in economic direction.

Education

Signatories to the UN Convention promise to 'make primary education compulsory and free to all',[14] but such promises have been swept aside in the rush to reduce public spending, which has forced schools to claw back ever-increasing amounts from hard-pressed parents. In Peru, one of the fiercest adjusters, per capita expenditure on education after the 1990 adjustment programme was less than a third of its 1985 figure, reaching only US$40 in 1993.[15]

In Jamaica (another keen adjuster), Alanzo Jones, principal of Bogue Hill All Age School near Montego Bay, has seen the impact on his pupils:

> We can see the literacy rate falling and exam results getting poorer. I think attendance patterns have got worse too – we have more problems with sleepy children, children without textbooks. Every year we get worse children to work with – in terms of their reading level and response. The GCSE results are deteriorating. We have seen a resurgence of the diseases we used to know in the 1960s: ringworm is back, along with mumps and measles. They had been kept down for years but all of a sudden they've come back in the last year or so.

According to Mr Jones, even though the Jamaican government's education budget has kept ahead of inflation, the impact has been undone by the broader impact of adjustment in increasing poverty. 'If you don't deal with the people's economics, it won't work', he concludes, 'you can't convert a hungry man.'

Rising poverty and the loss of many steady jobs in the public sector have combined to increase the number of street sellers, many of them children. A girl sells at the traffic lights in the Salvadorean capital of San Salvador.

Poverty and health

The debt crisis and structural adjustment have greatly increased both inequality and poverty in Latin America and the Caribbean. By 1993, the UN's Economic Commission for Latin America and the Caribbean, ECLAC, reported that the 1980s had seen 60 million new names join the grim roll-call of the poor, leaving 46 per cent of the population, nearly 200 million people,[16] living in poverty. Almost half of them were indigent, barely existing on an income of less than a dollar a day. Their numbers have continued to rise in the 1990s.

Poverty and child death go hand in hand. According to UNICEF, in 1990 nearly a million children under five died in Latin America and the Caribbean, three-quarters of them from preventable causes such as diarrhoea and malnutrition.[17] Of those who survived, six million were malnourished, a million of them severely so. Even then, UNICEF believes that 'these figures are no doubt underestimated'.[18]

Neglected sewage and water systems, victims of public spending cuts in the adjustment programmes of the 1980s, played an important role in allowing cholera to return to the continent in 1991, after an absence of over sixty years. According to official figures, which are underestimates due to under-reporting, by the end of 1995, 1.3 million people had been infected, of whom 11,000 had died.[19] Malaria and tuberculosis (TB) are also making a comeback in the new, structurally adjusted Latin America, exacting a heavy toll on future generations. TB alone killed 75,000 Latin Americans in 1995, mostly in Brazil and Peru.[20] The broader social cost of the new epidemics was revealed in an article which appeared in the Peruvian press under the headline 'Peru's most intelligent youth dies of tuberculosis':

> Nowadays to die of tuberculosis is dramatic. Some medicines and basic nutrition suffice to avoid such a death. However, medicine and bread, milk and eggs are not cheap in Peru, even less so with the 18 per cent VAT charged by the state … in Peru today, dying of tuberculosis is synonymous with poverty and misery; it is the reflection of a profound social crisis which permits the deaths of such human beings as Wilfredo Ruiz, a young genius who caused astonishment when he gained entrance to the Catholic University of Peru with the highest marks ever recorded in the whole history of that academic institution.[21]

Ironically, Wilfredo died in a year when Peru registered one of the highest economic growth rates in the world, following a particularly fierce brand of structural adjustment known as Fujishock, after its instigator, President

Alberto Fujimori. *The Economist* summed up the Alice-in-Wonderland nature of the economics of structural adjustment when it commented, 'There is a sense that Peru is doing well, but not the Peruvians.'[22]

In neighbouring Bolivia, the impact of adjustment on children's health has been equally harsh. 'I've seen far more serious malnutrition in children since [structural adjustment was introduced in] '85,' says Dr Ana María Aguilar of the Children's Hospital in La Paz. In El Alto, the slum city on the outskirts of La Paz, 96 per cent of babies have birthweights of less than the international standard for low birthweight, 5.5 lb.[23] By way of comparison, the figure for Ethiopia in 1990 was just 16 per cent.[24] As in Peru, tuberculosis is on the rise. In one of Dr Aguilar's wards, a 13-year-old boy stands protectively over the motionless form of his sister, whose brain is being attacked by TB meningitis. 'She can't say anything, but she knows I'm here,' he says quietly.

In the Caribbean, Jamaica has been taking the IMF medicine at regular intervals since 1977, with disastrous consequences for children, according to a 1995 UNICEF report:

> For the first time in almost a decade, the country does not face a major financial or macroeconomic imbalance. However these results were achieved by drastically retracting the role of government in the social services area and at a devastating social cost, as indicated by the decline of resources available to families, children and communities.[25]

UNICEF points out that poverty has risen almost continuously since adjustment began, and that four in ten Jamaican children now live in extreme poverty. Unemployment stood at 16 per cent nationally by 1993, but was higher among young people, while 'the quality of available jobs has deteriorated, compared to the pre-adjustment period, with rising underemployment and the shift to the less secure informal sector employment'.

UNICEF also found that the falling wages and rising food costs produced by adjustment 'show a dramatic correlation with hospital admissions of children for malnutrition'. The impact on children has been worsened by cuts in health and education spending – where there was one doctor for every 2700 Jamaicans in 1971, by 1988 the ratio had increased to one to 5240.

Fighting back

A period of poverty and hunger may be a bitter experience for any adult, but it is a permanent tragedy for children, stunting physical and mental

Without jobs, and in the absence of a functioning welfare system, entire families have been reduced to scavenging on rubbish dumps, collecting recyclable materials such as cardboard and metal. A mother and child on the dump in San Salvador.

development for a lifetime, as well as cutting short lives full of potential. According to SCF UK:

> Relatively short periods of malnutrition, which adults can withstand and suffer no long-term deficits, can permanently affect the early development of the child's capacities. Early childhood years are a crucial biological window of opportunity.[26]

Yet cuts in food subsidies and school feeding programmes, along with rising poverty, increased malnutrition among children. As the 1980s wore on, and the impact of adjustment on children became ever more apparent, the UN Children's Fund, UNICEF, took the lead in criticizing the impact of IMF and World Bank policies. In 1987 UNICEF published a landmark critique, *Adjustment with a Human Face*.[27] One of its principal findings was that, although structural adjustment had greatly increased poverty in the region, the international financial institutions' lending policies and conditions had paid 'almost no attention to the special problems of the poor' by the late 1980s.[28] One high-ranking World Bank economist confessed, 'we did not think that the human costs of these programmes could be so great, and the economic gains so slow in coming'.[29]

In 1990 the World Bank responded to such criticisms by adopting poverty alleviation as its main objective, formalizing its new commitment in that year's *World Development Report*. World Bank President Lewis Preston described sustainable poverty reduction as 'the over-arching objective of the World Bank. It is the benchmark by which our performance as a development institution will be measured.'[30] The new strategy aimed:

> to reduce poverty through broadly-based labour-intensive growth to generate jobs and income for the poor; social investment to improve poor people's access to education, nutrition, health care and other social services and social safety nets to protect the poorest and most vulnerable sections of society.[31]

However, the World Bank and IMF continue to insist that improving the lives of ordinary Latin Americans in terms of poverty, nutrition, health and education will essentially be an automatic by-product of economic growth. It is merely proposing some social programmes to ease the short-term pain of adjustment until the much trumpeted 'trickle down' of social and economic wellbeing comes on stream.[32]

In practice, this change of direction has meant World Bank pressure on Third World governments to maintain levels of health and education spending, an increase in loans for health, education and nutrition programmes, and finance for so-called 'safety net' welfare programmes which specifically target the most needy. The UK aid agency Oxfam is unimpressed, saying 'simply bolting-on social welfare provision to wider adjustment policies which are themselves exacerbating poverty, does not amount to a poverty-reduction strategy'.[33]

Seven years after the World Bank rediscovered poverty, it is still highly doubtful whether the change of rhetoric has changed the real-life impact of structural adjustment on Latin America's half billion citizens. Social issues still take a back seat compared to the harsher economic side of adjustment. In a wide-ranging survey of the issue in 1995, Oxfam noted that the World Bank often turns a blind eye when governments ignore its advice on social spending: 'non-compliance has been tolerated in a manner which would be inconceivable were it repeated in relation to, say, money supply or credit control.'[34] In the same year as the World Bank changed tack, Peru's 'Fujishock' adjustment programme cut teachers' wages by half,[35] yet Peru was portrayed as a model adjuster to other Latin American countries.

The World Bank's zeal for targeting is also open to question. Although, on the surface, aiming welfare measures at the most needy makes good sense, targeting can often act as a smokescreen for spending cuts, and targeted spending often fails to reach the poorest families. It is frequently used for political purposes, buying off political opposition to structural adjustment, rather than helping the poor. 'Whatever the country-specific experiences', states the report, 'social welfare safety-nets have inevitably proved inadequate in the face of the failure of structural adjustment programmes [to reduce poverty].'[36] Oxfam concluded:

> a vast gulf remains between public statements in favour of policies which benefit the poor, and the realities of structural adjustment. In practice, the costs of adjustment are still being borne by the most vulnerable sections of society.[37]

Agencies working specifically with children have also kept up the pressure. In 1995, to coincide with the UN's Social Summit in Copenhagen, SCF UK published *Towards a Children's Agenda*, laying out its findings on the impact of adjustment on children, and the need for change. It concludes:

> Current models of market-based economic growth exclude those with less power, wealth, assets and skills, and erode the traditional family and community support systems which provide help in times of need ... . Children will never have their rights secured when they and their parents are excluded in this way.

Towards a Children's Agenda states that much more than a mere change of policy at the top is required. Rather, a fundamental change of approach is needed as a 'precondition for economic reform ... enabling those who have less power to have more of a voice in decisions which affect them'. All this, SCF believes, calls for 'new economic models which put people at the centre'. At an international level, such models involve easing the debt burden on Third World countries, reforming international trade to give the Third World fairer prices for its products and reforming adjustment policies to help, rather than punish, the poor.[38]

While international economists and lobbyists debate the nature and purpose of development, and national politicians seek alternatives to the dead hand of structural adjustment, at the local level the daily struggle is usually more about survival than building a long-term alternative. Across the region, women are leading the struggle to survive the depredations of the market by organizing self-help programmes to feed and educate their children.

Although experiencing one of the harshest structural adjustment programmes, Peruvians have been able to count on a particularly strong tradition of grassroots organization, with historical roots in the communal organization of labour in the Andes dating back to Inca times. There are over 15,000 such organizations throughout the country, including mothers' clubs, neighbourhood soup kitchens and the 'Glass of Milk committees', which provide meals for the children and carry out immunization programmes and cholera prevention work. In Lima alone, the 7500 Glass of Milk committees reach over 650,000 people a day, most of them under-sixes or pregnant and lactating women. One in ten of the city's inhabitants relies on the 2500 'Popular Soup Kitchens' to keep them going.[39]

Moving beyond such 'survival strategies', there are numerous grassroots initiatives aiming to build a new kind of 'people-centred development'. As its name implies, this vision seeks to put people back at the centre of development, in particular women and children. Such initiatives concentrate on the nuts and bolts – water supplies, credit for family firms, crèches, growing enough food to eat, combating poverty or preserving the local environment. People-centred development strategies focus on the processes of economic planning, arguing that economic and political exclusion are mutually reinforcing, and trying instead to build new models based on public participation in economic decision-making.

Conclusion

Latin America and the Caribbean entered the debt crisis of the 1980s as the most unequal continent on earth, a land where spectacular wealth exists at a stone's throw from the sub-human shanty towns of the cities. Its economy was stagnant and vastly indebted, and some kind of adjustment was clearly required.

Yet the form that adjustment took was neither inevitable nor fair. It served the interests of the wealthy, be they in Latin America or outside, while forcing the poor, especially women and children, to carry the burden of economic change, even though they neither benefited from the previous model nor are likely to profit from the new free market Latin America.

Short-term economic goals such as reducing inflation have been achieved at an enormous social cost in the shape of a blighted generation of underfed, ill-educated children which is now growing up, undermining the region's chances of ever finding a worthwhile niche in the new cut-throat world economy that its governments are so keen to enter. These new generations feel excluded from the brave new consumer world they see flaunted in the shopping malls and on television. Resentment and a sense that they have nothing to lose goes a long way to explaining the epidemic of crime and social breakdown now afflicting much of the region.

Growing numbers of individuals and organizations are starting to criticize the new economic model, seeking for alternatives which treat people as the heart of development, rather than as an afterthought or unwitting victims. Unless these alternatives are found, with children at their centre, Latin America and the Caribbean's tragic tradition of underdevelopment and waste is set to continue.

Notes

1 Economist Intelligence Unit, *Nicaragua Country Profile 1995/6* (London), p. 35.

2 Trevor Evans, Carlos Castro and Jennifer Jones, *Structural Adjustment and the Public Sector in Central America and the Caribbean* (Managua, 1995), p. 179.

3 Karen Hansen-Kuhn, *Structural Adjustment in Nicaragua, Sapping the Social Fabric* (DGAP, Washington, 1995).

4 *Ibid*.

5 Ruth Mayne, *Report on Visit to Nicaragua* (mimeo) (Oxfam, September 1995).

6 Evans, Castro and Jones, *op. cit.*, p. 222; and CISAS, *Health and Structural Adjustment in Nicaragua* (Managua, February 1995).

7 CISAS, *op. cit.*, p. 20.

8 This section is based on Duncan Green, *Silent Revolution: The Rise of Market Economics in Latin America* (London, 1995).

9 William Ryrie, 'Latin America: a changing region', in *IFC Investment Review* (Washington, Spring 1992), pp. 4–5.

10 CEPAL, *Balance Preliminar de la Economía de América Latina y el Caribe 1993* (Santiago, December 1993), p. 47.

11 Laurie Richardson and Jean-Roland Chery, 'Haiti's not for sale', in *Covert Action Quarterly* (Washington, Winter 1995–6).

12 National Labor Committee, *The US in Haiti: How to Get Rich on 11 cents an Hour* (New York, 1996).

13 Caroline Moser, 'Adjustment from below: low-income women, time and the triple role in Guayaquil, Ecuador', in Sarah Radcliffe and Sallie Westwood (eds), *Viva: Women and Popular Protest in Latin America* (London, 1993).

14 UN Convention on the Rights of the Child (Geneva, 1989), Article 28.

15 Pedro Francke Ballve, *La Educación Pública, los Pobres y el Ajuste* (Lima, 1994), p. 33.

16 CEPAL, *Panorama Social de América Latina 1993* (Santiago), p. 100.

17 UNICEF, *Children of the Americas 1992* (Bogotá, 1992), p. 24.

18 *Ibid.*, p. 29.

19 www.paho.org/cgi-bin/pahosrch.cgi (17 March 1997).

20 *Noticias Aliadas* (Lima, 28 March 1996).

21 *Oiga*, No. 710 (Lima, 26 September 1994).

22 *The Economist* (London, 25 June 1994).

23 Ministerio de Previsión Social y Salud Pública, *Subsistema Nacional de Información de Salud 1991–92* (La Paz).

24 UNICEF, *The State of the World's Children 1994* (Oxford, 1994).

25 UNICEF Caribbean Area Office, *The Economics of Child Poverty in Jamaica* (May 1995).

26 SCF UK, *Towards a Children's Agenda: New Challenges for Social Development* (London, 1995), p. 32.

27 G.A. Cornia, R. Jolly and F. Stewart, *Adjustment with a Human Face* (Oxford, 1987).

28 Frances Stewart, *Protecting the Poor during Adjustment in Latin America and the Caribbean in the late 1980s: How Adequate was the World Bank Response?* (mimeo) (Oxford, 1991).

29 World Bank Chief Economist for Africa, quoted in Morris Miller, *Debt and the Environment: Converging Crises* (New York, 1991), p. 70.

30 Oxfam, *Embracing the Future ... Avoiding the Challenge of World Poverty* (mimeo) (Oxford, September 1994), p. 2.

31 Oxfam, *Structural Adjustment and Inequality in Latin America: How IMF and World Bank Policies Have Failed the Poor* (Oxford, 1994), p. 4.

32 David Woodward, *Children and Poverty* (mimeo) (Save the Children UK, 1995), p. 3.

33 Oxfam, *Structural Adjustment and Inequality in Latin America*, *op. cit.*, p. 17.

34 Kevin Watkins, *The Oxfam Poverty Report* (Oxford, 1995), p. 82.

35 Pedro Francke Ballve, *op. cit.*, p. 86.

36 Watkins, *op. cit.*, p. 85.

37 *Ibid.*, p. 108.

38 SCF UK, *Towards a Children's Agenda: New Challenges for Social Development* (London, March 1995), p. 46.

39 SCF UK, *Peru Draft Country Situation Analysis* (Lima, 1994), p. 42.

CHAPTER 7

The Next Generation

Health and Education

The rains came last night, two months late, and the fields are dotted with Indian families, planting potatoes in the rich brown earth of the village of Cuper Alto in the Peruvian Andes. The men pull hand-ploughs; the women hack at the larger clods with hoes, preparing the ground for planting. The children are working too, picking sticks and stones out of the freshly ploughed earth of a patchwork of plots belonging to different families in this Quechua-speaking community. The smell of the eucalyptus trees is strong after the rain, mixing with the chill smell of damp earth. In the distance hang the white Andean peaks, every detail clear in the mountain air.

Marcusa Pañehuara Huaittahuaman, 29, has the shiny frostbitten and sunburnt cheeks of an Andean peasant. It is only midday, but she looks exhausted. A lurid pink, blonde-haired doll with one eye missing sits on the windowsill of her mud hut as Marcusa plays with her two-year-old daughter, Ayde, a stunted, snot-nosed girl with a filthy face and matted straggly hair tied into two bunches.

> She gets sick every month – diarrhoea, fever. I use herbs to bathe her. If we catch it early, the herbs work, but if we leave it too late, we have to go to the health post. There's a nurse there but we have to pay for everything. When there's no money, death comes for the children. That's how I lost my first son – I had no money. I couldn't look after him properly. Two of my children died, the first at 15 months with fever, the second died within my womb.

> Health is our main worry. When it rains, the kids all get flu. We're just starting to organize latrines for the community – we used to get water from a spring but the animals use it and it's very dirty, and we have no money to buy chlorine.

Marcusa swings her toddler expertly onto her back and sets off to the fields, with Ayde's head poking contentedly out of the blanket in an image captured by a thousand tourist cameras. For Marcusa, the experience is not so idyllic: 'The baby makes my back ache but what can we do? We have to carry them up the mountain, wherever we go. That's why we want to start a crèche here this year.'

Health problems in Indian communities like Cuper Alto start even before birth, as malnourished women give birth to underweight and sickly babies prone to disease. They must then confront a hostile environment where the chief killer is dirty water. Losing a child is part of almost every mother's life.

Thanks to the vaccination campaigns of the last twenty years, those who survive to their first birthday are now less likely than their parents' generation to die of infectious childhood diseases such as measles and typhoid, but, beyond mere survival, their life chances remain grim. Run-down schools, staffed by teachers who in many cases speak no Quechua, combined with steadily rising school fees and hidden costs such as textbooks and uniforms, deter all but the most determined and talented of children from even reaching secondary school. Those who do must leave their villages for the nearest town and are unlikely to return, as Segundino, a stocky, hesitant 18-year-old who attends school in nearby Calca, explains:

I'm at third grade of night school. I study from 6–10pm and stay overnight in Calca with relatives, because the village is seven kilometres away. In the morning I walk home to start work by 8am, working with my father on the farm. We grow maize, potatoes, wheat, everything. I want to finish secondary and carry on studying. I don't want to stay here farming – it's pure sacrifice. Here in the community it's just work and study. We play the odd game of football, that's about it. I want to go to the city.

The evening sun lights up the plots of maize. A flock of parakeets cackle overhead. Dusk is full of the smells of eucalyptus and unknown herbs. Mountains rear up thousands of feet from the valley floor. And the children cannot wait to get out.

In Latin America and the Caribbean, perhaps more than in any other continent, life prospects are profoundly influenced by the accident of birth. Poor or rich, Indian, black or *mestizo*, male or female: the continent's multi-layered inequalities determine a child's access to health and education, and with them much of their future. Geography also matters – in rural Indian communities such as Cuper Alto, as many as four out of every five of the under-fives are malnourished, compared to one in seven in Lima.[1]

Individuals, through a combination of luck, determination and talent, may claw their way out, and, throughout the continent, communities of poor families from the shanty towns and rural villages are fighting back through a plethora of grassroots initiatives, covering everything from digging the trenches to bring water pipes into their neighbourhood or

Clean water is essential to child health and greatly reduces infant mortality rates. A child showers on the family banana farm in Honduras.

running soup kitchens and community schools for the children to opening a co-operative shop to sell handicrafts. As always, the most successful initiatives are often those which involve children themselves in programmes aimed at improving their lives.

Such examples offer genuine hope for the future, but, for now, the overall picture remains one of great and needless human waste, of lives blighted by hunger, poor-quality education and crumbling health services. All too often, governments have placed short-term economic priorities such as curbing inflation or satisfying the IMF before the overriding need to build a healthy, well-educated population. Unless they change their priorities, they risk condemning the next generation to the same poverty as their parents, reproducing the cycle of social and economic exclusion which has become so much a feature of the region.

Education

The heated arguments about how the next generation is formed are inevitably political: unequal education systems perpetuate unequal and wasteful societies which squander the talents of the poor. Reducing inequality in children's access to education can go a long way to reducing inequality in society.[2] Education's impact is not just economic, but social. Education affects health, nutrition and fertility. The World Bank calculates that one extra year of education of the mother means nine fewer dead babies per thousand. In Peru the average number of children is over six for an uneducated woman, falling to less than two for a woman with further education.[3]

At a national level, the benefits of education are indisputable, as a UNESCO document makes clear, albeit in rather bloodless terms:

> Education, especially basic education, contributes to growth by increasing the productivity of labour, by improving health, by reducing fertility, and by equipping people to participate fully in the economy and in society. For example, girls' education is associated with raising the age of marriage, use of contraceptives and use of health care systems, thus reducing the time of sick care or vision and hearing impairments.[4]

How and what children are taught is critical to what kind of citizens they become. Not so long ago, literacy itself was seen as highly dangerous and discouraged by the Andean landlords, who wanted to prevent new ideas from influencing 'their' Indians. In the 1960s and 1970s, educationalists such as Brazil's Paulo Freire promoted the idea of 'education for liberation', producing citizens ready to criticize and if necessary overthrow the *status quo*. In the market-dominated 1990s, the World Bank and other international bodies seem more comfortable referring to people (messy, unpredictable creatures), as 'human capital', converting them at a stroke to an abstract concept amenable to economic analysis. Schools and clinics have become sound investments, not tools for liberation.

Yet all sides of the political spectrum agree that what is going on in Latin America and the Caribbean is human waste on a grand scale, creating under-educated, undernourished generations and jeopardizing the region's future development. Everyone seems to want education and health reform, but, as always, the crucial question is what kind, and to whose benefit?

Under the UN Convention on the Rights of the Child, Latin American and Caribbean governments have committed themselves to providing free compulsory primary education, to making secondary education available to all children, to offering financial assistance to needy children, and to do their utmost to reduce drop-out rates.[5] In reality, they have made some progress on primary education, but have so far failed to comply with the other commitments.

Overall, the region's governments have managed to expand education coverage faster than population growth. Their most spectacular achievements have been in primary school education, where they have managed to incorporate an extra two million children every year since 1950, even during the 'lost decade' of recession and spending cuts in the 1980s. Across the region, about 94 per cent of 8–9-year-olds now attend school, producing close to total coverage in that age range.[6] Other areas of education have also expanded fast: between 1960 and 1988, pre-school education rose from one million to ten million children, although still only covering one in seven of the population, largely from the urban middle class; secondary school coverage rose from one in seven to more than half over the same period, while further education spread from 3 per cent to 19 per cent of the population.[7]

But as education has expanded, its overall quality has declined. Spending has failed to keep up with the rising numbers, and little attention is given to what children do once they are actually in the classroom. As a result, half of those who start school drop out before finishing primary school. Every second child repeats their first year, and, at any one time, one in three primary pupils are repeating the year. The average primary school pupil spends seven years in the system but only passes four grades.[8] Compared to Britain or the USA, children start school later (at 6 or 7), leave earlier (at 13 or 14), and work fewer hours while they are there. Half the students are not able to understand written messages at the moment of dropping out after six or more years of schooling.[9]

The economic crisis of the 1980s made matters worse. Average spending on primary education fell from US$164 per child in the early 1980s to

US$118 by the end of the decade.[10] Most affected were teachers' salaries, which dropped disastrously in almost every country, bringing the inevitable disruptions of strikes, absenteeism, the resignation of skilled staff, and teachers who depend on second or third jobs to make ends meet. Teaching is in danger of becoming the last resort of those unable to find jobs elsewhere. Another side effect of the crisis has been to introduce back-door charges to parents. Even though by law Latin American public education is free, in fact parents now pay up to one-third of the cost of schooling in the form of 'voluntary' contributions, transport, uniforms, shoes, bags, books, pads, pencils and other materials.[11]

Pressure of numbers and the lack of investment have forced schools to work a shift system, with separate shifts for mornings, afternoons and in some cases even evening shifts. The number of hours that pupils actually spend in the classroom has fallen steadily – in some areas, the school day is effectively three hours long.[12]

When the teacher is in the classroom, so-called 'frontal teaching' is the norm – four out of five Chilean teachers merely dictate classes to their students, who sit passively in rows.[13] This is what Paulo Freire condemned as the 'banking concept' of education, where teachers see children as empty receptacles in which they must deposit information. Creativity, children's own experience and knowledge and the ability to work in groups receive short shrift. Children who have never attended school are expected to adjust to hours of inactivity, sitting silent and motionless on pain of punishment. Frontal teaching is unable to cope with pupils who miss periods of time due to work commitments, for example during harvest time. Teachers are unable to deal separately with such children, helping them make up lost ground when they return to class. Not surprisingly, frontal teaching is seen as one of the chief causes of Latin America and the Caribbean's record drop-out and repetition rates.

Besides sterile teaching methods, the subject matter is often of little relevance to children's lives, as Domitila Chungara, a tin miner's wife from Bolivia, recalls:

> In school I learned to read, to write, and to get along. But I can't say that school really helped me to understand life. I think that education in Bolivia is an alienating education. For example, they make us see the motherland like a beautiful thing in the national anthem, in the colours of the flag, and all those things stop meaning anything when the motherland isn't well. The motherland, for me, is in every corner, it's also in the miners, in the peasants, in the people's poverty, their nakedness, their malnutrition, in their pains and their joys. That's the motherland, right? But in school they

teach us to sing the national anthem, to parade, and they say that if we refuse to parade we aren't patriotic, and, nevertheless, they never explain our poverty, our misery, our parents' situation, their great sacrifices and low wages, why a few children have everything and many others have nothing. They never explained that to me at school.[14]

Even such an education success story as Nicaragua under the Sandinistas often failed to break the mould of an education system which had little to do with the everyday lives of its children. In a country lauded by UNESCO and others for its literacy crusade, 11-year-old children in one Managua slum were to be found studying renaissance Europe, albeit with a revolutionary twist. In one notebook, the class question was 'what new classes grew up in the sixteenth and seventeenth century?'. The correct answer was 'the bourgeoisie and the proletariat'.[15]

The size of the education budget is not the main problem, but how it is spent. Compared to the size of their economies, Latin American countries outspend the successful nations of Southeast Asia, such as South Korea, yet the Asian 'tigers' have far more effective education systems.[16] The bulk of the money in Latin America goes on teachers' salaries – not because teachers are well paid, but because there are enormous numbers of them. In 1990, 98 per cent of Peru's education budget went on salaries, leaving minuscule amounts for investment, equipment and teaching materials. One study of 1000 schools showed that more than nine in ten pupils had no textbooks for the courses they were being taught.[17] When education spending levels recovered in the 1990s, the extra money was used to reduce the pupil/teacher ratio still further from 27 to 23.[18] Critics claim that the money would be better spent training teachers to teach (one in five teachers currently has no training at all[19]), providing pupils with textbooks, or raising teachers' wages to attract better-quality candidates.

Furthermore, despite their achievements in effectively providing universal primary education, Latin American governments spend too much of their education budgets on further education, which disproportionately benefits the middle classes, who send their children to university, rather than primary education, which benefits the poor. As one critic acerbically remarked, this may be because 'most public system managers send their children to private primary and secondary schools and then switch to free universities'.[20] The low quality of teaching itself squanders money – the 29 per cent of primary school children who are repeating the year are using up US$2.5 billion a year, a third of primary education spending.[21]

Up until the 1980s, at least those pupils who managed to finish secondary education could look forward to finding a steady job, often in the public sector, but the austerity programmes of the 1980s have ended even that. Many students leaving secondary school now find skilled jobs hard to come by. As an exhausted mother in a Chilean shanty town commented, 'why should kids read Neruda or go to the theatre if they're just going to end up picking oranges?'.[22] One UN study concluded that, in the 1990s, 'for the young people of Latin America, ... expectations are being increasingly thwarted'.[23]

Regional variations

Regional averages mask enormous variations between and within countries. In general, the larger countries such as Argentina and Mexico have better education systems, with the glaring exception of the largest country of all, Brazil. Nationally, only one in seven Brazilian 10–11-year-olds have completed their first four years of primary school. But the picture in rural areas is far worse – only two in every 100 rural children ever complete primary school.[24]

Disparities between countries are just as pronounced at secondary level; Uruguay has enrolment rates of 83 per cent of children of secondary school age, similar to the UK's, while in Guatemala less than one in four attends secondary school.[25]

The greatest variations are in the Caribbean, where Cuba has an education system which is the envy of the Third World, while Haiti invariably comes bottom of any educational league table. Despite the problems caused by its recent economic crisis and the US trade embargo, Cuba has the world's highest number of teachers per capita, 100 per cent primary school coverage, and minuscule drop-out and repetition rates. Every year throughout the 1980s, Cuban educationalists were developing, testing and printing some 800 new textbooks and teaching aids.[26] In Haiti, on the other hand, UNICEF believes that half the country's two million school-age children are not even enrolled, and estimates for the numbers completing primary school range as low as one in eight.[27]

Hope for the future

The inadequacy of the Brazilian education system, combined with that country's traditionally energetic and inventive grassroots movements, has produced some of the most inspiring attempts to place education at the service of the poor. Brazilian parents place great store on educating their children, struggling to make the sacrifices necessary to keep their children at school. Many have gone further, taking matters into their own hands by creating a parallel network of community schools. In 1992, 15,000 pupils attended 181 community schools in just one city, Recife,[28] the regional capital of Brazil's impoverished northeast.

Funded by the parents, donations and small hand-outs from local authorities, community schools aim both to prepare children from poor families for the culture shock they will experience when they start at a state school, and where necessary to provide an alternative form of education, rooted in the community and the children's own experience. A survey of parents in Recife revealed that the main reasons why they chose to send their children to community schools were the security that came with having a school near to their homes, teachers whom they knew, better education and avoiding the strikes that plague the state system.[29]

In the city of Salvador, capital of black Brazil, community schools are trying to combat the effects of racism, endemic in Brazilian society, giving black children in the shanty towns a positive self-image by encouraging Brazil's vibrant black culture, including the old slave dance form, *capoeira*.

The Paraguari Community School stands next to a large culvert full of plants and stagnant, foul water. Next door is a neat little private school, brilliant white in the sun. Although it is called the 'School of the Good Samaritan', it is only half full because few local people can afford the fees.

The Paraguari children are showing their paces with a capoeira show in the dirt yard next to the culvert. Congas are booming as four larger boys in white culottes, rough rope headbands and brooms and four girls in traditional *baiana* costume – off-the-shoulder full-length dresses, beads and headscarves – act out the 'washing ceremony', a hybrid of Catholic and African traditions.

As the drums pick up speed, groups of neighbours gather in their doorways to watch. Six boys in rope skirts appear and perform a dance with batons and rusty old machetes. The clang of machete on baton echoes over the favelas, mingling with the African drums. It is the sound of slavery and sugar from Brazil's black history. A strong smell of *cachaça* [cane spirit] floats across from somewhere. The dancers sing fishing songs to Iemanjá, goddess of the sea. Two Pentecostal Protestant women walk past, clutching Bibles, smile at the children and move on.

As the capoeira fight begins, a crowd gathers and everyone starts to laugh and get excited. The athleticism grows, as eight-year-old boys show their tricks – one-handed cartwheels, defying gravity, walking on their hands, backward flips. Each boy breaks into the circle, does his piece, and then retreats, grinning. Now it is the girls' turn, kicking and spinning like tops.

Bigger boys take over for the climax, kicking and wheeling at dizzying speed, clearing each others' heads by inches, never making contact.

Afterwards, a panting teenage performer explains:

The Cuban government has an exceptional record in providing health and education services. Two children at a primary and nursery school in Holguín province.

Capoeira's good – it's a sport and it's a show we can perform in schools and colleges. People love us! It's part of our culture – everyone can do it, you just have to love to dance. And you can use it to defend yourselves.

The capoeira teacher (who turns out to be the source of the cachaca smell) adds:

Capoeira came from Africa with the slaves. It started off as a form of self-defence, disguised as a dance, but then it was forbidden. It's perfect for the poor – it costs nothing, you don't need a special place to do it and it's getting more popular all the time.

The dancers drift off, laughing and chatting in the evening light, as a cool breeze ruffles the abandoned kites which litter the telegraph wires.

Community schools are largely an urban phenomenon, but rural communities are also trying to create better alternatives to a public system which is even worse in the countryside than in the city. One such attempt is providing a new kind of education for the rural children of the parched *sertão* scrublands of the northeast, home to three-quarters of Brazil's two million illiterate children.[30]

The school is run by the Caatinga environmental project, and has 160 students, aged from 4 to 54. The local community built the school, saying they wanted it to teach their kids not just to read and write, but how to survive in the sertão. Before, few children made the trek to the run-down state school in the nearest town, and most dreamed only of the day they could flee the sertão for the glittering promise of the city. Now, the school is seeking to educate children who will then stay in the region – a tough task, since rural education normally accelerates the speed of migration by expanding children's horizons to the new worlds on offer in the city.

'The main focus for the practical education is water – how to store it and keep it clean so the precious rains last longer,' explains teacher Isabel de Jesus Oliveira:

Wells, trench pits, roof-run-off cisterns – in the sertão, water is life. Before the project started, there were only wells which often ran dry, driving people to migrate. Now there is drinking water almost all year round. Another problem is how to feed their animals during the drought, how to gather and store feed without damaging the fragile scrub ecosystem. We show the kids how to collect firewood without destroying the source – we have practical classes out in the fields.

But life in the sertão remains harsh. Mariana is 28, with piercing hazel eyes. Her eldest son Flávio is nine. Every day he takes the two little ones – a girl of six and her seven-year-old brother – to school on his bike, nine kilometres there, and nine back. The state school is nearer, but the teachers often don't show up – 'the teaching is tired', complains Mariana.

> I've always lived here but I can barely read and write. The teaching was rubbish, always the same thing, and then I left to get married. I'm ashamed to try and write to a friend. Some people leave here, but my family has never left. I'm afraid it will happen with my children because there are not many jobs here. Life in the fields is too hard – it stops you developing. The kids go out to work as soon as they get home from school. I've never had any other life than plant, weed and sow. We put our kids into study so they could get a better job.

The environmental education given at the school has clearly influenced Mariana's husband Severino: 'In the old days you proved your manhood by chopping down everything. Now I know better. Now we respect nature.' But like so many other men from the northeast, Severino cannot stay with his family:

> I'm going to the [fruit farm] projects. We can't live from the millet and beans we grow here – it wouldn't keep us going for two months if I sold it. I'll go, but it's bad. In the evening you remember your kids, your wife. It's tough. I'm going until the rains come back.

And his departure will inevitably affect the children's education, according to Mariana:

> It's horrible, but we have no choice. I'll be alone here with the kids, looking after the animals, cutting feed. Survival comes first in the countryside, not education. They may have to miss a few days. But if they don't keep going to school they'll end up like their father and have to leave their loved ones.

Outside, battalions of slate-coloured clouds march across a vast sky, withholding every drop of water from the parched lands beneath. The brush is alive with birds, vivid yellows and reds. The late-afternoon sun is throwing long shadows across the yard from the chickens and the trees. The dirt is packed, without a speck of green. As the sun goes down, the temperature starts to drop into the sudden chill of the sertão night.

Learning to teach

Caatinga is one of innumerable attempts to improve Latin America and the Caribbean's dismal educational performance. Across the region, governments, private organizations and communities have been involved in many innovative experiments, some of which hold great potential for the region's children. In the Dominican Republic in 1983, a government project started putting out one-hour radio programmes for rural children from isolated areas, aided by local people who had volunteered for training as radio helpers. Within six years, studies showed pupils of the radio schools doing better than their peers in the dilapidated state system.[31]

The *Escuela Nueva* ('New School') programme is another successful government project that has been transforming rural education in Colombia. Started in 1975, it has made a serious attempt to end the antiquated and authoritarian teaching methods in Colombia's classrooms. Using student leaders elected by the classes, Escuela Nueva schools encourage group work and problem-solving, rather than 'frontal teaching' and rote-learning, allowing teachers to handle up to five grades simultaneously (a money-saving feature which endears it to the Colombian government). Students who drop out temporarily to work on their family farms are able to pick up their studies where they left off, greatly reducing drop-out and repetition rates. As in Caatinga, the schools have become conduits for health, sanitation and nutrition information for local families, who are now much more involved in running the schools. As in the Dominican Republic, subsequent studies show Escuela Nueva pupils out-performing children from traditional schools.[32] Similar programmes are now being tried out in Chile, Guatemala, Honduras, Paraguay and Argentina.[33]

In Brazil, the governor of the capital, Brasília, Cristóvam Buarque, has come up with a novel scheme to help working and poor children stay in school. Under the *bolsa-escola* scholarship programme, poor families who keep all their children in school receive a minimum wage every month. The money is lost if any child misses more than two days in a month, except through illness. In 1996 the programme was keeping 30,000 children in school at a cost of only 0.5 per cent of the total state budget, and the impact has been extraordinary. Repetition rates fell by 10 per cent in the first year of the programme, while absenteeism fell from 7 per cent to just 0.2 per cent. Brothers and sisters were even found to be policing their 'problem siblings', since all the children have to attend if the wage is to be earned.[34] The scheme is now being introduced in other cities in Brazil.

One particular challenge for educators is providing schools for the continent's 40 million indigenous people, many of whom are extremely poor and may not speak Spanish. In the past, when they have been taught at all, Indian children have been taught by non-Indian teachers in Spanish, leading to extremely high drop-out rates, while those who have succeeded have often ended up abandoning both their communities and their cultures.

All this is in clear contravention of Latin American and Caribbean governments' commitments under the UN Convention on the Rights of the Child, which states that 'a child who is indigenous shall not be denied the right … to enjoy his or her own culture … or to use his or her own language'.[35] Yet when well-intentioned NGOs in Bolivia began teaching Aymara Indians in their own language, they encountered mixed reactions. Some of the women valued recovering their culture: 'we learnt to tell the tales our grandmothers told and it helped us to see whether what we are doing now is following our ancestors or not'. However, most disagreed:

> It was not very useful. We have forgotten most of it because there is nothing to read in Aymara. What is the point of learning to read and write in Aymara? It is not used when we go and do business. It will not help us get a job or make money.

In the end, the project switched from Aymara to Spanish. As a speaker at a meeting on Bolivian teaching methods explained:

> Literacy is no use if it does not empower us. Spanish is the language of power and we must adopt it if we are to assert ourselves and seek change. The government has a glorified ideal of preserving our culture, but only we can do that and only from a position of power. We don't want to preserve our poverty.[36]

Elsewhere, the failures of the state education system have played an unexpected role in strengthening Indian identity:

> This process of educational empowerment is dramatically evident in the Ecuadorean Amazon. At 7.30 in the morning, as adults set off to tend their plots or pastures in a small river community in south-eastern Ecuador, barefoot children head for a palm-thatched hut in the middle of the village. There, sitting on wooden benches, they begin their lessons. The teacher, at the front of the class, is a bright-red portable radio. Beside the receiver is a teleauxiliar, a local person with primary education and some basic training who supervises lessons in reading, writing, maths and history. Every child in more than 400 communities, some with as few as 15 residents and more than a day's river trip from their nearest neighbour, attends five and a half hours of primary school a day. The lessons are broadcast from the Shuar-Achuar Federation's headquarters in the small town of Sucúa. Backed by the Ministry of Education in Quito, the scheme has become the most successful radio school in the world, playing a crucial role in making the Shuar one of the most effective defenders of indigenous territory in the Americas.[37]

Health

The patch of brown on a slight rise in the land is littered with countless wooden crosses. The peasant farmers who scrape a living on the banks of

The spread of primary education has been one of the key changes in Latin American society in recent decades. Children go to school in the Peruvian Amazon.

the Peruvian Amazon keep the site cleared of the all-engulfing forest undergrowth. In the centre is the chapel, a small palm-roofed shelter with branches lashed together to make a table on which to place coffins during the service. The cries of rainforest birds accentuate the stillness.

The size of the roughly nailed wooden crosses mirrors the size of the corpse beneath. There are many small ones. This hill is above the giant river's flood waters, so people come to bury their babies from miles up- and down-river. Hand-carved with date of death and name, hundreds of crosses protrude at crazy angles against the skyline. Many are already broken, leaving mouldering stumps sticking out of the soil in a scene of desolation and decay. The scene encapsulates the continuing, needless death-toll among Latin America's babies.

A million children die every year in Latin America and the Caribbean, 700,000 of them before their first birthday. Three-quarters of child deaths occur from causes that are largely preventable, such as diarrhoea and pneumonia, although mass vaccination campaigns in the 1980s have greatly reduced the impact of other killers like measles and tetanus. The last case of polio in Latin America and the Caribbean occurred in 1991.[38]

As elsewhere in the world, the figures have improved sharply in recent decades. Across Latin America and the Caribbean, the infant mortality rate – the number of children per thousand who die before reaching one year old – halved between 1960 and 1990, falling from 100 per 1000 live births to 47. The death-rate of children between the ages of one and five fell even faster, from 45 per 1000 to 16.[39]

In the Caribbean, Haiti and Cuba stand at opposite ends of the health spectrum.[40] In Haiti, nearly one in ten children die before their first birthday, with diarrhoea being the commonest cause of death. By the age of five, more than 40 per cent of children are permanently stunted through illness and malnutrition. Government health services reach less than half the population. By contrast, the renowned Cuban health system is built on primary health care, covering both preventive and curative medicine, and covers some 98 per cent of the population. More than nine out of ten one-year-olds are fully vaccinated against the major preventable childhood diseases such as tuberculosis, polio and measles. However, the island's economic difficulties in recent years have produced shortages and forced the government to cut back on prescriptions and introduce charges for most medicines.

World-wide, improvements in child health have been startling, as the World Bank acknowledges: 'Health conditions around the world have improved more in the past forty years than in all previous human history.'[41] One hundred years ago the infant mortality rate in the USA, the richest country in the world, was 180 per 1000 – higher than in even the poorest

165

countries today. The causes of such long-term improvements include rising incomes, advances in medical technology, better public health services and the spread of education. The World Bank believes that, of these, the spread of education, especially women's education, is the most important.[42]

One of the most important effects of education has been the fall in family size. From 1960 to 1990, the average number of births per woman in Latin America and the Caribbean fell from 5.9 to 3.2, faster than in any other region in the world. Besides improved education, greater access to contraceptives played a central role, as the proportion of women using some form of contraception rose from 11 per cent to 60 per cent over the same period.[43] Fewer children means more food and attention for the children who are born, and better maternal health.

One more sombre aspect of the panorama is that despite the general spread of contraception, more children are themselves giving birth. Research suggests that one-third of all abortions are carried out on adolescents, often using backstreet methods ranging from knitting needles to drugs such as the ulcer drug Citotec, the abortifacient of choice for thousands of Brazilian women. Such methods leave a terrible toll in the form of maternal death, internal bleeding and (in the case of Citotec) deformed babies. The Pan American Health Organization estimates that 1.2 million Brazilian adolescents have abortions every year.[44]

In recent years, a number of dangerous new developments have struck at child health. Cholera returned to the region in the early 1990s, and new drug-resistant strains have rekindled tuberculosis, killing 75,000 people in 1995,[45] and affecting a predicted 3.2 million people over the course of the 1990s.[46] Structural adjustment in many countries has brought deepening inequality and poverty and cuts in health services, undoing many of the benefits of technical and medical advances and falling fertility.

Furthermore, Latin America and the Caribbean's inexorable process of urbanization poses its own new threat – the growing health problem posed by urban pollution, as municipal governments fail to provide clean water, refuse disposal and sanitation for the influx of migrants from the countryside, and the steadily growing numbers of cars clog the city air with fumes. In Mexico City, children can catch hepatitis merely by breathing, as infected excrement on the streets is first dried by the sun, and then carried as faecal dust on the shanty town winds.

Death without weeping

Parades of heartening statistics are just averages. They hide the growing inequalities within Latin America and the Caribbean, where some countries have infant mortality rates approaching European levels, while others are closer to Africa. Even within countries, the inequalities of death have been widening. In the slums of São Paulo, children are five times more likely to die than in the richer central districts.[47]

Furthermore, statistical niceties obscure the abiding brutality of infant death. In *Death Without Weeping: The Violence of Everyday Life in Brazil*, US anthropologist Nancy Scheper-Hughes charted the impact of infant mortality on that most quintessential of emotions, mother love. Over a period of 25 years, Scheper-Hughes lived in, and revisited, a shanty town in the northeast of Brazil, a region which accounts for one in four of Latin America's child deaths.[48] At a time when the outside world saw Brazil going through an economic boom, Scheper-Hughes watched life and death in the blighted alleyways of Alto do Cruzeiro:

> Since 1964, and with little letup over the decade of the great economic miracle of Brazil, I have seen Alto children of one and two years who cannot sit up unaided, who do not or cannot speak, whose skin over the chest and upper part of the stomach is stretched so tightly that every curve of the breastbone and the ribs stands out. The arms, legs and buttocks of these children are stripped of flesh so that the skin hangs in folds. The buttocks are discoloured. The bones of the hungry child's face are fragile. The eyes have sunk back in the head. The hair is thin and wispy, often with patches of baldness, though the eyelashes can be exceptionally long. In some babies there is an extraordinary pallor, a severe anaemia, that lends the child an unnatural, waxen appearance that mothers see as a harbinger of death.[49]

Forced to witness the daily deaths of neighbours' babies, Scheper-Hughes expected the women to grieve over their loss. Instead, she wrote: 'What puzzled me was the seeming "indifference" of Alto women to the deaths of their babies and their willingness to attribute to their own offspring an "aversion" to life that made their deaths seem wholly natural.'[50] Mothers claimed their malnourished, sickly babies were born 'wanting to die'.

Scheper-Hughes discovered that women in Alto do Cruzeiro cope with the likelihood of infant death by loving differently from women in the USA or Europe. As one Alto woman explained:

> There is little sorrow for the death of an infant up until the age of eight or nine months. It is only after the baby is a year old that we begin to grieve. [Until then] the infant's story is not yet made up; it has no shape to it. And so the loss is not a big one.[51]

The lexicon of child death, known locally as 'child sickness' or 'child attack', or sometimes just referred to as 'the ugly disease', gives a sense of the horrors which lead to such radical differences in maternal behaviour.

Each condition has its own name: these include *gasto* (wasted, spent, passive), *batendo* (convulsed), *olhos fundos* (sunken eyes), *doença de cão* (frothing, raving madness), *pasmo* (witless), *roxo* (red), *pálido* (white), *susto* (soul-shocked), *corpo mole* (body soft, uncoordinated) and *corpo duro* (body rigid, convulsed).

At birth, women conduct a kind of subconscious triage, separating out the babies they judge likely to die from those deemed to have the 'courage' to survive. Sickly babies are effectively abandoned by the mothers, left alone in the hammock, withdrawing from human contact:

> They become fussy and profoundly unhappy creatures, difficult to engage and impossible to satisfy. Although slowly starving to death, such babies rarely demand to be fed or held. Many die alone and unattended, their faces set in a final, startled grimace, – an ultimate susto – that they will take with them into their tiny graves.[52]

For those who make it to their first birthday, 'mother love grows slowly, tentatively and fearfully.'[53] Scheper-Hughes concludes that:

> Learning how to mother on the Alto includes knowing when to let go of a child who shows that he wants to die. The other part is knowing just when it is safe to let oneself go enough to love a child, to trust him or her to be willing to enter the struggle that is this life on earth.[54]

If the child dies after the mother has decided to love her, the grief and bereavement is every bit as heart-rending as that prompted by a cot death in Europe or North America.

Over her 25 years visiting the Alto, Scheper-Hughes also witnessed what she termed 'the modernisation of child mortality', during which 'old' child killers, such as infectious diseases (which affected older children, across social classes), were replaced by the 'new' killers of malnutrition and diarrhoea-based dehydration, both related to bottle-feeding and poverty. 'Child death has retreated to the back streets, muddy roads and squalid hillsides of Brazil,' she concluded.[55]

She was herself an actor in the drama. When she first went to the Alto as a public health worker in the US Peace Corps in 1964, she sang the praises of the powdered milk being donated under the US Food for Peace Program, but local women refused to feed it to their children, preferring breast milk and goat's milk mixed with cereal. Over time, however, the aid fostered a powdered-milk dependency, which Nestlé and other companies took advantage of when the free distribution ended in the 1970s. Women's resistance was slowly eroded by the power of advertising, while the growing number of women working as temporary wage labourers had no other way of feeding their infants.

Powerful social stigmas also became attached to breast-feeding:

> The definition of father on the Alto do Cruzeiro is the man who arrives at least once a week bearing the prestigious purple-labelled can of Nestlé ... A mother who breast-feeds her infant is thought of either as an abandoned woman, or as a woman whose husband does not 'provide' for her and her offspring.[56]

Beneath it all, Scheper-Hughes detected women's growing mistrust of their own bodies, as they became convinced that breast milk is too weak, their bodies too wasted, to nourish their babies. But although hunger weakens children, dirty water kills them, and the rise of bottle-feeding greatly increased the death-toll. Studies in urban Brazil show that babies fed only on bottles are 14 times more likely to die than those fed only on breast milk. Besides the obvious danger of infection from dirty water, bottles and teats, impoverished women over-dilute the expensive milk powder, effectively starving their babies. Scheper-Hughes concluded that the spread of powdered milk is 'the commerciogenic plague of the current generation'.[57]

Surviving into childhood

Despite the horrors of places like Alto do Cruzeiro, 19 out of every 20 Latin American and Caribbean children now make it to their first birthday, but many have been marked for life by malnutrition, which afflicts one in seven of the survivors. Undernourishment lowers the child's resistance to infectious disease, and repeated bouts of ill-health and disease affect the appetite, digestion and absorption of food, increasing malnutrition further in a downward spiral. According to UNICEF, the damage inflicted on a child's growing body can never be undone. Malnutrition:

> strikes hardest in the last trimester of pregnancy and during the first twelve months after birth ... . Even if nutrition improves thereafter, the child is likely to suffer from below-normal growth, affecting physical and mental development and compromising the future of children and their nations.[58]

One long-term consequence of malnutrition can be seen in the Instituto Santa Maria de Guadalupe, a centre for disabled children in Lima. According to the deputy director, Javier Malpartida, poverty lies at the root of many of the children's disabilities, creating a combination of malnutrition and emotional neglect in the crucial early years. The results include physical/motor problems, partial hearing and mental retardation.

For Javier, the institute's greatest challenge is coping with the parents, not the children, specifically getting them to accept that their child is disabled. 'Even when the parents have accepted it, there's still the shame,' he says. 'Society is very hard on special needs kids. If parents see it as a cross they have to bear, they don't go out with their kids. But if they're positive about it, they take them to the park.' The institute tries to give the children skills which will enable them to find work when they leave, but Javier estimates that they only succeed with perhaps one in ten. The rest are more likely to stay stuck at home, being cared for by sisters and brothers, often resented as a burden on the family.

Peru's shock programme of structural adjustment, which itself has increased hunger and poverty, now threatens to close the very institute which cares for their victims. The Congress is debating a new education law which could mean that salaries are withdrawn from special needs schools. 'In an atmosphere of cost-cutting, special needs education doesn't have a hope. In all these changes the worst affected are the poor – of those, the worst affected are the kids; of those, the worst affected are special needs kids,' Javier says with anger. As a signatory to the UN Convention, the Peruvian government is obliged to 'recognise the right of the disabled child to special care' and to provide free assistance, wherever possible:

> to ensure that the disabled child has effective access to and receives education, training, health care services, rehabilitation services, preparation for employment and recreation opportunities in a manner conducive to the child's achieving the fullest possible social integration and individual development.[59]

Once again, a government's commitments under the Convention stand in bleak contrast to its behaviour in practice.

One important aspect of child rights, often ignored in the face of the more urgent problems of malnutrition and disease, is the right to play. The UN Convention states that signatory states should 'recognise the right of the child to rest and leisure, to engage in play and recreational activities … and to participate freely in cultural life and the arts'.[60] Adequate and safe facilities for play are essential to any child, providing exercise and a vital means of mental and social development, yet they are a rarity in most of the region. Instead, most children show their inventiveness by contriving to play in the most unpromising conditions, whether improvising toys out of paper, sticks, cardboard boxes or bottle-tops (the 'pogs' craze which swept through the school playgrounds of Britain and the USA in 1996 was based on a Latin American bottle-top game), or opting for more exciting, but dangerous, pastimes such as hopping rides on the fenders of passing cars.

HIV/AIDS

One serious new threat is HIV/AIDS. In the words of the World Bank, 'Historians will look back on the latter half of this century as having had one great medical triumph, the eradication of smallpox, and one great medical tragedy, AIDS.'[61] By mid-1995, Latin America and the Caribbean had an estimated two million HIV-positive people, double the US figure.[62] According to the Pan American Health Organization, the total number of cases of full-blown AIDS came to 146,000, and 67,000 had died by the end of 1995. The worst-hit countries were Brazil, where 38,000 people had died, Mexico (14,000), Venezuela (3000), Colombia (2900) and Argentina (2200).[63]

Although as a child killer it still lags far behind diseases of poverty such as diarrhoea and pneumonia, HIV/AIDS in Latin America and the Caribbean is spreading rapidly and affects growing numbers of children, largely because, as in Africa and Asia, the disease is becoming 'heterosexualized', striking women as much as men. Women are more at risk than men for both cultural and physiological reasons. Physiologically, women are at greater risk because a greater surface of mucus is exposed to infection during sex, and because semen carries a greater concentration of the virus than vaginal fluid.

The risk posed to women by AIDS is further heightened by the nature of their relations with men. Within a couple, even if a woman knows that her partner is unfaithful, it can be very hard to persuade him to use condoms. Men often take such a suggestion as a threat, both to their sexual satisfaction and to their power, as it involves the woman asserting her rights over her own sexuality. Furthermore, women commonly marry older men who have had more partners. UNICEF concludes, 'The growing AIDS threat to women and children will not diminish until women have more power to say no to sex, to choose their own partners, and to influence sexual behaviour.'

As more women become infected, so the impact on children increases. Children born to HIV-positive mothers have a 15–40 per cent chance of being born with the virus, and can also be infected by breast milk. In the Haitian capital of Port-au-Prince in 1991, over half the children under 18 months in orphanages were HIV positive.[64]

Rosanna Denegri's seven children have at least escaped infection, but their prospects are grim. Their mother, a strikingly young-looking 34-year-old Peruvian woman with an Afro hairstyle and trendy clothes, has the HIV virus:

> *I got infected from my husband, Armando. He got sick, diarrhoea, coughs, lost his job as an accountant. We went to the hospital and he took the news*

really badly. Imagine what I felt, with Jorge only four and the twins just two! When I found out they were negative I jumped in the air and thanked God. Armando never told me how he got it – he took the secret with him when he died on 11 May 1995.

Now I sell tamales, anything – you name it, I sell it. So far, all the kids are still in school except the ones who are too young. I am seropositive but I have no symptoms. I haven't told the kids yet – they wouldn't understand. I don't know how I'm going to tell them 'I've got this – I'm positive', but it's not time yet. My mum and dad know. They say they'll look after the kids.

In spite of everything, life goes on. God, I hope the symptoms don't come soon, not until my kids are big.

Armando died a week after begging me for forgiveness. It was terrible after he was diagnosed – we fought all the time. If my mum didn't support me, I'd be dead by now. When Armando died, I couldn't manage any more, so I moved in with them.

I never thought it would happen to me. When he came home late, I used to pull his leg and say 'Armando, careful of AIDS', and he'd say, 'No, woman, I'm well prepared.' Now it's touched me.

More than half of the children born with HIV in developing countries die before their first birthday, and AIDS-related deaths could increase infant mortality rates by half in coming years, reversing many of the gains of previous decades.[65] Those who do not contract the virus face the same grim future as Rosanna's children, as families lose breadwinners, sick mothers are unable to care for their children, and the children themselves, especially girls, find themselves forced to give up school to care for sick parents and relatives. As in Rosanna's case, the stigma and blame attached to AIDS often result in recrimination and family breakdown.

If there is no-one like Rosanna's parents to offer help, the children of parents with HIV/AIDS can end up on the street, themselves becoming a high-risk group. Street children typically become sexually active very early, and face so many more immediate threats, that preventing disease can often seem unimportant. Child prostitutes are frequently unaware of the risks involved or discount them, and are often under great pressure by men to have unprotected sex.

World-wide, HIV infection is spreading at a phenomenal rate. The World Health Organization predicts that numbers could double over the five years from 1995 to the end of the century, reaching 30 million people world-wide.[66] Besides the human suffering involved, AIDS is peculiarly destructive at a national level. As a sexually transmitted disease, it mainly strikes adolescents and young adults – the very people on whom society relies to maintain the population of children and the elderly.

Since no vaccine is in sight, only prevention can limit the spread – otherwise two million people will be dying every year by the end of the century.[67] Yet of the US$2 billion spent annually on AIDS prevention, only 10 per cent is spent in the developing world, where 85 per cent of infections occur.[68] The main kinds of prevention are sex education, in particular encouraging condom use, improving early detection to allow HIV-positive people to avoid infecting others, and early treatment of other sexually transmitted diseases, which can increase the likelihood of catching the HIV virus via genital ulcers and sores.

Fight for the future

Governments are generally doing better on health than education, switching resources to primary health care and away from expensive hospital treatments which disproportionately benefit the better-off, but there is still a long way to go: literally in the case of Peru, where more than 60 per cent of the poor have to travel for more than an hour to obtain primary health care, compared with less than 3 per cent of the better-off.[69]

In recent years, governments have continued to improve preventive work such as vaccination campaigns, oral rehydration campaigns against diarrhoea and the provision of clean water. Even during the economic crisis of the 1980s, mass vaccination campaigns across the region increased coverage for immunization against diseases like measles and tetanus from 60 per cent to 75 per cent.[70]

Access to safe drinking water rose from 66 per cent of the population to 79 per cent over the same period.[71] This had an enormous impact since, according to the World Health Organization, 60–80 per cent of all sickness in Latin America and the Caribbean stems from water and sanitation problems.[72] For those children still getting sick, help is at hand in the shape of oral rehydration therapy (ORT), a cheap and easy remedy for the dehydration caused by diarrhoea. In Mexico, from 1990 to 1993, a government programme trained five million mothers in the use of ORT. Many of the women went on to teach other women in their neighbourhood. The tuition was basic – three lessons on the themes of continued feeding, fluids and medical consultation when necessary. Mexico's annual production of ORT packets, which contain the essential ingredients for making up the rehydration fluid, leapt from nine million to 83 million packets in four years. The incidence of diarrhoea dropped by over a third, and the number of children dying fell by over half. UNICEF estimates that 30,000 young lives were saved.[73]

However, governments have also made things worse, by cutting state health spending, removing food subsidies, and other measures connected to structural adjustment programmes implemented across the region since the early 1980s. The result has been an increasingly two-tier system in which anyone who can afford it resorts to the private health and education system, leaving the poor to the frustration of an increasingly dilapidated and underfunded residual state sector. In many cases, local communities themselves have seized the initiative in finding solutions to their health needs, along with the region's burgeoning NGOs. In the shanty towns, women have set up soup kitchens to ensure that the children get at least one square meal a day. Poor communities are often at the forefront in demanding (and then digging the trenches for) water pipes to bring them life-giving clean water supplies.

When governments fail to act fast enough, as has so far been the case over HIV/AIDS, others have taken up the challenge. Some of the most successful programmes have been those which involve children themselves in educating and organizing for health. In Nicaragua, the Child-to-Child programme trains child health promoters who run workshops for other children in the shanty towns, using everything from puppet shows to videos to teach older children how to care for their infant brothers and sisters. Children organize clean-up campaigns to rid their barrios of stagnant water (a breeding ground for malaria and other diseases), and to turn garbage into compost for new tree-planting schemes.

In Peru, a similar scheme is training a new generation of community leaders in a school in one of Lima's shanty towns:

My granny first gave me a drink when I was three. The grown-ups all tell stories and laugh about kids getting drunk and falling down the stairs. But sometimes the parents get too drunk and beat up the kids, and then the kids go the same way, especially when the fathers take their sons drinking with them. Round here, the boys start boozing in their little gangs when they are 13.

Rocío is 14, a Peruvian schoolgirl sitting with her schoolmates, arms flung casually around each other's shoulders, as they discuss the drinking problems of their age group. Most of the girls have the stocky build and striking cheekbones of Peru's Indian population, millions of whom have migrated to Lima in recent decades, fleeing the violence and poverty of their Andean communities. Sitting in a stuffy classroom in their anonymous concrete block of a school, the girls are anything but giggly adolescents. They have volunteered for a training programme for youth leaders, in which they learn how to listen and offer advice to their classmates.

Girls set off to school from a shanty town in the Peruvian capital of Lima.

Elected by their peers, the girls receive an initial four days of training, followed by regular support from the Education and Health Institute (IES), a Peruvian organization which runs the programme. Once back among their classmates, they have plenty to discuss: domestic violence, sexual abuse, HIV/AIDS, teenage alcoholism, unwanted pregnancies – the full range of social and emotional problems facing young people inside the bleak adobe huts that cling to the hillsides outside Lima. They take it all in their stride, with a startling maturity and open-mindedness.

'Parents can't talk to their kids – there's a lack of confidence,' explains María, another leader. 'But we're adolescents too, so the kids aren't ashamed to talk to us.' The girls love the work. One says:

> We've had some good experiences, we had one girl who was pregnant and scared to tell her parents – she was going to have an abortion. We got her to talk to them, and she decided to have the baby. Now she's back at school. Another girl was being abused by her neighbour but was too ashamed to tell her parents. She was going out of her mind. We got her to tell them, and then they sorted it out.

The girls have to make up for the failings of school sex education: 'we've learned about sex, diseases like AIDS, and we can explain things better. They don't teach us these things in class – teachers are too ashamed, they think we're just little girls.'

One of their most popular activities is showing 'Love of my Life', a video about AIDS featuring a girl who catches the virus and has a baby. It leaves the audience in tears, but has been a big hit, generating requests for extra showings by youngsters in the neighbourhood.

The hours they have put in as voluntary youth counsellors have changed them, too. 'We've learned to build confidence with people, so they talk to us,' explains Rocío. At 14 and 15, they are already performing vital work in their communities, and show every sign of becoming the next generation of leaders in Lima's vibrant network of grassroots organizations.

Conclusion

Latin America and the Caribbean's failings in education and health care are both the symptom and the cause of its uniquely unequal society and growing levels of poverty. Poor people die younger, lose more babies, get sick more often and take longer to recover. They go to inferior schools and drop out earlier than the better-off. Their lack of education and ill-health means they earn less in later life, rearing their own families of poor children, and so on.

Building the next generation requires good schools and health care, breaking the cycle of deprivation and poverty. That needs money, for investment in new schools, teachers' salaries, vaccines and nurses. Whatever the new rhetoric from the World Bank and others about the importance of human capital, public spending is unlikely significantly to improve as long as Latin America and the Caribbean is in the grip of structural adjustment programmes. In the long term, the mind-set that puts economics before people must change.

But even within these constraints, much can be achieved. Technological advances have radically improved many aspects of health in recent decades, while the emphasis has started to shift away from costly curative medicine, which generally benefits the middle classes, to preventive and primary medicine which helps the poor. In education the panorama is more depressing, but there are innumerable initiatives which could transform Latin America and the Caribbean's wasteful, inefficient and irrelevant educational systems, if only governments have the imagination and political will to make use of them.

The tasks are urgent, whether they involve mass sex education to slow down or stop the rapacious spread of HIV/AIDS, or ensuring that the next generation does not drop out of school or emerge unable to read and write after years of sitting passively in front of untrained, underpaid and exhausted teachers. The first step must be to change the way in which decisions are taken. Against the odds, the poor are already coming up with ideas and answers. If education is to become relevant to people's lives, they must be involved in designing it, enabling governments to tap into the huge reserves of creativity, enthusiasm and energy that exist among the Latin American and Caribbean poor when it comes to providing for their children. Particularly in the case of education, a key resource in devising systems that work is the children themselves, who must be involved in designing, improving and running educational systems from the outset.

Notes

1 SCF UK, *Peru Draft Country Situation Analysis* (mimeo) (Lima, 1994), p. 3.

2 Kevin Watkins, *The Oxfam Poverty Report* (London, 1995), p. 25.

3 Pedro Francke Ballve, *La Educación Pública, los Pobres y el Ajuste* (Aprodeh/CEDAL, Lima, 1994).

4 Ernesto Schiefelbein, *Education Reform in Latin America and the Caribbean: An Agenda for Action* (mimeo) (UNESCO–OREALC, June 1995), p. 7.

5 UN Convention on the Rights of the Child (Geneva, 1989), Article 28.

6 CEPAL, *Education and Knowledge* (Santiago, 1992), p. 37.

7 *Ibid.*, p. 39.

8 *Ibid.*, p. 42.

9 Ernesto Schiefelbein, *School-related Economic Incentives used in Latin America for Reducing Drop-out and Repetition Mainly Linked to Child Labour* (draft, mimeo) (Santiago, August 1996), p. 2.

10 Watkins, *op. cit.*, p. 79.

11 Schiefelbein, *School-related Economic Incentives, op. cit.*, p. 5.

12 Schiefelbein *Education Reform in Latin America and the Caribbean, op. cit.*, p. 27.

13 *Ibid.*, p. 13.

14 Domitila Barrios de Chungara and Moema Viezzer, *Let Me Speak! Testimony of Domitila, a Woman of the Bolivian Mines* (New York, 1978), p. 56.

15 Author visit, 1986.

16 *Financial Times*, London (30 June 1994).

17 SCF UK, *op. cit.*, p. 19.

18 Schiefelbein, *Education Reform in Latin America and the Caribbean, op. cit.*, p. 16.

19 *Ibid.*, p. 26.

20 *Ibid.*, p. 12.

21 *Ibid.*, p. 16.

22 Duncan Green, *Silent Revolution: The Rise of Market Economics in Latin America* (London, 1995), p. 102.

23 CEPAL, *Social Panorama of Latin America 1993* (Santiago, 1993), p. 11.

24 UNICEF, *Children of the Americas* (Bogotá, 1992), p. 37.

25 CEPAL, 'El impacto de invertir más y mejor en la educación media', *Notas Sobre La Economía y el Desarrollo* No. 592/593 (Santiago, June/July 1996), p. 2.

26 SCF UK, *Sustaining Advances in Cuban Education: A Case for Support* (London, 1996).

27 Orla Quinlan, *Primary Education in Haiti* (mimeo) (April 1995).

28 Centro de Cultura Luiz Freire/Grupo Alternativas Educacionais, *Escolarização Básica das Camadas Populares na Região Metropolitana do Recife* (Olinda, November 1993), p. 21.

29 *Ibid.*, p. 144.

30 Instituto Brasileiro de Geografia e Estatística figures cited by Ana Dourado, SCF Brazil, in personal communication (26 November 1996).

31 'Radio education in the Dominican Republic', in Mary B. Anderson (ed.), *Education for All: What Are We Waiting for?* (UNICEF, 1992), p. 85.

32 Christopher Colclough and Keith M. Lewin, *Educating all the Children: Strategies for Primary Schooling in the South* (Oxford University Press, 1993), pp. 135–8.

33 Schiefelbein, *School-related Economic Incentives, op. cit.*, p. 8.

34 Andréa Barros e Policarpo Jr, 'Ajuda e até carinho fora do horror', *Veja* (São Paulo, 30 October 1996), p. 54.

35 UN Convention on the Rights of the Child, (Geneva, 1989) Article 30.

36 David Archer and Patrick Costello, *Literacy and Power: The Latin American Battleground* (London, 1990), pp. 163–6.

37 Phillip Wearne, *Return of the Indian: Conquest and Revival in the Americas* (London, 1996), p. 142.

38 UNICEF, *op. cit.*, p. 24.

39 UNICEF/CEPAL, *Mortalidad en la Niñez* (Santiago, 1995), p. 13.

40 SCF UK, *Caribbean Country Report* (mimeo) (London, 1996).

41 World Bank, *World Development Report 1993* (Washington), p. 21.

42 *Ibid.*, p. 39.

43 UNICEF, *State of the World's Children 1994* (New York), p. 8.

44 SCF UK, *Brazil Draft Country Situation Analysis* (Recife, 1995), p. 35.

45 *Noticias Aliadas* (Lima, 28 March 1996).

46 WHO, *Groups at Risk: WHO Report on the Tuberculosis Epidemic* (Geneva, 1996), p. 14.

47 UNICEF, *Children of the Americas, op. cit.*, p. 24.

48 Nancy Scheper-Hughes, *Death Without Weeping: The Violence of Everyday Life in Brazil* (Berkeley, 1992), p. 31.

49 *Ibid.*, p. 146.

50 *Ibid.*, p. 270.

51 *Ibid.*, p. 437.

52 *Ibid.*, p. 383.

53 *Ibid.*, p. 359.

54 *Ibid.*, p. 364.

55 *Ibid.*, p. 282.

56 *Ibid.*, p. 323.

57 *Ibid.*, p. 316.

58 UNICEF, *State of the World's Children 1994, op. cit.*, p. 16.

59 UN Convention on the Rights of the Child, (Geneva, 1989), Article 23.

60 UN Convention on the Rights of the Child, (Geneva, 1989), Article 31.

61 World Bank, *op. cit.*, p. 99.

62 Latin American Group on Women and Aids, Cuernavaca (mimeo) (Mexico, 1995).

63 PAHO, http://www.paho.org/english/aidtleng.htm, (31 October 1996).

64 Jo Boyden and Pat Holden, *Children of the Cities* (London, 1991), p. 86.

65 SCF UK, *HIV/Aids and Children: Some Facts and Figures* (mimeo) (London, June 1995).

66 *Ibid.*

67 UNICEF, *State of the World's Children 1995* (New York), p. 22.

68 *Ibid.*, p. 22.

69 World Bank, *op. cit.*, p. 4.

70 UNICEF, *Children of the Americas, op. cit.*, p. 26.

71 UNICEF, *State of the World's Children 1996* (New York), p. 63.

72 UNICEF, *Children of the Americas, op. cit.*, p. 43.

73 UNICEF, *State of the World's Children 1995 op. cit.*, p. 24.

CHAPTER 8

Rights and Wrongs

Child Rights and the UN Convention on the Rights of the Child

In a community hall in the Nicaraguan town of Estelí, a band called 'Tempranal' is deafening rows of dazed-looking parents with a heavy rock version of a popular toddlers' song. This is a children's concert with a difference – *by* children, as well as *for* them. Toddlers mill around, babies dressed up in party frocks and frilly socks are passed from adult to adult.

The band, all aged 12–15, are heavily electric, sporting US street fashion in the shape of reversed baseball caps and enormous trainers. Sofia, the 12-year-old singer, is vamped up in heels and miniskirt, pouting and cool and having the time of her life. As well as being deafening, their songs are political: 'there's too much poverty, too much crime, we want to study, not just work'.

Working the crowd like professionals, Tempranal build up to a final crescendo, and their even-younger groupies whoop and scream as their favourite songs are introduced. They join hands and sway on the slower numbers (invariably sung off-key, but no-one seems to care). *La bamba* starts and they're on their feet, holding up posters of their heroes. The two coolest boys in the band leap down off stage and break into a high-energy dance, driving their fans to fever pitch.

While the crowd roars, two street kids sneak their way into the hall and wend their way through the tables. They do not dance and most of the time do not even watch the music, staring intently at the leftover tacos on people's plates and wolfing down any offerings.

Tempranal is the flagship for *Los Cumiches*, a child-run radio programme which has taken the children of Estelí by storm. Their work is at the cutting edge of the growing child rights movement in Latin America and the Caribbean, which has taken off in the wake of the ratification by all the region's governments of the 1989 UN Convention on the Rights of the Child. The movement is promoting both respect for more traditional notions of child rights, such as the right to education and health care, and a more radical and controversial set of children's rights to have a genuine say in the decisions which affect them, and, more generally, to participate in social development. By ensuring that policies are more effective, and harnessing the boundless energy and enthusiasm of children, child participation could play a crucial part in devising a more just and effective development model for Latin America and the Caribbean.

Back at the studio, this week's *Los Cumiches* is being made. Children surround the microphone, laughing and jostling as they fluff their lines and argue with a portly, patient adult producer. In the four years since they began work, the children have become polished radio announcers, with classic Latin American machine-gun delivery and rolled 'r's. To cover a story, they send out squads of reporters, two or three to a BMX bike, tearing round Estelí's cobbled streets, tape-recorders slung over shoulders, thrusting their mikes into adult faces like real professionals. They stand on tiptoe to record the views of a particularly tall doctor or chat to working children amid the noise and chaos of the market or the bus terminal. For a piece on a children's strike at a secondary school in demand of more chairs, the children head off to doorstep an uncomfortably defensive mayor, who promises to try harder.

News and features are interspersed with music. Sofia, Tempranal's starlet, sings a number about how just because girls play with boys, it does not mean that they are slags. But she loses her cool when asked why she never smiles on stage – 'because my tooth's just fallen out'. Child stardom brings its own special problems.

Manuel, a 14-year-old veteran at the radio station, describes how it all works:

> We started in August 1991 with four kids. Now there are eighty Cumiches who act as correspondents and journalists in the different schools in Estelí. Anyone can join. The programme goes out in three parts, for the 7–10, 10–13 and 14-and-over age groups.

> We meet on Sundays and plan the themes in the three sections. We choose who will do the interviews, then record on Friday to go out on Saturday – we don't feel ready to do it live! The programme goes out again on Monday. We also do two ten-minute news programmes every day. At the moment an aid agency helps us buy air-time on a commercial radio station, Radio Liberación, which covers the whole of the region, but we want to open our own station.

> Our main theme is child rights. We run campaigns, working with the schools, about the right to health, education, recreation and so on. We support the health ministry in areas like prevention. We have programme sections on the environment, sport, poetry, gossip, stories and music – we play techno, rock, US music.

We ask kids to write in on the problems they are facing at school – we get piles of letters! No desks, no water, toilets that don't work, that kind of thing. We send a team of journalists to investigate, then lobby the Education Ministry. We also work with the street kids – we don't want them to feel left out. We meet them and peasant kids to exchange ideas. The street kids always say they like the way we call on the parents to treat their children better! We do a lot of work with them – they're the worst treated.

Once we saw a kid being hit by a policeman and lodged a complaint with the local police chief. The policeman got five days in jail – next time we see him, we'd better run! One kid came to the radio saying his mum had chucked him out, so we went with him to his house, advised him he should behave better and invited him to join the radio. A lot of kids who are badly treated come to us. A few days ago we had a girl who was working as a maid who'd been sacked without pay, so we went to the house and sorted it out and talked about it on the programme.

All the children agree that working on the programme has changed them, as 13-year-old Sara explains:

We like doing it and we learn about defending our rights – it's not about becoming journalists; it's about learning to express ourselves better and understand the lives of other children. You get to know new places, and to talk to other kids about human rights. And our parents have treated us better since we got involved! Now we feel able to stand up and talk in front of 300 people. We're used to everything now.

The experience of these children highlights many of the benefits produced when children actively participate in running any of the numerous social projects going on around Latin America. Children can talk to other children in a way that adults never can, they more easily identify with and understand each other's situations and difficulties, and they are more likely to come up with solutions that work for the children concerned. The Estelí social services department now regularly calls on these children to act as a go-between with children in difficult circumstances and their families. Along the way, the children participating in the project not only have a lot of fun, but acquire new skills and self-confidence, as well as a real, and probably life-long, commitment to their communities.

Child rights and changing views of childhood

The growing importance of child rights is bound up with the changing views of childhood during the course of the nineteenth and twentieth centuries. As child rights proponents Judith Ennew and Brian Milne explain:

The question of children's rights was not an issue for the French Declaration of the Rights of Man in 1780. Children were regarded as a residual category of persons, lacking full human rights. At that time, European society simply thought of children as the property of their parents. According to legal commentaries in England, for instance, child stealing was not theft unless the child was wearing clothes. Otherwise child theft was like theft of a corpse. The body was not inhabited by a legal person in either case.[1]

The notion of children as innocents in need of protection is also comparatively recent, in historical terms. Up until the eighteenth century, they were more likely to be seen as innately evil, inheritors of original sin in need of correction, as John Wesley, the founder of Methodism, made blood-curdlingly clear:

> Break their wills betimes. Begin this work before they can run alone, before they can speak plain, perhaps before they can speak at all. Whatever pains it costs, break the will if you would not damn the child. Let a child from a year old be taught to fear the rod and to cry softly; from that age, make him do as he is bid, if you whip him ten times running to effect it. Break his will now, and his soul shall live, and he will probably bless you to all eternity.[2]

Since then, starting with the British Factory Act of 1833, which limited the working day for 9–13-year-olds to eight hours,[3] there has been a steadily growing public acceptance that children have both rights as individual human beings, and additional rights as children (for example, to protection or education). The debate has been almost entirely conducted in the rich countries of the North, and its conclusions are often at odds with the realities of life in the poorer countries of the South, but in Latin America and the Caribbean, the changing conceptions of child rights have been spread both through international law and the Westernized views of the ruling élites.

One of the pioneers of this work was Eglantyne Jebb, a redoubtable English woman who, as a result of her experiences working with the Macedonian Relief Fund during the Balkan War, declared herself a pacifist during World War I. Jebb stood firm against the tide of jingoism which swept across Britain, declaring 'all wars, just or unjust, disastrous or victorious, are waged against the child'.[4] In 1919 she was the driving force behind setting up the Save the Children Movement, dedicated to child protection, whose Declaration of Child Rights was taken over, almost without alteration, by the Geneva Declaration of the Rights of the Child, adopted by the League of Nations in 1924 and the United Nations in 1959.[5]

Children are often more effective than adults in discussing issues such as sexuality and AIDS prevention with their peers. Volunteers train in AIDS education in a school in a Lima shanty town.

Such declarations largely depicted children as passive, helpless dependants in need of protection by both state and family, but the prevailing view remained that children 'should be seen and not heard'. Investigators researching the lives of children talked to parents or teachers, but not the children themselves. But as the twentieth century has worn on, a second current in the debate over child rights has become increasingly important. Children have come to be seen as actors and givers, as subjects of rights, actively involved, along with adults, in struggling for a better future, rather than mere passive receivers, in need of protection. The growth of such notions lies at the heart of some of the new perceptions enshrined in the 1989 UN Convention on the Rights of the Child.

The notion that children have a right to a voice is still deeply controversial. As revealed by the heated public debate in the UK over whether parents should be allowed to smack their children, adults find the notion that children have rights, even to protection against physical punishment, disturbing when it encroaches on one of their most precious and basic functions – being a parent. The idea that children should also have the right to a voice, including to dissent, is even more threatening, and often provokes both ridicule and hostility.

This is nothing new. In one of the more memorable examples of children's participation, the Children's Crusade in the thirteenth century, a 12-year-old boy named Stephen entered Paris at the head of a crowd of 30,000 children. The Bishop of Paris gave a classic adult's response to the threat:

> My child, you claim to serve God's natural order better than we do, but you are mistaken. For in this order parents command children, priests bless, knights fight, peasants labour and children obey. If we let children preach and command, do you not see that the order is reversed? The devil has led you into a trap and you have fallen into it.[6]

The many defenders of child rights in Latin America also come under attack, suffering everything from death threats to official harassment. When the Covenant House project in Honduras went to the InterAmerican Court of Human Rights in 1996 to condemn the practice of holding children in adult jails, the government responded with a press campaign threatening to remove its legal status and, referring to the Covenant House's North American director, Bruce Harris, muttered darkly about foreign interference in Honduran affairs.[7]

Those who believe that children's opinions need not be taken into account usually base their arguments on two connected strands: first, that children are not rational and capable of making reasoned and informed decisions; and second, that children lack the wisdom born of experience and so make mistakes. Any parent will have experienced situations where their child insists on going out in the middle of winter dressed only in a T-shirt and shorts, or demands ice-cream for breakfast, lunch and dinner. So, the argument goes, children do not know what is best for them and adults should protect them by taking decisions on their behalf.

Supporters of child rights point out that, whether in the school playground or at home, children show enormous intelligence and guile in making decisions on everything from dealing with the school bully to how to cadge another biscuit from their parents. This is even more the case in Latin America and the Caribbean, where poor children go out to work or learn to fend for themselves from an early age. Furthermore, adults themselves frequently prove irrational – they smoke, or drink and drive – or make mistakes, yet this does not disqualify them from citizenship. Some degree of double standards is clearly involved.[8]

Child rights advocates also believe that the inexperience argument is self-fulfilling – denying children the right to take responsibility keeps them in a dependent state for longer than is necessary. First World parents astonished by the 'precocious' maturity of Third World children as they work in the market or look after the home should perhaps reflect on whether it is their own children who have been kept in a state of immaturity by being denied responsibility and the chance to learn from their mistakes.

One of the chief uncertainties is the age at which children acquire the capacity to reason and make decisions. Children are not a homogeneous group with the same needs and abilities. A newborn baby is largely helpless, while a 17-year-old is often a more concerned citizen than many adults, despite not having the right to vote. The view of the UN Convention is that children's views should be taken into account in all decisions that affect their lives, 'in a manner consistent with the evolving capacities of the child'. This gradual transformation from helplessness to reason takes place at different ages for different children, but it seems clear that most children, at least in the North and middle-class Latin America, are kept in dependence long after they need to be.

Participation

Confusion also surrounds what precisely is meant by 'participation'. The UN convention on the Rights of the Child is not much help, demanding only that states:

> shall assure to the child who is capable of forming his or her own views the right to express those views freely in all matters affecting

the child, the views of the child being given due weight in accordance with the age and maturity of the child.

In practice, child participation can mean anything from a token presence at a conference (often performing songs or plays before an adult audience), to a largely child-run programme like *Los Cumiches*, although even this has an adult who is in charge of the budget.

One author, Barbara Franklin, has devised a 'ladder of participation' to show the different possible levels of children's involvement.[9] At the bottom of the ladder stand 'adult rule' and 'adults rule kindly', devoid of any child participation. Next come 'manipulation, decoration and tokenism', where children are used to provide a veneer of involvement, but in practice have no power or voice in decision-making. The higher rungs of the ladder pass through various forms of consultation to joint decision-making and, finally, children in charge.

It is worth considering a few of the typical institutions in which children lead their lives – schools, the family, working for an adult – to see how few rungs up the ladder their level of 'participation' reaches.

The children's projects which reach the highest rungs are usually those involving street and working children, who have already gained formidable experience and independence in their fight for survival on the streets. Organizations like Brazil's MNMMR or Peru's Movement of Working Children and Adolescents from Working-Class Christian Families (MANTHOC) are at the forefront of using child-led approaches in working with children and their families at a community level.

MNMMR played a crucial role in pressing for child rights to be included in the landmark Brazilian Child and Adolescent Statute in 1990, while MANTHOC has argued forcefully against the abolition of child work, instead demanding that children's right to work be respected.[10] However, the organizations are usually run by charismatic adults, raising suspicions that the children may to some extent be manipulated into adopting radical political stances.

Children world-wide are particularly concerned about their environment, and many programmes now involve them directly in trying to combat the region's growing environmental crisis. Children are often themselves involved in environmentally damaging practices such as collecting firewood or over-grazing, and often prove more open to new ideas on areas such as sustainable development and soil conservation. Moreover, children are often more susceptible than adults to environmental degradation such as air and water pollution or the lack of playing areas.

Haiti has the most devastated environment in the Americas, with land denuded of trees, long since cut down for firewood, or to make way for farming.[11] Shorn of tree cover, some 40 million tons of soil are washed away each year. Agricultural yields have fallen, and much of the countryside lives on the brink of starvation. But one child-centred project is trying to reverse the damage.

Benita Louis is 14 years old and lives with her family on a small farm in the Jacmel area of southern Haiti. Her day begins at 5 a.m., when she gets up to help her mother around the house. Since the age of 10, Benita has also worked on her father's fields, weeding them and helping to plant yams, and looking after the family's few goats and pigs. At 9 a.m., she goes to school.

Several months ago, Benita received four fruit trees from a Haitian environmental organization, ASSODLO, as part of a project to reforest the valley round her home. After two or three years, they will yield a crop which may provide enough income to keep Benita in school. In a few months, she will get another six trees to plant on a piece of land given to her by her father:

> I was really excited when I was told about the project. We were told about the importance of trees to our environment and then shown how to plant and water them and how to protect them from animals that want to eat them. In three years' time I will sell the fruit in our local market and pay for my education out of the money I earn.

> These trees will not only help us with our school fees. They will send an important message to other children and our parents that trees are important and that one of the reasons why our soil gets washed away every year and our crops are declining is because we have cut them down. Now if I see someone cutting down a tree, I tell them that their actions affect all of us.

There are now 900 children between the ages of 5 and 15, all tending their trees. They are divided into groups, each of whom has elected a representative to monitor and support their care of the trees.

Child-to-child

One of the most innovative programmes is 'child-to-child', a community health programme that started in Britain in 1978. Child-to-child started off teaching older children how to look after their little brothers and sisters, for example dealing with infant diarrhoea, but has moved on to broader development tasks, such as trying to involve children in improving their local environments. An example of the new approach is taking place in the Nicaraguan town of El Viejo, according to three teenage 'health promoters', Juan, 16, Armando, 14, and Lucho, 12:

Manuel, the local child-to-child organizer, sold it to us, got us excited, so we joined in. We went to a health workshop and they taught us how to solve the rubbish problem, that we could turn it into rich compost for the trees. We got interested and decided to form a barrio committee and carried out a survey. It showed the main problems were rubbish, malnutrition and malaria. We decided to start with the rubbish, turning it into organic fertilizer. We want kids in future to play in clean streets, and we want to give every family a tree and five kilograms of fertilizer to plant trees all over the barrio. People used to dump their rubbish right next to the school, so we organized a clean-up day and went round telling people not to dump there — they stopped.

Child-to-child means passing on knowledge. We call meetings on Saturdays — sometimes the kids say 'why are you doing this?' and we say 'so you can play in clean streets with shade', and they love it! We make sure it's fun — lots of jokes. If the kids get bored, we do a quick game to wake them up again.

On a personal level, we want to achieve health for both the community and ourselves. We want fruit and shade. Before, I just used to play around. Now I like work and study. Study helps us develop personally, the project helps us develop as a community — they go together.

Child-to-child exemplifies many of the benefits of child participation, both to children themselves and to the wider community. In *Great Expectations*, Charles Dickens wrote 'In the little world in which children have their existence, there is nothing so finely perceived and so finely felt as injustice.'[12] In these kinds of programmes, children can channel that sense of injustice and idealism into improving their communities, gaining self-esteem from being treated as responsible participants.

Children and young people are often best-placed to work with other young people because they speak the same language, share the same culture and experience the same difficulties. In Colombia, young rap stars can reach teenagers who have long given up on the politicians:

The 17th century theatre in Bogotá's historic Candelaria district has played host to thousands of performances — but never one like this. On a sparsely set stage, scruffy young rap singers in baggy jeans and baseball caps enact a Colombian 'social cleansing'. A death squad murders the leader of a popular rap group. His friends take the corpse on a hallucinogenic journey through modern Colombia: police corruption, drug abuse, political assassinations, kidnappings. Death, leering through a white mask, insists that life in such a country is not worth living. The singers take a more redemptive view: rapping for tolerance, they carry their fallen hero to the sea for a symbolic resurrection. The teen audience watching 'Opera Rap', as the show is called, cheers wildly.[13]

Child-to-child techniques also make sense in practical terms, providing a large and enthusiastic force of volunteers with intimate knowledge of the local community and conditions. Many health projects in Latin America and the Caribbean during the wave of cholera outbreaks in 1992 used this approach, and it could be argued that the prevention of a large-scale epidemic throughout the continent was achieved by its children.[14]

The UN Convention

The changing understanding of child rights has been reflected in a stream of national and international legislation. Cruelty to children became a criminal offence in the UK in 1889, some sixty years after similar legislation outlawed cruelty to animals.[15] In 1924, the League of Nations approved a Declaration of the Rights of the Child. In 1959, the UN issued its first Declaration of the Rights of the Child, announcing young people's entitlements to adequate nutrition, free education and medical care, as well as rights against exploitation and discrimination. In 1979 there was the International Year of the Child, which prompted calls for a Convention. Unlike a Declaration, which is little more than a statement of good intentions, a Convention has to be ratified by signatory states, once they have brought their own legislation into line with its contents. After that, other UN member states have the right to treat the provisions of the Convention as a 'matter of legitimate concern' for intervention to ensure the Convention is upheld.[16] For the ratifying states, the Convention constitutes international law.

As is the way with international bureaucracies, drafting the Convention took 10 years of delicate negotiations, but in November 1989 the child rights movement achieved its finest hour when the UN General Assembly approved the UN Convention on the Rights of the Child.

The UN Convention has become something of a phenomenon in the field of international human rights law. Within a year, it had been ratified by over 130 countries, and by April 1996, 187 of the world's 193 countries had become parties to the convention. Haiti became the last country in Latin America and the Caribbean to ratify in June 1995. Two of the six non-ratifying countries, Switzerland and the USA (both, ironically, home to the main UN organizations working on children's issues), have signed but not yet ratified the Convention, meaning that it is not legally binding. Both claim that their constitutions already set higher standards than the Convention.

The four countries yet to sign or ratify are the Cook Islands, Oman, Somalia and the United Arab Emirates. The speed and breadth of

Across the world, children are often more concerned than adults about environmental issues. Two new recruits receive training in a child-run reforestation scheme in Haiti.

ratification far outstrips any previous piece of international legislation, leading UNICEF to conclude: 'Before this century is out, there is every possibility that the Convention will become the first universal law of mankind.'[17] The full text of the Convention is given in the Appendix.

The vision of the Convention

Four of the Convention's 54 articles encapsulate its distinctive vision:[18]

Article 2 establishes that all rights described in the Convention apply to all children, without any discrimination on the grounds of gender, race, language, religion or other basis. It obliges governments to 'take all appropriate measures to ensure that children are protected from all forms of [such] discrimination'.

Article 3 states that 'in all actions concerning children, the best interests of the child shall be a primary consideration'. This places children squarely at the centre of state policy-making. A government or other organization can no longer take decisions without considering their impact on children.

Article 6 requires that states 'shall ensure to the maximum extent possible the survival and development of the child'. Thus governments are obliged to guarantee not just the lives of children, but their broader development, entailing economic, social and cultural rights. Although the phrase 'to the maximum extent possible' offers a form of get-out clause, it is strongly worded by the standards of international law, insisting that priority be given to child survival and development at all times.

Article 12 insists that parties shall 'assure to the child who is capable of forming his or her own views the right to express those views freely in all matters affecting the child, the views of the child being given due weight in accordance with the age and maturity of the child'. This guarantees active consultation with and participation by children, increasing as they grow older, in the decisions which affect their lives.

Taken overall, the Convention constitutes a substantial shift in the accepted understanding of the nature and role of children, and their relationship to the adult world. By stressing that children are individual human beings with rights and the same inherent value as adults, the Convention shifts the emphasis from a benefactor state which helps children to a child's basic and intrinsic rights to protection, to health, education and housing, and to a voice. In the process, power shifts from the state to the child, who is no longer seen as passive and helpless, but active and involved.[19]

The Convention even ventures onto the political and emotional minefield of parents' relations with their children – one of the most controversial issues surrounding child rights. In Article 18, it establishes that parents or legal guardians have the primary responsibility for the upbringing and development of the child and that 'the best interests of the child will be their basic concern'. Elsewhere the Convention talks of parents and guardians' duties 'to provide direction to the child in the exercise of his or her right [to freedom of thought, conscience and religion] in a manner consistent with the evolving capacities of the child'.[20] Thus the acceptable degree of parental control depends on the emotional and mental development of the individual child – a far cry from the notion that a child 'belongs' to his or her family that was so prevalent, even at the beginning of the twentieth century.

What the Convention says

The articles covering children's right to be consulted and involved form a minor part of the Convention, whose contents are often broken down into the '3 Ps': protection, provision and participation.

Under the general category of protection, the Convention obliges states to protect children from abuse and neglect, from drugs, from sexual or any other form of exploitation, from torture or incarceration along with adults, from taking part in armed hostilities under the age of 15, and from work that threatens their health, education or development, to protect refugee children and those without a family, and to protect children from all forms of discrimination.

The articles on provision are just as sweeping, obliging states to provide all children with access to health-care services, especially primary health care, to provide compulsory primary education for all (in their own language in the case of indigenous populations), to make secondary education available to every child, and to provide disabled children with access to special care.

Compared to these, there are relatively few articles covering the third 'P', participation. These guarantee children's rights to freedom of thought, conscience, religion and association, and to express their opinions freely, and to have that opinion taken into account in any matter affecting the child.

The impact of the Convention

The finely honed wording of the Convention, thrashed out over 10 years in interminable negotiations within the UN system, may seem a long way from the daily lives of poor children across Latin America and the Caribbean, but the Convention has had an impact in several important areas.

One of the most significant has been in changing national laws. A number of Latin American and Caribbean governments have had to revise their child laws to make them compatible with their new commitments under the Convention. Having ratified the Convention in 1991, the Jamaican government, with help from UNICEF, carried out a review of existing legislation concerning children in Jamaica. They found that there were large gaps – for example, Jamaica had no specific legislation dealing with children and armed conflicts, the right to play or children's rights to express their opinions and have them taken into account. A new 'Child Protection Act' was drawn up to fill in the missing pieces.

In Latin America, the need to bring national legislation into line with the Convention has led to a spate of new 'children's codes' in countries such as Brazil, Guatemala, Peru and Honduras.

In Brazil, the new Child and Adolescent Statute (ECA) was drawn up with unprecedented levels of child participation, thanks to the work of MNMMR. Within each project, then later at state and national level, MNMMR child activists discussed the draft for the statute and selected delegates to go to a national conference in Brasília. There, they made national headlines by invading the national Congress and presenting their demands. In the words of one of the conference organizers, João de Deus:

> The day the children occupied the senate was the most important day of my life. They ducked under the arms and between the legs of policemen who tried to stop them. The senate security tried to keep them out but they got in every way they could. There was a session going on. The children made a statement denouncing the attitude of a judge who had tried to stop them meeting in Brasília and denouncing the killings of children by vigilantes in Recife. It was very strong. There were congressmen crying who gave up their seats to the children.[21]

At the time the ECA was drawn up, Brazil had recently returned to civilian rule after 20 years of military government and Brazilians were enthusiastic about their new freedoms and democratic duties. The ECA reflects that enthusiasm, creating a vast network of children's rights councils (*conselhos de direitos*) and guardianship councils (*conselhos tutelares*) in all of the country's nearly 5000 municipalities. The rights councils, made up of representatives from NGOs and government institutions, are responsible for implementing the ECA, by monitoring policy-making and law enforcement. The guardianship councils function as local advocates for children, intervening when abuses occur and acting rather like child-specific social workers.[22]

While the legislative spree has sometimes meant little more than fat fees for lawyers, some changes have made a real difference. In Peru, Article 45 of the new Children's Legal Code of 1993 stated that any public or private institution could establish 'defence offices' for children and adolescents. Local and international NGOs have seized the opportunity.

The offices, known as Demunas (*Defensoría Municipal para Niños y Adolescentes*), began work in Lima and, by late 1996, had 160 centres all over Peru, and had dealt with well over 20,000 cases in their first three years. About 40 per cent of cases involved maltreatment, including sexual abuse. Other important areas included maintenance payments and the failure to register newborn children.[23] Offices do both case work and public education on child rights at community level. They are staffed by university students, usually lawyers on work experience.[24]

A case is initially denounced by neighbours, teachers, children themselves or relatives. Demuna representatives then investigate the allegations, giving priority at all times to resolving the dispute outside the court system. However, if a serious crime is involved, the case is immediately referred to the police. Demuna lawyers try and get both parties to a meeting and sign a contract/agreement on child maintenance, access and so on. If the agreement is repeatedly broken, the Demuna passes the case over to the criminal justice system.

Demuna's wider education role is similar to preventive work in health. Demuna teams work with local authorities, local radio stations, parents' associations and schools to organize events such as campaigns to register children without birth certificates, or to raise awareness of domestic abuse.

David Herrera Quispe and Haymet Aguilar Villa are two young law students doing their year's compulsory social service in a Defensoría in a small town just outside the former Inca capital city of Cusco. Their office is a bare room above a school, furnished with a couple of dilapidated benches; their windows look out on a fertile valley floor and scrubby Andean slopes dotted with eucalyptus. The dirt streets of the town are daubed with election graffiti. In animated tones, David and Haymet describe their work:

Our main area is domestic abuse. In a peasant community like this, people are very reluctant to denounce their relatives, and if someone does, everyone soon knows who talked. For that reason, most of our work is preventive, rather than judicial, mainly giving talks in primary and secondary schools, both to children and their parents. We also do some conciliation work, usually in cases where the father leaves and refuses to provide for his family. We contact the father, read him the law, and try and persuade him to cough up. We agree how much, whether he should pay in cash or in kind, and how it should be channelled. We sign an agreement and then follow it up.

We get involved trying to sort out domestic violence, since it indirectly affects the kids – women have been known to tell their husbands, 'don't hit me or I'll go to the defensoría'!

Sitting outside the office is today's first client, Ana Lucía, 15, a quiet, angry girl in a grey school uniform:

My father left eleven years ago – he went off with another woman and had four kids with her. He sent us food at first, but he soon stopped. I'm the oldest of five. Mum works in the market in Cusco, selling milk and stuff. I go and help her around 2pm, after I finish school. I'm in 3rd grade of secondary.

We brought a case against him but had to drop it – the lawyers were asking too much money. We've asked him to come here for conciliation, but he won't come, so now we're going to trial.

My mum doesn't want a trial – Dad gave her a bit of land where she grows maize and potatoes, and she's happy with that. But the land only gives enough food for three months of the year.

He's a real machista – he's got no heart, no love. I'm really angry with him. He looks after his other kids and not us. I've talked to him and he says he's got no money, but I know he's sold some of his crops.

When I finish school I'd like to study law. I may have kids some day, but I don't think their lives will be much different from mine. I'd like to get out of here, maybe to Mexico or the US.

Making the Convention work

In general, the real test of the Convention comes after it has been ratified and subsequent legislation has been passed. Latin American and Caribbean governments are renowned for their inability or unwillingness to enforce their own laws and constitutions, making the determination of the rest of what is known as 'civil society' pivotal in ensuring that the Convention becomes a set of real commitments rather than a series of pious hopes. Local scrutiny and pressure, from citizens' groups, NGOs, the media and other groups play a vital role in monitoring the authorities' performance and pressing for improvements.

Local NGOs and others have been helped in their work by a novel aspect of the Convention: the mechanisms it establishes to ensure compliance. The drafters of the Convention tried to learn from the inadequate mechanisms for ensuring the implementation of previous international legislation, and laid down that each state must present a report to a newly established Committee on the Rights of the Child, based in Geneva, within two years of the date of ratification, and every five years thereafter. The report must give details of the measures that the state has taken to ensure the effective and progressive fulfilment of the rights laid down in the Convention.

To prevent the government report becoming a whitewash, the Committee is allowed to collect information from other sources, such as UN bodies and NGOs, to compare with the official report. It is allowed to reject, partially or wholly, poor reports by signatory states and can oblige them to submit new reports in a relatively short time-scale, as it has in the case of Sweden and the UK.

The new role conferred upon local NGOs by the Convention has in some cases had a galvanizing effect. Jamaica's 'Coalition on the Rights of the Child' grew out of two conferences held in 1989 to raise awareness of the Convention. It comprises 15 NGOs, together with UNICEF. After wide consultations, it produced a supplement to the government's report to the UN Committee, and in October 1994 met the Committee to discuss its findings in more detail. NGO representatives also attended the Jamaican government's meeting with the Committee in order to highlight their areas of concern. The Coalition has proved to be an influential mechanism for promoting child rights issues through public education and for lobbying both the government and the UN Committee.[25]

Elsewhere, working together to compile an alternative report to take to Geneva has been a productive experience for many NGOs. According to one Honduran activist:

> It got people in NGOs to reflect on wider issues, not just what to do about 'their' 200 children. The document that emerged now forms the basis for our future work on children – it's an overview of the situation of kids in Honduras and the key areas of our work.[26]

Criticisms of the Convention

Given the enormous hopes aroused by the Convention, it is hardly surprising that it has not always lived up to expectations, in terms of both its contents and its impact in practice. Judith Ennew, a specialist on street children and one of the Convention's more trenchant, while constructive, critics, believes that:

> In the juxtaposition of the Convention and the image of the street child the entire discourse on children's rights stands revealed. The Convention, in the drafting process, the resulting text and in its implementation, takes as its starting point Western, modern

The right to play is a crucial aspect of the UN Convention. Children in the war-torn region of Chalatenango, El Salvador.

childhood, which has been 'globalised' first through colonialism and then through the imperialism of international aid.[27]

The Convention, Ennew believes, takes the Western, nuclear family as the norm. Article 5 of the Convention speaks of the child's 'right to know and be cared for by his or her parents', while Article 18 states that 'Parents or, as the case may be, legal guardians, have the primary responsibility for the upbringing and development of the child.' There is no mention of the role of extended families or the protection and companionship of other children (especially important for street children), implicitly invalidating the lives of poor, working and street children who do not fit the Western stereotype, and who thereby risk being branded an aberration in need of cure or correction.

Within Latin America and the Caribbean, the growing official acknowledgement that children have the right to be protected and to participate has been controversial. The social and cultural gulf between the poor majority and the élite of politicians and opinion-formers has meant that child rights have often provoked public hostility. While the élite may accept Northern views on issues such as child labour or the 'normality' of the nuclear family, this is very far from the experience of many poor families, who often believe that children should go out to work as part of their education, and who live in communities where nuclear families have never been the norm.

Furthermore, the recent legislation guaranteeing child rights has often proved unpopular with adults. For example, by granting legal impunity to children under the age of 18, Brazil's new Code of the Child and Adolescent is seen by much of the public as encouraging child crime, producing a backlash against child rights and increasing support for death squad attacks on alleged child criminals. Isa Ferreira, SCF UK's programme co-ordinator in Brazil, fears that the Code has become a scapegoat for public concern over crime levels, and that NGOs and other organizations are diverting too much time into defending it, distracting them from their primary task of working with children.[28]

Nevertheless, optimists among the child rights movement believe that the public education work of numerous government bodies and NGOs is making ground in persuading people to 'revalue' children, and believe that the tide of public opinion is now turning in their favour. In the absence of much hard empirical evidence, they point to much more supportive media coverage and the work of the Demunas and other innovative bodies, claiming these are producing a 'drip' effect on public opinion, slowly raising the level of acceptance for the notion of children's rights.

Tomás Andino, a specialist on child rights working for SCF UK in Honduras, believes that the Convention does not go far enough in encouraging children's participation:

> *The Convention is very weak on participation, and very conditioned, politically. There are three articles referring to the right to free expression, organization and movement, which are conditional as long as they don't threaten the security of the state – but that can mean almost anything!*[29]

A further weakness lies in the Convention's definition of a child. While setting an upper limit of 18 (lower in cases where children attain their majority earlier), the Convention ducks the issue of a *lower* limit, thereby ducking difficult debates over whether life begins at conception, birth, or somewhere in between. While such a fudge was clearly necessary to achieve consensus, it means that the Convention has little to say on crucial areas like teenage abortion and sexuality.

Amnesty International has also aired doubts, pointing out that while signatory governments must submit reports, the Committee on the Rights of the Child has no direct powers to enforce the rights contained in the Convention. Furthermore, Amnesty International is disappointed that the Convention does not specify which rights can never be suspended, for example during states of emergency.[30]

Despite such criticisms, most authors and activists praise the Convention's principles as a leap forward in international law. To date, most doubts surround its performance in practice. Many child rights activists who initially welcomed the Convention and its new role for NGOs are now beginning to feel drained by the bureaucracy of the UN system, as Arnulfo Ochoa from Honduras reveals:

> *It's frustrating. All that work, then raising the money to go to Geneva, and all you see is the report. Then five years without anything really changing, and another trip to Geneva and another report. What for? That level of disillusionment with the Geneva process is already quite generalized in Latin America. Maybe the main success of the Convention was to get us the new Children's Code, and that's what we have to work on now – getting our own laws implemented.*[31]

Tomás Andino agrees:

> *The UN hasn't given us much in the way of results so far. The UN system is a great big dinosaur, that moves very slowly, with little co-ordination, very diplomatic, respectful and so on. We feel pretty disillusioned with all this. In general, the UN responds better to political human rights violations – coups d'etats, cases of torture etc., and to occasional high profile child issues*

that make the headlines, like the sale of organs. But on low-level violations suffered by most children, daily, systematically, that are linked to typical state policies like economic policy or penal policy – then there's very little movement.

In Honduras we were very active as NGOs, and we managed to get the UN Committee to understand, we even brought one of its members here. That man saw everything, and as he was Peruvian, he understood the situation here. We left mountains of documents and videos in Geneva, and in spite of all that, the final declaration was pretty soft. So what happens when a country doesn't have a well-organized NGO system?

The Committee approved some resolutions on Honduras, but then the government leaves the meeting and there's no way to enforce them until the country comes back to the committee in five years time and it all happens again, the committee makes the same resolutions and so on. It could go on for ever! It's an ineffective bureaucratic mechanism.

In theory, in very serious cases, the Committee can call the government to extraordinary meetings, but is has to be like Somalia or Bosnia. Otherwise the Committee meets only three times a year, for two weeks each time. There are very few people on it, for the work it has. Each year the Committee has to receive twenty countries' reports.

So we need something more practical, more immediate – that's the wish of the NGOs right now. The Committee's resolutions, however weak, help legitimize our work, our demands within the country. And that's where the real fight is – you mustn't forget that. The real challenge for us is to mobilize national public opinion around these resolutions.[32]

In Brazil, the new children's statute, the ECA, has been both a blessing and a curse, according to child rights activist Isa Ferreira. Those working on children's issues have been forced to devote much of their time to defending the statute from attempts by right-wing politicians to amend it. On the other hand, it is one of Brazil's most popular and best-known laws, and it has played a vital role in changing the way in which government works at both national and local level. Since the ECA was passed, Isa has seen an attitude shift in the authorities, which now take children into account when formulating policy to a far greater extent than in the past.[33]

Above all, the Convention cannot yet be said to have made an enormous change in the lives of most of Latin America and the Caribbean's children. There are more children living in poverty than when the Convention was approved in 1989, more children going out to work, education systems are still crumbling and governments are still pursuing economic policies which in their impact on children often seem diametrically opposed to the vision of the Convention.

Yet even those frustrated with slow results believe that, despite all the bureaucracy and the lack of progress on the ground, the Convention still represents an enormous advance. It is part of a wider recognition that children have rights that is permeating through much of Latin American and Caribbean society: 'The problems of children are now an important political issue,' says Brazilian children's activist Rodrigo Gonzalez. 'Groups working with kids can today go to a government office and get an appointment. Eight years ago, we would have waited all day and no one would have seen us.'[34] Some adults working with children believe this change of attitude has also affected the children: 'You can hear kids on the street today say they're going to the [child rights] council to complain. You can hear kids detained by the police demand to know the charges against them,' says Ulisses Guirgel of the São Paulo Archdiocese. 'You can hear kids cite you chapter and verse about their right to live on the street if they have no other place to go. You never heard this ten years ago. There's a beginning of a change in consciousness.'[35]

Internationally, the Convention has established a benchmark of child rights that is rapidly approaching the status of the world's first universal law. Optimists see it as a watershed, claiming that the spread in public awareness and acceptance of child rights today resembles the mood just before the abolition of slavery in the last century, or apartheid in recent years.[36] Others compare children's previous 'invisibility' to that of women some decades ago[37] and argue that the Convention and the legitimacy it gives to notions of child rights can enable children to become the new focus of better models of social and economic development.

Conclusions

For those concerned with the future of Latin America and the Caribbean, the region's children constitute one of the greatest priorities and challenges. Huge obstacles must be overcome, if the next generation of adults is to fulfil its potential. Children must be part of the effort, and that can only happen if they are actively involved in the process of charting a new course for the region. Unleashing the energy of the most enthusiastic, idealistic members of society could hold the key to the region's development dilemma.

Over the course of recent years, the adult world has made great strides in recognizing children's rights as human beings. At first that meant respecting 'passive' rights, such as those to protection from abuse, or to access to welfare services. But it has become increasingly clear that children's 'active' rights, to a voice, to participation, are equally important to their development and that of society. That is easier to say in theory than to implement in practice, but numerous projects and organizations across the region are involved in exploring the area of children's participation, and in exchanging views and ideas. The UN Convention lies at the heart of the process, acting both as a benchmark for how far the concept of child rights has come, and legitimizing the next stage, which must be to broaden and deepen child participation.

Notes

1 Judith Ennew and Brian Milne, *The Next Generation* (London, 1989), p. 12.

2 Quoted in Martin Hoyles, *The Politics of Childhood* (London, 1989), p. 63.

3 Allison James and Alan Prout (eds), *Constructing and Reconstructing Childhood* (Basingstoke, 1990), p. 41.

4 Quoted in Dorothy Buxton and Edward Fuller, *The White Flame* (London, 1931), p. 5.

5 Ennew and Milne, *op. cit.*, p. 12.

6 Quoted in Hoyles, *op. cit.*, p. 67.

7 *El Heraldo* (Tegucigalpa, 15 October 1996).

8 Bob Franklin, 'The case for children's rights: a progress report', in Bob Franklin (ed.), *The Handbook of Children's Rights* (London, 1995), p. 10.

9 Devised by Barbara Franklin as an alternative to Roger Hart's version of the ladder of participation. Permission for use granted on her behalf by Judith Ennew and Brian Milne, 20 March 1997.

10 Giangi Schibotto and Alejandro Cussianovich, *Working Children: Building an Identity* (Lima, 1990), p. 54.

11 Information and interview by Chris McIvor, SCF UK, Kingston, 1996.

12 Quoted in Hoyles, *op. cit.*, p. 67.

13 *Newsweek* (Washington, 28 October 1996).

14 Judith Ennew, *Street and Working Children: A Guide to Planning* (London, 1994), p. 121.

15 Bob Franklin, 'The case for children's rights: a progress report', *op. cit.*, p. 5.

16 Ennew and Milne, *op. cit.*, p. 13.

17 *Unicef Information Sheet* (London, 24 June 1996).

18 Preface to Bob Franklin (ed.), *op. cit.*

19 Teresa Albánez, 'Human rights and the child', in *CEPAL Review* 57 (Santiago, December 1995), p. 38.

20 UN Convention on the Rights of the Child (Geneva, 1989), Article 14.

21 Anthony Swift, *Brazil: The Fight for Childhood in the City* (Florence, 1991), p. 20.

22 Daniel Hoffman, 'The struggle for citizenship and human rights', in *Nacla Report on the Americas* (New York, May/June 1994), p. 19.

23 Leif Lahne and Rädda Barnen, personal communication (Lima, 21 November 1996).

24 Based on Rädda Barnen, Justice Ministry pamphlets on the Demuna system, 1995.

25 SCF UK, *Implementation of the Convention on the Rights of the Child in Jamaica: Caribbean Country Report* (mimeo) (London, May 1996).

26 Arnulfo Ochoa, Author Interview (Coiproden, July 1996).

27 Judith Ennew, 'Outside childhood: street children and rights', in Bob Franklin (ed.), *op. cit.*

28 Author interview (London, November 1996).

29 Author interview (Tegucigalpa, June 1995).

30 Amnesty International, *Amnesty* (London, July 1995).

31 Author interview (London, July 1996).

32 Author interview (Tegucigalpa, June 1995).

33 Author interview (London, November 1996).

34 *Latinamerica Press* (Lima, 6 March 1997), p. 3.

35 *Ibid.*

36 Teresa Albánez, *op. cit.*, p. 40.

37 SCF UK, *Towards a Children's Agenda: New Challenges for Social Development* (London, 1995), p. 5.

Conclusions

Children in Latin America and the Caribbean worry adults. Parents agonize constantly about how to feed, clothe and educate their own children; shoppers walk in fear of diminutive muggers and pickpockets, or skirt in distaste and contempt around the clumps of glue-sniffers and down-and-outs in public squares and on street corners; right-wing politicians clamour for a 'clean-up' of the streets, often with sinister implications; others decry the 'exclusion' of the majority of the continent's children from social and economic well-being. Beyond the region, mute images of street children and child labourers create the impression of a continent of helpless, destitute children.

The first step in finding any solutions to the problems facing children is to understand the real nature of the issue. What are children's lives really like? The best way to find out is to ask them, something which astonishingly few people do. The vast majority of books, research papers or journalism on the subject have only the most cursory scattering of quotes from children. Yet if we place children at the centre of the picture, and ask them how *they* see their situation, and what would improve their lives, the results are often radically different from the kind of analysis and solutions routinely offered up by adults.

One of the first stereotypes to fall is that of the nuclear family unit. Families take many of the most important decisions in a child's early life: when they go out to work, when they go to school, whether they are beaten or encouraged to play, even (in the case of northeast Brazil) whether they live or die. The family is the main channel through which broader social and economic processes affect the child, the crucible in which values are inculcated and the next generation of citizens is created.

To determine whether government policies and other measures benefit or harm children, we must start with their impact on the family, and in Latin America and the Caribbean the real, rather than imagined, family is varied, complex and fluid. In many countries, most children have never grown up in 'normal' nuclear families, but in a range of different kinds of structures, often headed by women, whether mothers, aunts or grandmothers. Recent social change, such as migration to the cities and the impact of structural adjustment, have, if anything, accentuated that pattern.

Some family arrangements provide children with a range of loving, supportive adult carers, whereas in others they fall through the cracks of ever-changing family structures and end up on the streets. If governments, aid agencies and others want to help the children who lose out, they must design policies aimed at real families. In practice, that means supporting women, who increasingly combine the roles of breadwinner, parent and community activist in order to raise their children.

Other aspects of the conventional view of Third World children also evaporate once children are handed the microphone. Many children see paid work very differently from officially sanctioned views of child labour as an evil which should be swiftly abolished. Children often *want* to work, valuing the confidence and self-esteem that their contribution brings them, as well as the cash. They work in an astonishing range of jobs, usually for extremely little money, but their earnings often keep them and their families above the bread-line.

What matters is not to condemn, but to listen, in order better to understand the costs and benefits, both short term and long term, which work brings to children. The next step is to strengthen the benefits, whether by trying to improve wages and working conditions or by encouraging children to organize in the workplace. Minimizing the damaging impact of work on children means outlawing dangerous jobs and ensuring that the education system adapts to the reality that many children have to work as well as study. Throughout, the participation of working children, who are often extremely confident and articulate, is essential to ensure that the measures taken actually benefit them.

Passing laws is the easy (and often least effective) part. Children work at least partly because their families are poor, and the education system has little to offer them. Unless these underlying causes are dealt with, children will continue to go out to work, and some will be damaged for life. If Latin America and the Caribbean one day achieves the economic and social development that has so far eluded the region for 500 years, it may become both possible and desirable to abolish child labour, but, as yet, that day is not even in sight. Until it comes, children will continue to work in Latin America and the Caribbean.

Street children exercise a particular fascination for the public outside the region, and here again, allowing the children to speak for themselves produces a panorama which is barely recognizable from the standard charity fundraising image of the cowering, helpless child. Millions of children spend part of their day on the street, but their relationship with it varies enormously. Most work there, but return at night to sleep in their shanty town homes. Only a comparatively small number are 'of' the street, night and day.

Street children, like all others, make choices and take difficult decisions, albeit within a range of unpalatable options. The vast majority have families, but have chosen to be on the streets because they fear beatings or worse at home or simply because the street, for all its undoubted dangers, is more fun. On the street, many become skilled survivors, establishing a network of contacts for food, shelter, entertainment and mutual defence against the dangers that surround them. They may even end up better nourished, or happier, than their brothers and sisters who have remained at home.

Life on the streets should not be romanticized, however. Glue and violence claim their share of victims, maiming many street children for life and prompting compassion and the urge to help among adults both at home and in the West. But well-intentioned projects which seek only to 'rescue' children from the street are in many cases doomed to failure before they start – the children do not want to be rescued if it means returning to the grim homes from which they have fled. As with child labour, real help must start with the causes – poverty, domestic violence, boredom – which have driven children onto the street. Moreover, prevention is both better and cheaper than cure – it may have less missionary appeal than 'saving' street children, but supporting poor families where one child has already left for the street in order to help their brothers and sisters stay at home may be more effective in the long run. Like working children, street children are often independent and articulate, and any project which does not involve them is both wasting an invaluable source of advice, and likely to fail.

Those seeking to help children in Latin America and the Caribbean must first listen to the children, and then try to understand how the broader processes of economic, political and social change under way in the region filter down to them through their impact on the family, working conditions, or life (and sometimes death) on the street. Violence, whether political, domestic or criminal, is an increasing feature of contemporary life in the villages and shanty towns of Latin America and the Caribbean, and its impact on children's lives can be devastating. Whether driven from their homes by paramilitaries, seduced by the excitement of urban gang warfare, beaten senseless by drunken relatives or shot down in the middle of the night as they sleep in city centre doorways, children grow up in a violent world in which they are both victims and participants.

To turn the tide of violence means first understanding, and then dealing with, its root causes: the economics and politics of exclusion that condemn half of Latin America to rot on the margins of society, the inept and brutal judicial system which gives impunity to killers while locking children up alongside hardened criminals, and the widespread acceptance of the authoritarian use of force, both inside and outside the home. Putting the genie of violence back in the bottle is a huge task, involving measures to reduce poverty and redistribute income, making the criminal justice system function in the interests of its citizens, ending abuses by the military and police forces, and launching an enormous effort at public re-education to make domestic violence socially unacceptable.

Reversing the process of exclusion and social disintegration which characterizes contemporary Latin America and the Caribbean means changing the way in which governments govern, replacing the economics of the balance sheet with policies which put people, and above all children, first. It means creating jobs, and getting it right for the next generation, by making sure that the education system educates and the health system cures and prevents disease. To date, the role of outside forces such as Western governments and the IMF has largely been negative, as they have insisted on austerity and structural adjustment programmes which have only exacerbated poverty and inequality. If people in the West want to help Latin America's children, they should be demanding a radical change of approach from their governments and representatives on the IMF and World Bank.

Another error frequently committed by outsiders and governments alike is to try and start from scratch, ignoring the dynamic and creative self-help movement within Latin American and Caribbean communities. Latin Americans have never been able to rely on the state for anything except trouble, and have developed a rich tradition of community organizing, a few examples of which have been included in this book. The self-help movement in Latin America and the Caribbean is a particularly appropriate means of reaching children, because it is dominated by women, who in most families are the key providers for children. Governments and NGO programmes which ignore these community-based structures frequently end up failing

Grassroots organizations are a good way of reaching children, but going directly to the children themselves is even better. If lasting progress is to be achieved, children must be placed at the centre of the process, their hidden lives understood. Their voices must be listened to, their rights respected, and their involvement sought. Isolated acts of charity are not enough. What is needed is a profound change in the way children are seen, transforming them from voiceless objects of sympathy and charity to active participants in building their futures. Adults have little reason to be proud of their record and every reason to ask children for their help. In the words of Bertolt Brecht:

So all I can do, who have so
Wasted my life, is tell you
To obey not a single command that comes
From our rotten mouths and to take
No advice from those
Who have failed so badly, but
To decide for yourselves what is good for you
And what will help you
To cultivate the land which we let go to ruin and
To make the cities
Which we poisoned
Places for people to live in.[1]

Note

1 Bertolt Brecht, from 'The Dying Poet's Address to Young People', *Poems 1913–56*, translated by Christopher Middleton (London, Methuen, 1976), p. 229.

Appendix

The UN Convention on the Rights of the Child

Text

Preamble

The States Parties to the present Convention,

Considering that, in accordance with the principles proclaimed in the Charter of the United Nations, recognition of the inherent dignity and of the equal and inalienable rights of all members of the human family is the foundation of freedom, justice and peace in the world,

Bearing in mind that the peoples of the United Nations have, in the Charter, reaffirmed their faith in fundamental human rights and in the dignity and worth of the human person, and have determined to promote social progress and better standards of life in larger freedom,

Recognizing that the United Nations has, in the Universal Declaration of Human Rights and in the International Covenants on Human Rights, proclaimed and agreed that everyone is entitled to all the rights and freedoms set forth therein, without distinction of any kind, such as race, colour, sex, language, religion, political or other opinion, national or social origin, property, birth or other status,

Recalling that, in the Universal Declaration of Human Rights, the United Nations has proclaimed that childhood is entitled to special care and assistance,

Convinced that the family, as the fundamental group of society and the natural environment for the growth and well-being of all its members and particularly children, should be afforded the necessary protection and assistance so that it can fully assume its responsibilities within the community,

Unofficial summary of main provisions

Preamble

The preamble recalls the basic principles of the United Nations and specific provisions of certain relevant human rights treaties and proclamations. It reaffirms the fact that children, because of their vulnerability, need special care and protection, and it places special emphasis on the primary caring and protective responsibility of the family. It also reaffirms the need for legal and other protection of the child before and after birth, the importance of respect for the cultural values of the child's community, and the vital role of international cooperation in securing children's rights.

Recognizing that the child, for the full and harmonious development of his or her personality, should grow up in a family environment, in an atmosphere of happiness, love and understanding,

Considering that the child should be fully prepared to live an individual life in society, and brought up in the spirit of the ideals proclaimed in the Charter of the United Nations, and in particular in the spirit of peace, dignity, tolerance, freedom, equality and solidarity,

Bearing in mind that the need to extend particular care to the child has been stated in the Geneva Declaration of the Rights of the Child of 1924 and in the Declaration of the Rights of the Child adopted by the United Nations on 20 November 1959 and recognized in the Universal Declaration of Human Rights, in the International Covenant on Civil and Political Rights (in particular in articles 23 and 24), in the International Covenant on Economic, Social and Cultural Rights (in particular in article ten) and in the statutes and relevant instruments of specialized agencies and international organizations concerned with the welfare of children,

Bearing in mind that, as indicated in the Declaration of the Rights of the Child, "the child, by reason of his physical and mental immaturity, needs special safeguards and care, including appropriate legal protection, before as well as after birth,"

Recalling the provisions of the Declaration on Social and Legal Principles relating to the Protection and Welfare of Children, with Special Reference to Foster Placement and Adoption Nationally and Internationally; the United Nations Standard Minimum Rules for the Administration of Juvenile Justice ("The Beijing Rules"); and the Declaration on the Protection of Women and Children in Emergency and Armed Conflict,

Recognizing that, in all countries in the world, there are children living in exceptionally difficult conditions, and that such children need special consideration,

Taking due account of the importance of the traditions and cultural values of each people for the protection and harmonious development of the child,

Recognizing the importance of international cooperation for improving the living conditions of children in every country, in particular in the developing countries,

Have agreed as follows:

PART I

Article 1
For the purposes of the present Convention, a child means every human being below the age of 18 years unless, under the law applicable to the child, majority is attained earlier.

Definition of a child
A child is recognized as a person under 18, unless national laws recognize the age of majority earlier.

Article 2
1. States Parties shall respect and ensure the rights set forth in the present Convention to each child within their jurisdiction without discrimination of any kind, irrespective of the child's or his or her parent's or legal guardian's race, colour, sex, language, religion, political or other opinion, national, ethnic or social origin, property, disability, birth or other status.

2. States Parties shall take all appropriate measures to ensure that the child is protected against all forms of discrimination or punishment on the basis of the status, activities, expressed opinions, or beliefs of the child's parents, legal guardians, or family members.

Non-discrimination
All rights apply to all children without exception. It is the State's obligation to protect children from any form of discrimination and to take positive action to promote their rights.

Article 3
1. In all actions concerning children, whether undertaken by public or private social welfare institutions, courts of law, administrative authorities or legislative bodies, the best interests of the child shall be a primary consideration.

2. States Parties undertake to ensure the child such protection and care as is necessary for his or her well-being, taking into account the rights and duties of his or her parents, legal guardians, or other individuals legally responsible for him or her, and, to this end, shall take all appropriate legislative and administrative measures.

3. States Parties shall ensure that the institutions, services and facilities responsible for the care or protection of children shall conform with the standards established by competent authorities, particularly in the areas of safety, health, in the number and suitability of their staff, as well as competent supervision.

Best interests of the child
All actions concerning the child shall take full account of his or her best interests. The State shall provide the child with adequate care when parents, or others charged with that responsibility, fail to do so.

Article 4
States Parties shall undertake all appropriate legislative, administrative, and other measures for the implementation of the rights recognized in the present Convention. With regard to economic, social and

Implementation of rights
The State must do all it can to implement the rights contained in the Convention.

cultural rights, States Parties shall undertake such measures to the maximum extent of their available resources and, where needed, within the framework of international cooperation.

Article 5

States Parties shall respect the responsibilities, rights and duties of parents or, where applicable, the members of the extended family or community as provided for by local custom, legal guardians or other persons legally responsible for the child, to provide, in a manner consistent with the evolving capacities of the child, appropriate direction and guidance in the exercise by the child of the rights recognized in the present Convention.

Article 6

1. States Parties recognize that every child has the inherent right to life.

2. States Parties shall ensure to the maximum extent possible the survival and development of the child.

Article 7

1. The child shall be registered immediately after birth and shall have the right from birth to a name, the right to acquire a nationality and, as far as possible, the right to know and be cared for by his or her parents.

2. States Parties shall ensure the implementation of these rights in accordance with their national law and their obligations under the relevant international instruments in this field, in particular where the child would otherwise be stateless.

Article 8

1. States Parties undertake to respect the right of the child to preserve his or her identity, including nationality, name and family relations as recognized by law without unlawful interference.

2. Where a child is illegally deprived of some or all of the elements of his or her identity, States Parties shall provide appropriate assistance and protection, with a view to speedily re-establishing his or her identity.

Article 9

1. States Parties shall ensure that a child shall not be separated from his or her parents against their will,

Parental guidance and the child's evolving capacities

The State must respect the rights and responsibilities of parents and the extended family to provide guidance for the child which is appropriate to her or his evolving capacities.

Survival and development

Every child has the inherent right to life, and the State has an obligation to ensure the child's survival and development.

Name and nationality

The child has the right to a name at birth. The child also has the right to acquire a nationality and, as far as possible, to know his or her parents and be cared for by them.

Preservation of identity

The State has an obligation to protect, and if necessary, re-establish basic aspects of the child's identity. This includes name, nationality and family ties.

except when competent authorities subject to judicial review determine, in accordance with applicable law and procedures, that such separation is necessary for the best interests of the child. Such determination may be necessary in a particular case such as one involving abuse or neglect of the child by the parents, or one where the parents are living separately and a decision must be made as to the child's place of residence.

2. In any proceedings pursuant to paragraph 1 of the present article, all interested parties shall be given an opportunity to participate in the proceedings and make their views known.

3. States Parties shall respect the right of the child who is separated from one or both parents to maintain personal relations and direct contact with both parents on a regular basis, except if it is contrary to the child's best interests.

4. Where such separation results from any action initiated by a State Party, such as the detention, imprisonment, exile, deportation or death (including death arising from any cause while the person is in the custody of the State) of one or both parents or of the child, that State Party shall, upon request, provide the parents, the child or, if appropriate, another member of the family with the essential information concerning the whereabouts of the absent member(s) of the family unless the provision of the information would be detrimental to the well-being of the child. States Parties shall further ensure that the submission of such a request shall of itself entail no adverse consequences for the person(s) concerned.

Separation from parents

The child has a right to live with his or her parents unless this is deemed to be incompatible with the child's best interests. The child also has the right to maintain contact with both parents if separated from one or both.

Article 10

1. In accordance with the obligation of States Parties under article 9, paragraph 1, applications by a child or his or her parents to enter or leave a State Party for the purpose of family reunification shall be dealt with by States Parties in a positive, humane and expeditious manner. States Parties shall further ensure that the submission of such a request shall entail no adverse consequences for the applicants and for the members of their family.

2. A child whose parents reside in different States shall have the right to maintain on a regular basis, save in exceptional circumstances personal relations and direct contacts with both parents. Towards that end and in accordance with the obligation of States Parties under

Family reunification

Children and their parents have the right to leave any country and to enter their own for purposes of reunion or the maintenance of the child-parent relationship.

article 9, paragraph 1, States Parties shall respect the right of the child and his or her parents to leave any country, including their own, and to enter their own country. The right to leave any country shall be subject only to such restrictions as are prescribed by law and which are necessary to protect the national security, public order (ordre public), public health or morals or the rights and freedoms of others and are consistent with the other rights recognized in the present Convention.

Article 11

1. States Parties shall take measures to combat the illicit transfer and non-return of children abroad.

2. To this end, States Parties shall promote the conclusion of bilateral or multilateral agreements or accession to existing agreements.

Illicit transfer and non-return

The State has an obligation to prevent and remedy the kidnapping or retention of children abroad by a parent or third party.

Article 12

1. States Parties shall assure to the child who is capable of forming his or her own views the right to express those views freely in all matters affecting the child, the views of the child being given due weight in accordance with the age and maturity of the child.

2. For this purpose, the child shall in particular be provided the opportunity to be heard in any judicial and administrative proceedings affecting the child, either directly, or through a representative or an appropriate body, in a manner consistent with the procedural rules of national law.

The child's opinion

The child has the right to express his or her opinion freely and to have that opinion taken into account in any matter or procedure affecting the child.

Article 13

1. The child shall have the right to freedom of expression; this right shall include freedom to seek, receive and impart information and ideas of all kinds, regardless of frontiers, either orally, in writing or in print, in the form of art, or through any other media of the child's choice.

2. The exercise of this right may be subject to certain restrictions, but these shall only be such as are provided by law and are necessary:

(a) For respect of the rights or reputations of others; or

(b) For the protection of national security or of public order (ordre public), or of public health or morals.

Freedom of expression

The child has the right to express his or her views, obtain information, make ideas or information known, regardless of frontiers.

Article 14

1. States Parties shall respect the right of the child to freedom of thought, conscience and religion.

2. States Parties shall respect the rights and duties of the parents and, when applicable, legal guardians, to provide direction to the child in the exercise of his or her right in a manner consistent with the evolving capacities of the child.

3. Freedom to manifest one's religion or beliefs may be subject only to such limitations as are prescribed by law and are necessary to protect public safety, order, health or morals, or the fundamental rights and freedoms of others.

Freedom of thought, conscience and religion

The State shall respect the child's right to freedom of thought, conscience and religion, subject to appropriate parental guidance.

Article 15

1. States Parties recognize the rights of the child to freedom of association and to freedom of peaceful assembly.

2. No restrictions may be placed on the exercise of these rights other than those imposed in conformity with the law and which are necessary in a democratic society in the interests of national security or public safety, public order (ordre public), the protection of public health or morals or the protection of the rights and freedoms of others.

Freedom of association

Children have a right to meet with others, and to join or form associations.

Article 16

1. No child shall be subjected to arbitrary or unlawful interference with his or her privacy, family, home or correspondence, nor to unlawful attacks on his or her honour and reputation.

2. The child has the right to the protection of the law against such interference or attacks.

Protection of privacy

Children have the right to protection from interference with privacy, family, home and correspondence, and from libel or slander.

Article 17

States Parties recognize the important function performed by the mass media and shall ensure that the child has access to information and material from a diversity of national and international sources, especially those aimed at the promotion of his or her social, spiritual and moral well-being and physical and mental health. To this end, States Parties shall:

(a) Encourage the mass media to disseminate information and material of social and cultural benefit to the child and in accordance with the spirit of article 29;

Access to appropriate information

The State shall ensure the accessibility to children of information and material from a diversity of sources, and it shall encourage the mass media to disseminate information which is of social and cultural benefit to the child, and take steps to protect him or her from harmful materials.

(b) Encourage international cooperation in the production, exchange and dissemination of such information and material from a diversity of cultural, national and international sources;

(c) Encourage the production and dissemination of children's books;

(d) Encourage the mass media to have particular regard to the linguistic needs of the child who belongs to a minority group or who is indigenous;

(e) Encourage the development of appropriate guidelines for the protection of the child from information and material injurious to his or her well-being, bearing in mind the provisions of articles 13 and 18.

Article 18

1. States Parties shall use their best efforts to ensure recognition of the principle that both parents have common responsibilities for the upbringing and development of the child. Parents or, as the case may be, legal guardians, have the primary responsibility for the upbringing and development of the child. The best interests of the child will be their basic concern.

2. For the purpose of guaranteeing and promoting the rights set forth in the present Convention, States Parties shall render appropriate assistance to parents and legal guardians in the performance of their child-rearing responsibilities and shall ensure the development of institutions, facilities and services for the care of children.

3. States Parties shall take all appropriate measures to ensure that children of working parents have the right to benefit from child-care services and facilities for which they are eligible.

Parental responsibilities

Parents have joint primary responsibility for raising the child, and the State shall support them in this. The State shall provide appropriate assistance to parents in child-raising.

Article 19

1. States Parties shall take all appropriate legislative, administrative, social and educational measures to protect the child from all forms of physical or mental violence, injury or abuse, neglect or negligent treatment, maltreatment or exploitation, including sexual abuse, while in the care of parent(s), legal guardian(s) or any other person who has the care of the child.

2. Such protective measures should, as appropriate, include effective procedures for the establishment of

Protection from abuse and neglect

The State shall protect the child from all forms of maltreatment by parents or others responsible for the care of the child and establish appropriate social programmes for the prevention of abuse and the treatment of victims.

social programmes to provide necessary support for the child and for those who have the care of the child, as well as for other forms of prevention and for identification, reporting, referral, investigation, treatment and follow-up of instances of child maltreatment described heretofore, and, as appropriate, for judicial involvement.

Article 20

1. A child temporarily or permanently deprived of his or her family environment, or in whose own best interests cannot be allowed to remain in that environment, shall be entitled to special protection and assistance provided by the State.

2. States Parties shall in accordance with their national laws ensure alternative care for such a child.

3. Such care could include, inter alia, foster placement, Kafala of Islamic law, adoption, or if necessary placement in suitable institutions for the care of children. When considering solutions, due regard shall be paid to the desirability of continuity in a child's upbringing and to the child's ethnic, religious, cultural and linguistic background.

Protection of a child without family

The State is obliged to provide special protection for a child deprived of the family environment and to ensure that appropriate alternative family care or institutional placement is available in such cases. Efforts to meet this obligation shall pay due regard to the child's cultural background.

Article 21

States Parties that recognize and/or permit the system of adoption shall ensure that the best interests of the child shall be the paramount consideration and they shall:

(a) Ensure that the adoption of a child is authorized only by competent authorities who determine,in accordance with applicable law and procedures and on the basis of all pertinent and reliable information, that the adoption is permissible in view of the child's status concerning parents, relatives and legal guardians and that, if required, the persons concerned have given their informed consent to the adoption on the basis of such counselling as may be necessary;

(b) Recognize that inter-country adoption may be considered as an alternative means of child's care, if the child cannot be placed in a foster or an adoptive family or cannot in any suitable manner be cared for in the child's country of origin;

(c) Ensure that the child concerned by intercountry adoption enjoys safeguards and standards equivalent to those existing in the case of national adoption;

Adoption

In countries where adoption is recognized and/or allowed, it shall only be carried out in the best interests of the child, and then only with the authorization of competent authorities, and safeguards for the child.

(d) Take all appropriate measures to ensure that, in intercountry adoption, the placement does not result in improper financial gain for those involved in it;

(e) Promote, where appropriate, the objectives of the present article by concluding bilateral or multilateral arrangements or agreements, and endeavour, within this framework, to ensure that the placement of the child in another country is carried out by competent authorities or organs.

Article 22

1. States Parties shall take appropriate measures to ensure that a child who is seeking refugee status or who is considered a refugee in accordance with applicable international or domestic law and procedures shall, whether unaccompanied or accompanied by his or her parents or by any other person, receive appropriate protection and humanitarian assistance in the enjoyment of applicable rights set forth in the present Convention and in other international human rights or humanitarian instruments to which the said States are Parties.

2. For this purpose, States Parties shall provide, as they consider appropriate, cooperation in any efforts by the United Nations and other competent intergovernmental organizations or non-governmental organizations co-operating with the United Nations to protect and assist such a child and to trace the parents or other members of the family of any refugee child in order to obtain information necessary for reunification with his or her family. In cases where no parents or other members of the family can be found, the child shall be accorded the same protection as any other child permanently or temporarily deprived of his or her family environment for any reason, as set forth in the present Convention.

Refugee children

Special protection shall be granted to a refugee child or to a child seeking refugee status. It is the State's obligation to co-operate with competent organizations which provide such protection and assistance.

Article 23

1. States Parties recognize that a mentally or physically disabled child should enjoy a full and decent life, in conditions which ensure dignity, promote self-reliance, and facilitate the child's active participation in the community.

2. States Parties recognize the right of the disabled child to special care and shall encourage and ensure the extension, subject to available resources, to the eligible child and those responsible for his or her care, of assistance for which application is made and which is

Disabled children

A disabled child has the right to special care, education and training to help him or her enjoy a full and decent life in dignity and achieve the greatest degree of self-reliance and social integration possible.

appropriate to the child's condition and to the circumstances of the parents or others caring for the child.

3. Recognizing the special needs of a disabled child, assistance extended in accordance with paragraph 2 of the present article shall be provided free of charge, whenever possible, taking into account the financial resources of the parents or others caring for the child, and shall be designed to ensure that the disabled child has effective access to and receives education, training, health care services, rehabilitation services, preparation for employment and recreation opportunities in a manner conducive to the child's achieving the fullest possible social integration and individual development, including his or her cultural and spiritual development.

4. States Parties shall promote, in the spirit of international cooperation, the exchange of appropriate information in the field of preventive health care and of medical, psychological and functional treatment of disabled children, including dissemination of and access to information concerning methods of rehabilitation, education and vocational services, with the aim of enabling States Parties to improve their capabilities and skills and to widen their experience in these areas. In this regard, particular account shall be taken of the needs of developing countries.

Article 24

1. States Parties recognize the right of the child to the enjoyment of the highest attainable standard of health and to facilities for the treatment of illness and rehabilitation of health. States Parties shall strive to ensure that no child is deprived of his or her right of access to such health care services.

2. States Parties shall pursue full implementation of this right and, in particular, shall take appropriate measures:

(a) To diminish infant and child mortality;

(b) To ensure the provision of necessary medical assistance and health care to all children with emphasis on the development of primary health care;

(c) To combat disease and malnutrition including within the framework of primary health care, through inter alia the application of readily available technology and through the provision of adequate nutritious foods and clean drinking water, taking into consideration the dangers and risks of environmental pollution;

Health and health services

The child has a right to the highest standard of health and medical care attainable. States shall place special emphasis on the provision of primary and preventive health care, public health education and the reduction of infant mortality. They shall encourage international cooperation in this regard and strive to see that no child is deprived of access to effective health services.

(d) To ensure appropriate pre-natal and post-natal health care for mothers;

(e) To ensure that all segments of society, in particular parents and children, are informed, have access to education and are supported in the use of basic knowledge of child health and nutrition, the advantages of breast-feeding, hygiene and environmental sanitation and the prevention of accidents;

(f) To develop preventive health care, guidance for parents and family planning education and services.

3. States Parties shall take all effective and appropriate measures with a view to abolishing traditional practises prejudicial to the health of children.

4. States Parties undertake to promote and encourage international cooperation with a view to achieving progressively the full realization of the right recognized in the present article. In this regard, particular account shall be taken of the needs of developing countries.

Article 25
States Parties recognize the right of a child who has been placed by the competent authorities for the purposes of care, protection or treatment of his or her physical or mental health, to a periodic review of the treatment provided to the child and all other circumstances relevant to his or her placement.

Periodic review of placement

A child who is placed by the State for reasons of care, protection or treatment is entitled to have that placement evaluated regularly.

Article 26
1. States Parties shall recognize for every child the right to benefit from social security, including social insurance, and shall take the necessary measures to achieve the full realization of this right in accordance with their national law.

Social security

The child has the right to benefit from social security including social insurance.

2. The benefits should, where appropriate, be granted, taking into account the resources and the circumstances of the child and persons having responsibility for the maintenance of the child, as well as any other consideration relevant to an application for benefits made by or on behalf of the child.

Article 27
1. States Parties recognize the right of every child to a standard of living adequate for the child's physical, mental, spiritual, moral and social development.

2. The parent(s) or others responsible for the child have the primary responsibility to secure, within their abilities and financial capacities, the conditions of living necessary for the child's development.

3. States Parties, in accordance with national conditions and within their means, shall take appropriate measures to assist parents and others responsible for the child to implement this right and shall in case of need provide material assistance and support programmes, particularly with regard to nutrition, clothing and housing.

4. States Parties shall take all appropriate measures to secure the recovery of maintenance for the child from the parents or other persons having financial responsibility for the child, both within the State Party and from abroad. In particular, where the person having financial responsibility for the child lives in a State different from that of the child, States Parties shall promote the accession to international agreements or the conclusion of such agreements, as well as the making of other appropriate arrangements.

Standard of living

Every child has the right to a standard of living adequate for his or her physical, mental, spiritual, moral and social development. Parents have the primary responsibility to ensure that the child has an adequate standard of living. The State's duty is to ensure that this responsibility can be fulfilled, and is. State responsibility can include material assistance to parents and their children.

Article 28

1. States Parties recognize the right of the child to education, and with a view to achieving this right progressively and on the basis of equal opportunity, they shall, in particular:

(a) Make primary education compulsory and available free to all;

(b) Encourage the development of different forms of secondary education, including general and vocational education, make them available and accessible to every child, and take appropriate measures such as the introduction of free education and offering financial assistance in case of need;

(c) Make higher education accessible to all on the basis of capacity by every appropriate means;

(d) Make educational and vocational information and guidance available and accessible to all children;

(e) Take measures to encourage regular attendance at schools and the reduction of drop-out rates.

2. States Parties shall take all appropriate measures to ensure that school discipline is administered in a manner consistent with the child's human dignity and in conformity with the present Convention.

Education

The child has a right to education, and the State's duty is to ensure that primary education is free and compulsory, to encourage different forms of secondary education accessible to every child and to make higher education available to all on the basis of capacity. School discipline shall be consistent with the child's rights and dignity. The State shall engage in international co-operation to implement this right.

3. States Parties shall promote and encourage international cooperation in matters relating to education, in particular with a view to contributing to the elimination of ignorance and illiteracy throughout the world and facilitating access to scientific and technical knowledge and modern teaching methods. In this regard, particular account shall be taken of the needs of developing countries.

Article 29

1. States Parties agree that the education of the child shall be directed to:

(a) The development of the child's personality, talents and mental and physical abilities to their fullest potential;

(b) The development of respect for human rights and fundamental freedoms, and for the principles enshrined in the Charter of the United Nations;

(c) The development of respect for the child's parents, his or her own cultural identity, language and values, for the national values of the country in which the child is living, the country from which he or she may originate, and for civilizations different from his or her own;

(d) The preparation of the child for responsible life in a free society, in the spirit of understanding, peace, tolerance, equality of sexes, and friendship among all peoples, ethnic, national and religious groups and persons of indigenous origin;

(e) The development of respect for the natural environment.

2. No part of the present article or article 28 shall be construed so as to interfere with the liberty of individuals and bodies to establish and direct educational institutions, subject always to the observance of the principles set forth in paragraph 1 of the present article and to the requirements that the education given in such institutions shall conform to such minimum standards as may be laid down by the State.

Article 30

In those States in which ethnic, religious or linguistic minorities or persons of indigenous origin exist, a child belonging to such a minority or who is indigenous shall not be denied the right, in community with other members of his or her group, to enjoy his or her own culture, to profess and practise his or her own religion, or to use his or her own language.

Aims of education

Education shall aim at developing the child's personality, talents and mental and physical abilities to the fullest extent. Education shall prepare the child for an active adult life in a free society and foster respect for the child's parents, his or her own cultural identity, language and values, and for the cultural background and values of others.

Children of minorities or indigenous populations

Children of minority communities and indigenous populations have the right to enjoy their own culture and to practise their own religion and language.

Article 31

1. States Parties recognize the right of the child to rest and leisure, to engage in play and recreational activities appropriate to the age of the child and to participate freely in cultural life and the arts.

2. States Parties shall respect and promote the right of the child to participate fully in cultural and artistic life and shall encourage the provision of appropriate and equal opportunities for cultural, artistic, recreational and leisure activity.

Leisure, recreation and cultural activities

The child has the right to leisure, play and participation in cultural and artistic activities.

Article 32

1. States Parties recognize the right of the child to be protected from economic exploitation and from performing any work that is likely to be hazardous or to interfere with the child's education, or to be harmful to the child's health or physical, mental, spiritual, moral or social development.

2. States Parties shall take legislative, administrative, social and educational measures to ensure the implementation of the present article. To this end, and having regard to the relevant provisions of other international instruments, States Parties shall in particular:

(a) Provide for a minimum age or minimum ages for admissions to employment;

(b) Provide for appropriate regulation of the hours and conditions of employment;

(c) Provide for appropriate penalties or other sanctions to ensure the effective enforcement of the present article.

Child labour

The child has the right to be protected from work that threatens his or her health, education or development. The State shall set minimum ages for employment and regulate working conditions.

Article 33

States Parties shall take all appropriate measures, including legislative, administrative, social and educational measures, to protect children from the illicit use of narcotic drugs and psychotropic substances as defined in the relevant international treaties, and to prevent the use of children in the illicit production and trafficking of such substances.

Drug abuse

Children have the right to protection from the use of narcotic and psychotropic drugs, and from being involved in their production or distribution.

Article 34

States Parties undertake to protect the child from all forms of sexual exploitation and sexual abuse. For these purposes, States Parties shall in particular take all appropriate national, bilateral and multilateral measures to prevent:

(a) The inducement or coercion of a child to engage in any unlawful sexual activity;

(b) The exploitative use of children in prostitution or other unlawful sexual practises;

(c) The exploitative use of children in pornographic performances and materials.

Article 35

States Parties shall take all appropriate national, bilateral and multilateral measures to prevent the abduction of, the sale of or traffic in children for any purpose or in any form.

Article 36

States Parties shall protect the child against all other forms of exploitation prejudicial to any aspects of the child's welfare.

Article 37

States Parties shall ensure that:

(a) No child shall be subjected to torture or other cruel, inhuman or degrading treatment or punishment. Neither capital punishment nor life imprisonment without possibility of release shall be imposed for offences committed by persons below 18 years of age;

(b) No child shall be deprived of his or her liberty unlawfully or arbitrarily. The arrest, detention or imprisonment of a child shall be in conformity with the law and shall be used only as a measure of last resort and for the shortest appropriate period of time;

(c) Every child deprived of liberty shall be treated with humanity and respect for the inherent dignity of the human person, and in a manner which takes into account the needs of persons of his or her age. In particular every child deprived of liberty shall be separated from adults unless it is considered in the child's best interest not to do so and shall have the right to maintain contact with his or her family through correspondence and visits, save in exceptional circumstances;

(d) Every child deprived of his or her liberty shall have the right to prompt access to legal and other appropriate assistance, as well as the right to challenge the legality of

Sexual exploitation

The State shall protect children from sexual exploitation and abuse, including prostitution and involvement in pornography.

Sale, trafficking and abduction

It is the State's obligation to make every effort to prevent the sale, trafficking and abduction of children.

Other forms of exploitation

The child has the right to protection from all forms of exploitation prejudicial to any aspects of the child's welfare not covered in articles 32, 33, 34 and 35.

Torture and deprivation of liberty

No child shall be subjected to torture, cruel treatment or punishment, unlawful arrest or deprivation of liberty. Both capital punishment and life imprisonment without the possibility of release are prohibited for offences committed by persons below 18 years. Any child deprived of liberty shall be separated from adults unless it is considered in the child's best interests not to do so. A child who is detained shall have legal and other assistance as well as contact with the family.

the deprivation of his or her liberty before a court or other competent, independent and impartial authority, and to a prompt decision on any such action.

Article 38

1. States Parties undertake to respect and to ensure respect for rules of international humanitarian law applicable to them in armed conflicts which are relevant to the child.

2. States Parties shall take all feasible measures to ensure that persons who have not attained the age of 15 years do not take a direct part in hostilities.

3. States Parties shall refrain from recruiting any person who has not attained the age of 15 years into their armed forces. In recruiting among those persons who have attained the age of 15 years but who have not attained the age of 18 years, States Parties shall endeavour to give priority to those who are oldest.

4. In accordance with their obligations under international humanitarian law to protect the civilian population in armed conflicts, States Parties shall take all feasible measures to ensure protection and care of children who are affected by an armed conflict.

Article 39

States Parties shall take all appropriate measures to promote physical and psychological recovery and social reintegration of a child victim of: any form of neglect, exploitation, or abuse; torture or any other form of cruel, inhuman or degrading treatment or punishment; or armed conflicts. Such recovery and reintegration shall take place in an environment which fosters the health, self-respect and dignity of the child.

Article 40

1. States Parties recognize the right of every child alleged as, accused of, or recognized as having infringed the penal law to be treated in a manner consistent with the promotion of the child's sense of dignity and worth, which reinforces the child's respect for the human rights and fundamental freedoms of others and which takes into account the child's age and the desirability of promoting the child's reintegration and the child's assuming a constructive role in society.

Armed conflicts

States Parties shall take all feasible measures to ensure that children under 15 years of age have no direct part in hostilities. No child below 15 shall be recruited into the armed forces. States shall also ensure the protection and care of children who are affected by armed conflict as described in relevant international law.

Rehabilitative care

The State has an obligation to ensure that child victims of armed conflicts, torture, neglect, maltreatment or exploitation receive appropriate treatment for their recovery and social reintegration.

Administration of juvenile justice

A child in conflict with the law has the right to treatment which promotes the child's sense of dignity and worth, takes the child's age into account and aims at his or her reintegration into society. The child is entitled to basic guarantees as well as legal or other assistance for his or her defence. Judicial proceedings and institutional placements shall be avoided wherever possible.

2. To this end, and having regard to the relevant provisions of international instruments, States Parties shall, in particular, ensure that:

(a) No child shall be alleged as, be accused of, or recognized as having infringed the penal law by reason of acts or omissions that were not prohibited by national or international law at the time they were committed;

(b) Every child alleged as or accused of having infringed the penal law has at least the following guarantees:

(i) To be presumed innocent until proven guilty according to law;

(ii) To be informed promptly and directly of the charges against him or her, and, if appropriate, through his or her parents or legal guardians, and to have legal or other appropriate assistance in the preparation and presentation of his or her defence;

(iii) To have the matter determined without delay by a competent, independent and impartial authority or judicial body in a fair hearing according to law, in the presence of legal or other appropriate assistance and, unless it is considered not to be in the best interest of the child, in particular, taking into account his or her age or situation, his or her parents or legal guardians;

(iv) Not to be compelled to give testimony or to confess guilt; to examine or have examined adverse witnesses and to obtain the participation and examination of witnesses on his or her behalf under conditions of equality;

(v) If considered to have infringed the penal law, to have this decision and any measures imposed in consequence thereof reviewed by a higher competent, independent and impartial authority or judicial body according to law;

(vi) To have the free assistance of an interpreter if the child cannot understand or speak the language used;

(vii) To have his or her privacy fully respected at all stages of the proceedings.

3. States Parties shall seek to promote the establishment of laws, procedures, authorities and institutions specifically applicable to children alleged as, accused of, or recognized as having infringed the penal law, and, in particular:

(a) the establishment of a minimum age below which children shall be presumed not to have the capacity to infringe the penal law;

(b) whenever appropriate and desirable, measures for dealing with such children without resorting to judicial proceedings, providing that human rights and legal safeguards are fully respected.

4. A variety of dispositions, such as care, guidance and supervision orders; counselling; probation; foster care; education and vocational training programmes and other alternatives to institutional care shall be available to ensure that children are dealt with in a manner appropriate to their well-being and proportionate both to their circumstances and the offence.

Article 41
Nothing in the present Convention shall affect any provisions which are more conducive to the realization of the rights of the child and which may be contained in:

(a) The law of a State Party; or

(b) International law in force for that State.

PART II: IMPLEMENTATION AND MONITORING

Article 42
States Parties undertake to make the principles and provisions of the Convention widely known, by appropriate and active means, to adults and children alike.

Article 43
1. For the purpose of examining the progress made by States Parties in achieving the realization of the obligations undertaken in the present Convention, there shall be established a Committee on the Rights of the Child, which shall carry out the functions hereinafter provided.

2. The Committee shall consist of 10 experts of high moral standing and recognized competence in the field covered by this Convention. The members of the Committee shall be elected by States Parties from among their nationals and shall serve in their personal capacity, consideration being given to equitable geographical distribution, as well as to the principal legal systems.

3. The members of the Committee shall be elected by secret ballot from a list of persons nominated by States

Respect for higher standards

Wherever standards set in applicable national and international law relevant to the rights of the child that are higher than those in this Convention, the higher standard shall always apply.

Implementation and entry into force

The provisions of articles 42-54 notably foresee:

(i) the State's obligation to make the rights contained in this Convention widely known to both adults and children.

(ii) the setting up of a Committee on the Rights of the Child composed of 10 experts, which will consider reports that States Parties to the Convention are to submit two years after ratification and every five years thereafter. The Convention enters into force – and the Committee would therefore be set up – once 20 countries have ratified it.

(iii) States Parties are to make their reports widely

Parties. Each State Party may nominate one person from among its own nationals.

4. The initial election to the Committee shall be held no later than six months after the date of the entry into force of the present Convention and thereafter every second year. At least four months before the date of each election, the Secretary-General of the United Nations shall address a letter to States Parties inviting them to submit their nominations within two months. The Secretary-General shall subsequently prepare a list in alphabetical order of all persons thus nominated, indicating States Parties which have nominated them, and shall submit it to the States Parties to the present Convention.

5. The elections shall be held at meetings of States Parties convened by the Secretary-General at United Nations Headquarters. At those meetings, for which two thirds of States Parties shall constitute a quorum, the persons elected to the Committee shall be those who obtain the largest number of votes and an absolute majority of the votes of the representatives of States Parties present and voting.

6. The members of the Committee shall be elected for a term of four years. They shall be eligible for re-election if renominated. The term of five of the members elected at the first election shall expire at the end of two years; immediately after the first election, the names of these five members shall be chosen by lot by the Chairman of the meeting.

7. If a member of the Committee dies or resigns or declares that for any other cause he or she can no longer perform the duties of the Committee, the State Party which nominated the member shall appoint another expert from among its nationals to serve for the remainder of the term, subject to the approval of the Committee.

8. The Committee shall establish its own rules of procedure.

9. The Committee shall elect its officers for a period of two years.

10. The meetings of the Committee shall normally be held at United Nations Headquarters or at any other convenient place as determined by the Committee. The Committee shall normally meet annually. The duration of the meetings of the Committee shall be determined, and reviewed, if necessary, by a meeting available to the general public.

(iv) The Committee may propose that special studies be undertaken on specific issues relating to the rights of the child, and may make its evaluations known to each State Party concerned as well as to the UN General Assembly.

(v) In order to "foster the effective implementation of the Convention and to encourage international co-operation," the specialized agencies of the UN – such as the International Labour Organisation (ILO), World Health Organization (WHO) and United Nations Educational, Scientific and Cultural Organization (UNESCO) – and UNICEF would be able to attend the meetings of the Committee. Together with any other body recognized as 'competent', including non-governmental organizations (NGOs) in consultative status with the UN and UN organs such as the United Nations High Commissioner for Refugees (UNHCR), they can submit pertinent information to the Committee and be asked to advise on the optimal implementation of the Convention.

of the States Parties to the present Convention, subject to the approval of the General Assembly.

11. The Secretary-General of the United Nations shall provide the necessary staff and facilities for the effective performance of the functions of the Committee under the present Convention.

12. With the approval of the General Assembly, the members of the Committee established under the present Convention shall receive emoluments from the United Nations resources on such terms and conditions as the Assembly may decide.

Article 44
1. States Parties undertake to submit to the Committee, through the Secretary-General of the United Nations, reports on the measures they have adopted which give effect to the rights recognized herein and on the progress made on the enjoyment of those rights:

(a) Within two years of the entry into force of the Convention for the State Party concerned,

(b) Thereafter every five years.

2. Reports made under the present article shall indicate factors and difficulties, if any, affecting the degree of fulfilment of the obligations under the present Convention. Reports shall also contain sufficient information to provide the Committee with a comprehensive understanding of the implementation of the Convention in the country concerned.

3. A State Party which has submitted a comprehensive initial report to the Committee need not in its subsequent reports submitted in accordance with paragraph 1(b) of the present article repeat basic information previously provided.

4. The Committee may request from States Parties further information relevant to the implementation of the Convention.

5. The Committee shall submit to the General Assembly, through the Economic and Social Council, every two years, reports on its activities.

6. States Parties shall make their reports widely available to the public in their own countries.

Article 45

In order to foster the effective implementation of the Convention and to encourage international cooperation in the field covered by the Convention:

(a) The specialized agencies, the United Nations Children's Fund and other United Nations organs shall be entitled to be represented at the consideration of the implementation of such provisions of the present Convention as fall within the scope of their mandate. The Committee may invite the specialized agencies, the United Nations Children's Fund and other competent bodies as it may consider appropriate to provide expert advice on the implementation of the Convention in areas falling within the scope of their respective mandates. The Committee may invite the specialized agencies, the United Nations Children's Fund and other United Nations organs to submit reports on the implementation of the Convention in areas falling within the scope of their activities;

(b) The Committee shall transmit, as it may consider appropriate, to the specialized agencies, the United Nations Children's Fund and other competent bodies, any reports from States Parties that contain a request, or indicate a need, for technical advice or assistance, along with the Committee's observations and suggestions, if any, on these requests or indications;

(c) The Committee may recommend to the General Assembly to request the Secretary-General to undertake on its behalf studies on specific issues relating to the rights of the child;

(d) The Committee may make suggestions and general recommendations based on information received pursuant to articles 44 and 45 of the present Convention. Such suggestions and general recommendations shall be transmitted to any State Party concerned and reported to the General Assembly, together with comments, if any, from States Parties.

Article 46

The present Convention shall be open for signature by all States.

Article 47

The present Convention is subject to ratification. Instruments of ratification shall be deposited with the Secretary-General of the United Nations.

Article 48

The present Convention shall remain open for accession by any State. The instruments of accession shall be deposited with the Secretary-General of the United Nations.

Article 49

1. The present Convention shall enter into force on the thirtieth day following the date of deposit with the Secretary-General of the United Nations of the twentieth instrument of ratification or accession.

2. For each State ratifying or acceding to the Convention after the deposit of the twentieth instrument of ratification or accession, the Convention shall enter into force on the thirtieth day after the deposit by such State of its instrument of ratification or accession.

Article 50

1. Any State Party may propose an amendment and file it with the Secretary-General of the United Nations. The Secretary-General shall thereupon communicate the proposed amendment to States Parties, with a request that they indicate whether they favour a conference of States Parties for the purpose of considering and voting upon the proposals. In the event that, within four months from the date of such communication, at least one third of the States Parties favour such a conference, the Secretary-General shall convene the conference under the auspices of the United Nations. Any amendment adopted by a majority of States Parties present and voting at the conference shall be submitted to the General Assembly for approval.

2. An amendment adopted in accordance with paragraph 1 of the present article shall enter into force when it has been approved by the General Assembly of the United Nations and accepted by a two-thirds majority of States Parties.

3. When an amendment enters into force, it shall be binding on those States Parties which have accepted it, other States Parties still being bound by the provisions of the present Convention and any earlier amendments which they have accepted.

Article 51
1. The Secretary-General of the United Nations shall receive and circulate to all States the text of reservations made by States at the time of ratification or accession.

2. A reservation incompatible with the object and purpose of the present Convention shall not be permitted.

3. Reservations may be withdrawn at any time by notification to that effect addressed to the Secretary-General of the United Nations, who shall then inform all States. Such notification shall take effect on the date on which it is received by the Secretary-General.

Article 52
A State Party may denounce the present Convention by written notification to the Secretary-General of the United Nations. Denunciation becomes effective one year after the date of receipt of the notification by the Secretary-General.

Article 53
The Secretary-General of the United Nations is designated as the depositary of the present Convention.

Article 54
The original of the present Convention, of which the Arabic, Chinese, English, French, Russian and Spanish texts are equally authentic, shall be deposited with the Secretary-General of the United Nations. In witness thereof the undersigned plenipotentiaries, being duly authorized thereto by their respective Governments, have signed the present Convention.

Further Reading

There is a vast and constantly expanding literature on this area, ranging from dry academic studies to heart-on-sleeve accounts. I have selected some of the English-language publications I have found most useful in writing this book.

General overviews
UNICEF produces an annual *State of the World's Children*, published by Oxford University Press, which is stuffed full with the latest economic and social statistics, and selects a different focus each year – the 1996 edition looked at the impact of war on children. On Latin America, UNICEF published *Children of the Americas* (Bogotá, 1992), while the UN's Economic Commission for Latin America and the Caribbean, based in Santiago, releases the annual *Social Panorama of Latin America*. UNICEF's International Child Development Centre, based in Florence, churns out a vast range of reports on specific topics such as country studies, and discussions of child labour. For a full catalogue write to the UNICEF International Child Development Centre, Piazza S.S. Annunziata 12, 50122 Florence, Italy.

For a well-written overview of child-related issues world-wide, try Annie Allsebrook and Anthony Swift, *Broken Promise: The World of Endangered Children* (Sevenoaks, 1989). Jo Boyden, *Children of the Cities* (London, 1991), provides an evocative picture of life for the urban child. For a provocative and highly enjoyable account of child rights and the history of childhood, read Martin Hoyles, *The Politics of Childhood* (London, 1989).

Family life
The best portraits of childhood are often contained in some of the powerful autobiographies of Latin American women, most notably Carolina Maria de Jesus, *Beyond All Pity: The Diary of Carolina Maria de Jesus* (London, 1990) and Elisabeth Burgos-Debray (ed.), *I Rigoberta Menchú: An Indian Woman in Guatemala* (London, 1984). Oscar Lewis' famous and controversial study, *The Children of Sánchez: Autobiography of a Mexican Family* (Harmondsworth, 1961), gives a gruelling account of family life in a Mexican slum, while Nancy Scheper-Hughes, *Death Without Weeping:*

The Violence of Everyday Life in Brazil (Berkeley, 1992), provides a unique insight into life at the bottom of the heap in the world's most unequal society.

Working children

Rachel Marcus and Caroline Harper, *Small Hands: Children in the Working World* (Save the Children UK Working Paper #16, London, 1996), contains an excellent and even-handed summary of the issues surrounding working children, as does Judith Ennew, *Street and Working Children: A Guide to Planning* (Save the Children UK Development Manual 4, London, 1994). For an extreme example of the right-to-work approach, try Giangi Schibotto and Alejandro Cussianovich, *Working Children: Building an Identity* (Lima, 1994). More nuanced treatments can be found from the ILO in Assefa Bequele and Jo Boyden (eds), *Combating Child Labour* (Geneva, 1988), and from UNICEF in William E. Myers (ed.), *Protecting Working Children* (London, 1991) or Judith Ennew (ed.), *Learning or Labouring? A Compilation of Key Texts on Child Work and Basic Education* (Florence, 1995).

Street children

There are numerous accounts by well-meaning outsiders of their encounters with street children, but much less in the way of objective analysis or interviews with the children themselves. One exception is Judith Ennew, *Street and Working Children: A Guide to Planning* (Save the Children UK Development Manual 4, London, 1994). Another fascinating anthropological account is contained in Lewis Aptekar, *Street Children of Cali* (Durham NC, 1988).

Child criminals and social cleansing

For an unbeatable portrait of the lives and dreams of adolescent gangsters, read Alonso Salazar, *Born to Die in Medellín* (London, 1992). For the opposite portrayal of child-as-victim, see Gilberto Dimenstein's powerful book, *Brazil: War on Children* (London, 1991). Human Rights Watch has published some damning reports on violence against children, notably *Final Justice: Police and Death Squad Homicides of Adolescents in Brazil* (New York, 1994).

Political violence

Human Rights Watch has produced an important report in *Generation Under Fire: Children and Violence in Colombia* (New York, 1994). For a general look at the impact of war on children, see Garbarino, Kostelny and Dubrow, *No Place to Be a Child: Growing up in a War Zone* (Lexington MA, 1991).

Children and economic change

For an overview of recent developments in the Latin American economy, see Duncan Green, *Silent Revolution: The Rise of Market Economics in Latin America* (London, 1995). For a more general survey of the connection between economic change and social deprivation, see Kevin Watkins, *The Oxfam Poverty Report* (Oxford, 1995).

Health and education

Both UNICEF and the UN Economic Commission for Latin America and the Caribbean have published excellent reports on Latin America's dilapidated education system and the need for reform. See, for example, ECLAC, *Education and Knowledge* (Santiago, 1992). For regional health issues, consult the Pan American Health Organization (PAHO), which has an excellent website on www.paho.org.

Child rights and participation

There are several good discussions of the issues raised by the UN Convention on the Rights of the Child. See, for example, Judith Ennew and Brian Milne, *The Next Generation: Lives of Third World Children* (London, 1989) or Save the Children, *Towards a Children's Agenda: New Challenges for Social Development* (London, 1995). A more technical exploration of policy and practice is contained in Bob Franklin (ed.), *The Handbook of Children's Rights* (London, 1995) and the quarterly *International Journal of Children's Rights* (Kluwer Academic Publishers, Dordrecht, Netherlands). Also worth consulting are Phil Treseder, *Empowering Children and Young People: Promoting Involvement in Decision-Making* (Children's Rights Office/Save the Children UK, London, March 1997) and Roger Hart, *Children's Participation* (London, 1997).

Save the Children UK and Rädda Barnen

This book is co-published with Save the Children UK and Rädda Barnen.

Save the Children UK

Save the Children

Save the Children works to achieve lasting benefits for children within the communities in which they live by influencing policy and practice based on its experience and study in different parts of the world. Save the Children endeavours to put the reality of children's lives at the heart of all programmes, championing the right of all children to childhood and, together with children, helping to build a better world for present and future generations.

In Latin America and the Caribbean, Save the Children works with partners in the Caribbean (Cuba, Jamaica, Haiti), Central America (Guatemala, El Salvador, Nicaragua, Honduras) and South America (Colombia, Peru, Brazil). Save the Children's approach to work emphasizes the inclusion and participation of children in all project work. Priority areas of work include education, working children, child rights, HIV/AIDS, disability, children and the environment, and children and violence.

Through working in partnership with local organizations, Save the Children aims to facilitate the sharing of experience between partners across the whole region, as well as giving support on capacity building, monitoring and assessment and advocacy to secure long-term benefits for children and adolescents.

Rädda Barnen
(Swedish Save the Children)

Rädda Barnen is a non-governmental organization that fights for the rights of children, in Sweden and around the world. Activities are designed to improve conditions for children at risk. Rädda Barnen acts by itself and in co-operation with others by:

- *identifying and analysing problems and potential courses of action*
- *sponsoring practical development and support programmes and sharing the experience gained*
- *influencing public opinion*

Rädda Barnen publishes books itself, and with others, primarily for people who work with children. Its goal is to disseminate knowledge concerning the situation of children and to provide guidance and impetus for new ideas.

Contact Organizations

There are hundreds of development and aid organizations working either partly or exclusively on children's issues. The main international networks are the United Nations Children's Fund (UNICEF) and the International Save the Children Alliance, and for reasons of clarity and space, I have restricted this section to those two networks. More information about both networks can be obtained from their websites on www.unicef.org and www.savechildren.or.jp/alliance respectively.

The International Save The Children Alliance

Australia
Save the Children Australia
P.O. Box 1281, Collingwood
Victoria 3066
scfa@scfa.asn.au

Austria
Rettet Das Kind
Pouthongasse 3
A-1150 Wien
rettkind@magnet.at

Canada
Save the Children Canada
3080 Yonge Street, Suite 6020
Toronto
Ontario M4N 3P4
sccan@web.apc.org

Denmark
Red Barnet
Rantzausgade 60
DK-2200 Copenhagen N
redbarn@inet.uni-c.dk

Dominican Republic
Fundación para el Desarrollo
    Comunitario
EPS #X-10397 FUDECO
P.O. Box 02-5261, Miami,
Florida 33102-5261
fudeco@codetel.net.do

Egypt
Egyptian Save the Children
P.O. Box 5854
Heliopolis West, 1771 Cairo

Faroe Islands
Barnabati
Margarinfabrikkin Magnus
    Heinasonargöta 12
Postboks 1052, FR-110 Torshavn

Finland
Pelastakaa Lapset Ry
P.O. Box 177
00181 Helsinki

France
Enfants et Développement
13, rue Jules Simon
F-75015 Paris
eedparis@worldnet.fr

Greece
Save the Children Greece
54 Papadiamandopoulou St
GR-157 71 Zografou, Athens

Guatemala
Alianza para el Desarrollo Juvenil
    Comunitario
Apdo P.O. stal 2903
Guatemala City
adejucsc@guate.net

Iceland
Barnaheill
Soltún 24 (Sigtún 7)
105 Reykjavik
barnaheill@treknet.is

Japan
Save the Children Japan
510 Kondo Building
4-4-12 Nishitenma, Kita-ku
Osaka 530
tsuruta@yo.rim.or.jp

Jordan
Jordanian Save the Children
P.O. Box 927370
Amman, 11181 Jordan

Korea
Save the Children Korea
C.P.O. Box 1193
Seoul

Mauritius
Save the Children Mauritius
Sivananda Avenue
Vacoas

Mexico
Fundación Méxicana de Apoyo
    Infantil
Callejón de Arias No. 11
Col. la Palmita
C.P. 37700 San Miguel de Allende
Guanajuato
faiac@www.ecsanet.net

The Netherlands
Save the Children The Netherlands
P.O. Box 30470, 2500 GL
The Hague

New Zealand
Save the Children New Zealand
P.O. Box 6584, Marion Square
Wellington
info@scfnz.org.nz

Norway
Redd Barna
P.O. Boks 6200
Etterstad
N-0602 Oslo 6
pro.rb@normail.no

Sweden
Rädda Barnen
Torsgatan 4
S-10788 Stockholm
lennart.lindgren@rb.se

United Kingdom
Save the Children
17 Grove Land
London SE5 8RD
f.howden@scflondon.ccmail.compuse
    rve.com

United States
Save the Children Federation
54 Wilton Road
Westport
Connecticut
awillliam@savechildren.org

**Save the Children Alliance
    Secretariat**
59, Chemin Moïse Deboule
1209 Geneva
Switzerland
alliance@iprolink.ch
alliance home page:
    http://www.savechildren.or.jp/allia
    nce

Unicef

Unicef has a world-wide network of regional offices, given here, as well as national offices in the industrialized nations which work to publicize Unicef's work and raise money. There is a field office in most countries in the developing world. Details of all these, along with a vast amount of information on Unicef's work, child rights and other topics, are available on the Unicef website, on www.unicef.org.

Headquarters
3 UN Plaza
New York
NY 10017
USA

Geneva Office
Palais des Nations
CH-1211 Geneva 10
Switzerland

Regional Office for Central and Eastern Europe/ Commonwealth of Independent States
5–7 Avenue de la Paix
Geneva
Switzerland

Regional Office for Eastern and Southern Africa
P.O. Box 44145
Nairobi
Kenya
unicef.esaro@unicef.unon.org

Regional Office for West and Central Africa
P.O. Box 443
Abidjan 04
Côte d'Ivoire
wcaro@unicef.org

Regional Office for the Americas and the Caribbean
Apartado Aereo 7555
Santa Fé de Bogotá
Colombia

Regional Office for East Asia and the Pacific
P.O. Box 2-154
Bangkok 10200
Thailand
unicef_eapro.unescap@un.org

Regional Office for the Middle East and North Africa
P.O. Box 811721
11181 Amman
Jordan

Regional Office for South Asia
P.O. Box 5815
Lekhnath Marg
Kathmandu
Nepal
unicefrosa@uncrosa.mos.com.np

Index